Palestine
Yesterday, today and tomorrow

Dr. Tareq M. Suwaidan

Author: Dr. Tareq M. Suwaidan
Project Director: Ahmad A. Shurbaji
Coordination: Dr. Bahige Mulla Huech
Sources & Language Consultant: Dr. Teresa Lesher
Design & Production: Didaco Co. Spain
Printing: Egedsa
ISBN: 978-84-96557-32-1
D.L.:B-37605-2005

January 2006

الإبـداع الفكري

Kuwait – P.O. Box 28589 Safat 13146
Tel.: +965 2404883 / 54
Fax: +965 2404852
E-mail: info@ebdaaco.com
www.ebdaaco.com

Palestine
Yesterday, today and tomorrow

Contents

Table of contents

Detailed Table of Contents

Prologue

Prologue

Since the dawn of history, the Palestinian issue has been the focal point of national and international conflicts in the Middle East. However, the historical realities of Palestine in general, and of Jerusalem in particular, have been manipulated, adulterated and even hijacked for one specific reason or another.

The various accounts of events, taken out of their historical context and used for political, ethnic, religious and sectarian purposes, have spread confusion and uncertainty in contemporary culture, to such an extent that people today view the socio-historic situation of Palestine as fraught with insurmountable hurdles that prevent a correct understanding of the "Palestinian Problem".

In the two years of lectures I have given on Palestine, I have verified that, by presenting history "from the outside looking in", in a logical, chronological sequence, one can gain a better understanding of historical realities, because it enables one to analyse historical facts reliably and impartially. By applying this methodology, I have rearranged the content of the above-mentioned lectures in this book, so as to put within reach of the average reader a well-documented, and comparatively comprehensive treatise.

This book contains two distinct parts—the first deals with the
history of Jerusalem, from the dawn of time to well into the
modern age; that is, up to the time of the Ottoman empire. In
contrast, the second part focuses on demographic and political
events from the fall of the Ottoman empire, and the subsequent
colonial invasion, to the present time; in other words, from the
end of the First World War to the death of Yasir Arafat in late 2004.

The aim of this book is not merely to provide an account of
historical events in a region that is the focus of world attention,
but to explain—through data, facts, documents and the
biographies of prominent figures who have played a leading role
in shaping Palestine—the undeniable realities that should be
taken into account in building the future of Palestine on the
basis of law and legality, and not on the basis of ethno-political
claims tainted by fanatical or dogmatic stances.

I hope that this compendium fulfils the objectives I have
outlined, which are intended solely to lay bare the unmasked
realities of the Palestinian situation to those readers interested
in knowng what is happening in that part of the world.

December 2005
Dr. Tareq M. Suwaidan
Author

The importance of Palestine in the life of a Muslim

The excellence of the place where Jerusalem is sited has been proven not only historically but also in numerous texts of the Koran (or Qur'an) and the Sunna (Prophetic tradition). This excellence undoubtedly goes back to ancient times because it was where many prophets grew up and died. It was where they received inspiration and where many messages were revealed to them that would mark the course of most events in ancient history.

The Koran (Textual Revelation)

1. The Koranic text emphasizes the sacred nature of this land and its great importance throughout the course of history. The blessing bestowed upon it extends not only to the Al-Aqsa Mosque but also to its surroundings. *(Al-Isra', 1)*

2. The Holy Land referred to in the Koran covers the whole of Palestine, including Jerusalem, formerly known as "Ilia", or the Land of God *(Al-Ma'ida, 21)*. The Koran underlines the holy or sacred epithet understood not only as exaltation, blessing and great importance, but also as a place of spiritual purity.

3. There are many passages in the Koran that narrate Abraham's emigration from the land of the Chaldeans in Iraq to as far as Syria. (See *Al-Anbiya', 71*)
These passages tell how God saved Abraham from being burnt at the stake and ordered him to emigrate to the land of Syria where the Holy Land is located. According to Qataadah's version, Abraham was in Iraq and God, who sent him to Syria, saved him. It was then said that it would be the land of the Congregation and Resurrection of men and where Jesus Christ would be resurrected and the Antichrist would die.

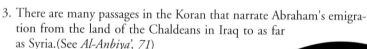

4. Many interpreters of the Koran understand that the blessed land is Syria. *(Al-Anbiya', 81)*
Historians are also most concerned about understanding the borders of the former Syria. Some extended them from Turkey in the north as far as the Arabian Peninsula, including Iraq. Others narrowed them down to only Palestine and its surroundings. In any case, Jerusalem is located within the greater Syrian territory, according to all historians and scholars. This is the most common version in the majority of the texts and accounts.

5. The allusion of the Koran to the change in the *qibla* – the direction which Muslims face to say their prayers – from Jerusalem to Mecca *(Al-Baqara, 144),* or from Al-Masjidu-l-Aqsa (the Sacred Mosque of Jerusalem) to Al-Masjidu-l-Haram (the great Mosque of Mecca), has been ratified repeatedly by numerous hadiths, or sayings of the prophet Muhammad.
This means that the orientation towards Jerusalem lasted almost fourteen months. During this time, the Prophet multiplied his additional prayers and his pleas to God so that he could be directed towards the Kaaba, which is Abraham's *qibla*. God attended his prayers and ordered him to go towards the old building. It is said that the first prayer he uttered facing the direction of the new *qibla* was Al-Asr (the afternoon prayer), as given in As-Sahihayn, two outstanding and reliable sources of prophetic traditions in Sunni Islam. More than one exegete confirmed that the reorientation of the *qibla* was revealed to the Prophet when he had just completed half of the midday prayer at the Bani Salmah mosque, later known as the Masjidu-l-Qiblatayn (the mosque of the two *qiblas,* which was built first in Medina). As for the people of Qobaa', the news did not reach them until the dawn prayer the following day, as stated in As-Sahihayn.

6. We should remember that there are numerous verses in different chapters of the Koran that emphasize the excellence of the Holy Land and its surroundings. The fact of stressing the direction of prayer towards Jerusalem before this was changed highlights its great importance and its holiness.

"The *qibla* is the direction which Muslims face to say their prayers."

Palestine

The Sunna (Conceptual Revelation)

The Prophet himself often alluded to the excellence of the Holy Land. He said: "The places that are worthy of pilgrimage are: Al-Masjidu-l-Haram (the Great Mosque of Mecca), my mosque of Al-Medina and Al-Masjidu-l-Aqsa (the Mosque of Jerusalem)".

1. Tradition holds that the reward for worshipping at the three mosques multiplies according to their rank. Praying at the Great Mosque of Mecca is equivalent to one hundred thousand prayers. At the Mosque of the Prophet in Medina it is equivalent to one thousand prayers and, at the Mosque of Jerusalem, five hundred. So God placed the latter in third position and multiplied the divine recompense.

2. The Mosque of Jerusalem is the second place of worship built on Earth after the Great Mosque of Mecca.

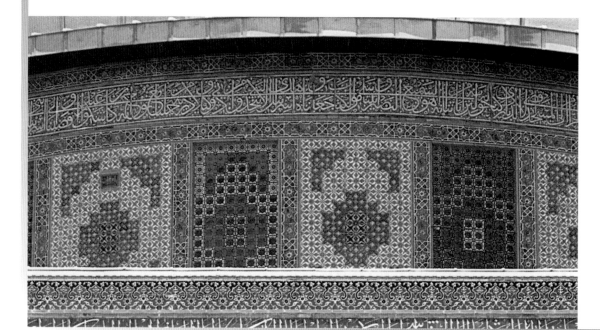

3. Zayd Ibn Thabit recounted that he heard the Prophet say: "Blessed be Syria … Blessed be Syria!" They asked him: "Why are you praising Syria?" He said: "Because the angels have spread their wings over Syria".

4. Al-Bukhari and Muslim mention that it was Al-Baraa' Ibn 'Azib who said: "We prayed with the Prophet facing Jerusalem for sixteen or seventeen months, and then we changed towards Mecca".

5. Jerusalem was the goal of the Prophet's night-time trip and the starting point of his ascension to heaven.

6. In his invocation to God, Moses exalted Jerusalem and the Holy Land, and on his deathbed he asked God to bring him closer.

7. They are many quotations (hadiths) by the Prophet that beseech God's blessing for Syria.

8. Ahmad and At-Tirmidhi quote Salim Ibn 'Abdillah as saying he heard the Prophet state: "Fire will come from Hadramaut; that is to say, at the end of time, the doors of hell will open and the people will congregate". We said: "God's messenger—so, what are your orders?" He replied: "You must go to Syria".

9. Numerous exegetes and scholars, including Al-Qurtubi and Ibn al-Juzi, agreed on the exegesis of the Koranic verse that reads: "Listen on the day the town crier calls from somewhere nearby" Qaf (41). It was Israfil, standing on the rock of Jerusalem, from where the Prophet's Ascension began, calling the people to go to the final judgment. That is where all the dead would start to congregate and that is what Imam Ahmad says in his collection, when he quotes Maimunah Bintu Saad, the Prophet's wife, who said: "Prophet of God! Is our end in Jerusalem?" The Prophet answered: "Land of the congregation of the dead, and of their Resurrection".

Some Muslims exaggerate by venerating the Rock. Its exaltation, accor-

ding to Ibn Taymiyyah, is considered to be a heretical invention, as there is no text that justifies its consecration. Even some people believe that it is suspended in air without any support and this is not the case. In fact, there is a cave underneath it and whoever goes inside it gets the sensation that the rock is hanging.

10. Many of the Prophet's companions, such as the scholars and the devout, visited Jerusalem. They prayed within its boundaries, thus heeding the call made by Muhammad in this respect. Among the companions who visited Jerusalem were: 'Umar Ibn al-Khattab, Abu Ubaydah, Amir Ibn al-Jarrah, the mother of the believers and wife of the Prophet Safya bint Hayi, Mu'adh Ibn Jabal, Abdullah Ibn 'Umar, Khalid Ibn al-Walid, Abu Dharr al-Ghafari, Abu Ad-Dardaa', Salman al-Farisi, Amr Ibn al-'As and Said Ibn Zayd of the ten foretold to be going to Paradise besides Abu Hurayra, together with Abdullah Ibn Amr Ibn al-'As, among others.

PART ONE
Palestine before Islam

PART ONE
Palestine before Islam

CHAPTER ONE
The Ancient History of Palestine

"The first inhabitants of Palestine were tribes that moved there from Arabia."

The Ancient History of Palestine

1. The first inhabitants

Nobody knows exactly when the land of Palestine was first inhabited and there is no proof allowing a date to be determined. However, initial indications and archaeological remains lead us to believe it was the *Natoufiyyun* who settled in Palestine in the 10th Century BC. They were a group of tribes whose vestiges speak about them. But does anyone know who they were or where they came from?

Jericho

Dating from the 8th Century BC, the earliest archaeological data reveal vestiges of a city that is currently called Jericho. Some researchers believe it is the oldest city in the world. Before then, people led a nomadic life, roaming in search of fertile land and water. Nevertheless, the sedentary life that began in antiquity left its first traces in Jericho, but we do not know who its original inhabitants were or where they came from.

The Canaanites

The first known archaeological discoveries in Palestine date back to the Canaanites and the Amorites. These two people were tribes that emigrated from Arabia towards the north and settled in the land of Sham (Syria) and, specifically, in Palestine. This is clearly demonstrated in the history of Palestine and not only the eastern but also the western historians confirm this. Therefore, the initial historical recording about the first inhabitants of Palestine dates back to the Arab Canaanites and the Amorites. As for the Jews, there was no reference to them here. Even more, they first appeared on the scene very much later—several centuries later—as shall be demonstrated with correlative historical evidence.

The Jebusites

There are numerous Arab tribes from the Arabian Peninsula who emigrated towards the north. There, they dispersed between Syria and Iraq (Mesopotamia). Some of them moved to Egypt. Among them were the Canaanites, who settled in the valleys of Palestine. Others, the Jebusites, established themselves in the Al-Quds area (Jerusalem), before it was built. Other people broke away and settled in the mountains. They were called the Phoenicians and the Amorites. This is how the land of Palestine was divided among these tribes. History books based on archaeological documents and on evident reality mention the names of all these people according to their geographical distribution in the habitat of Palestine.

> "Palestine is known among archaeologists as the land of Canaan, in reference to the Canaanites."

The "Land of Canaan" is clearly mentioned in the Old Testament and in the New Testament, as well as in the history books of that time, but there is no explicit reference to the Israelites.

"The origin of the name of Palestine dates back to the people who lived in the Baalist area, in southern Palestine."

Map of Jerusalem made out of mosaics found in the city of Ma'daba, in Jordan.

2. The origin of the name of Palestine

Baalists

The name of Philistine is attributed above all to people who hailed from Mediterranean islands, especially Crete. It seems that the people from these islands suffered from famine or some specific circumstances that forced them to repeatedly attack the coasts of Syria and Egypt. They were first driven back by Ramses III in the famous battle of Luzin that took place in Egypt. Ramses did not want them to settle in Egypt. Following negotiations, they ended up emigrating to Palestine. There, Ramses ordered them to settle in the south, in a region called Baalist. This is recorded in history books and Holy Scriptures, where the name Baalist is mentioned. Hence, the people who lived there belong to the lineage of *Al-balistiniyyun* (Philistines). The name of Palestine comes from here because it was then known as Baalistine. Over time it changed to Palestine. However, these people became neighbours not only of the Canaanites but also of the *Yabusiyyun* (Jebusites) who were the first inhabitants in that region. From there, their languages interchanged and mixed, and they merged with the original people who were also the most numerous and civilized. In time, the Philistines intermarried with the "Canaanites". This removed distinct signs of their original identities, therefore leaving no historical reference.

This information reveals why, up until then, there is not even one single mention of the Jews. Where were they in that epoch? How did they get to the land of Palestine? All the archaeological documents, history books and Holy Scriptures, in addition to western books, corroborate that the original inhabitants of Palestine were the Canaanites and the Jebusites.

PART ONE
Palestine before Islam

CHAPTER TWO
The Israelites in Palestine

The Israelites in Palestine

Tomb of the prophet Abraham and the prophet Jacob, at the Sanctuary of Abraham in Hebron. Palestine.

1. Emigration of the Israelites to Palestine

Jacob

History tells us that Abraham's two sons, Isaac and Ishmael, were born in Palestine. Nevertheless, they came from an emigrant family and did not belong to the well-settled residents. Jacob, who was also called Israel, was the son of Isaac. Joseph was among his children. The Koran refers to Joseph as a man who came to Egypt as a slave, until God provided him with wisdom and the capability to interpret dreams. He became a viceroy of Egypt holding the position of finance minister for the country. This was when he sent for his father and all his family so that they could join him in Egypt. *(Yusuf, 93)*

This is how Jacob gathered all his family and children together and finally settled in Egypt. Their long journey from Palestine put an end to their status as emigrants. It therefore goes without saying that Jacob belonged to the

Palestinian race or at least that is where he originated. History and all the books agree in confirming the accuracy of these facts. Jacob's descendants did not live for even one generation in Palestine. So, how can the Israelites claim that Palestine is their land and use Jacob's residence there for a certain time as a pretext?

Moses

Another emigration to Palestine by the Israelites was that of Moses when, together with his people, the children of Israel, he emigrated from Egypt, fleeing from the Pharaoh and his soldiers. So we see that the Israelites only went into Palestine as emigrants. As for the true inhabitants of Palestine, they were the Canaanites. As far as I could verify, not in Arab sources but in sacred and western books, the Israelites emigrated mainly from Egypt to Palestine. This was because Palestine was administratively dependent on Egypt and also politically and historically since the temple founded by Jacob was built there. In that period the Pharaohs had started expanding into that land and had occupied Palestine, specifically the area under the rule of the Hyksos. When it was taken over by Egypt, it never became clear that the Israelites made it their land, nor that they settled there for a long period of time. They were short emigrations, but what is absolutely definitive is that the land first belonged to the Canaanites and the Jebusites.

Let's return to Moses' flight from Egypt and God's intervention to save the Israelites by drowning the followers of the Pharaoh and his soldiers in the sea. This episode provides a position and a consideration in revealing who the Israelites actually are, in respect of their history with their prophet Moses—I aim to provide examples and advice for anyone who wishes to discover the falsehood of their cause and see them as they really are.

> "The Israelites were not the original inhabitants of Palestine, but were always sporadic emigrants."

Pharaoh.

1250 BC

2. Moses and the Israelites

Moses in Egypt

The appearance of Moses on the scene took place in Egypt. Such an event goes back to 1250 BC. God helped him with many impressive miracles. It began when his mother was inspired to throw him into the open water and from hence to be raised in the house of the tyrant Pharaoh, who was oppressing the people of Egypt. The Koran relates that, when he grew up, Moses mistakenly killed an Egyptian and took refuge in Madian, escaping from the Pharaoh and his council of dignitaries. Then he was inspired by a mission that God ordered him to fulfil so that the people would stop worshipping the Pharaoh and only worship God, and in order for the children of Israel to leave Egypt where they were suffering the oppression of the Pharaoh, reinforcing his cause with miracles. One of these miracles was that of the staff that was transformed into a snake and that of the white hand, thus demonstrating his great magical skills. The story is very well known. Moses defied the Pharaoh in front of a multitude of Israelites and before the assembly of his people. The Pharaoh called for his sorcerers to confront the challenge. As a result, many Israelites and many sorcerers believed in his mission and in the Lord of Moses and Aaron, and ceased believing in the Pharaoh and his following. Then God revealed to Moses that Pharaoh was going to deceive them, so they fled from Egypt in the direction of Palestine. Pharaoh pursued them and was on the verge of catching them on the banks of one of the Red Sea inlets, the western one to be precise. There, God parted the waters for Moses and his followers to cross over on dry land. When Pharaoh and his soldiers reached the water, they were drowned. This is how God granted safety and peace to Moses' people, after having been persecuted and terrorized.

The people of the Pharaoh and his soldiers drowning in the sea.

Moses in Sinai

When Moses and his people reached Sinai, they encountered a people who worshipped idols. His companions said to him: "Appoint us gods like theirs". Moses was surprised by their attitude and treated them as ignoramuses. How could it be that, after having showed them ten miracles, including the emergence of dry land through the parting of the seas, they were asking him to adore something other than God, he who had asked them to venerate Him? This indicated how the lack of conviction of their faith was rooted in their souls. Moses and his brother Aaron were perplexed. In fact, the Israelites were tinged with the ungratefulness and subjugation acquired during the many centuries spent in the service of the Pharaohs in Egypt.

Mount Sinai

Moses decided to go ahead of his people and climb Mount Sinai (Jabal at-Tor) to speak to the Lord. He was away for forty days, during which he appointed his brother Aaron to be in command. As soon as he returned, he found them adoring a golden calf instead of God. Such disobedience was the greatest sin and the most burdensome. God punished them by subjecting their repentance to suicide, since their canonical laws stipulated that repentance for associating other beings with God and for ungratefulness was linked to suicide. Suicide was the penance that led to Paradise. In spite of all this, they refused. So he told them: "Listen and obey". They answered: "We have listened but we disobey". Then they received a divine warning threatening them with punishment. They saw how Mount Sinai was being completed raised above their heads. Moses said to them: "Listen and obey" and they were forced to reply: "We listen and shall obey".

It was then that Moses chose seventy of the best men from his people to meet God on Mount Sinai in order to apologize before his Lord for the disobedience incurred by those who had gone astray, after having seen with their own eyes the eleventh miracle of the minor earthquake of the mountain. When they heard Moses speaking with God, they came to tell him that they were not going to believe it until they saw God face to face. The response was that they were struck by lightning. However, Moses then begged the Lord as these men were the best of his people and God revived them due to his generosity towards Moses. This was to be the twelfth miracle. And this is how the miracles of

Moses occurred before his people without forgiveness for their arrogance and ungratefulness.

Moses in the Holy Land

When the people of Moses reached the gates of Palestine, he notified them that God had ordered them to enter Jerusalem. Their reply was that the people there were mighty and they were not going to go in until they had left. Moses and Aaron advised them to enter all the same, as God had guaranteed their victory. They continued to refuse and told Moses that he and his God should fight for them as they had no intention of complying with God's commands. *(Al-Ma'ida, 24).* That attitude cost them severe divine punishment in life and on the final judgment day. Their sentence was to wander for forty years, during which they had to live miserably, without knowing what direction to take. *(Al-Ma'ida, 26)*

The story of the Israelites' Cow

During their long journey, the story of the cow they were ordered to slaughter took place. They started repeating one question after another, rebelling tenaciously against fulfilling any divine commands transmitted via their prophet. Hardly had they killed the cow when Moses took hold of a chunk of it and threw it onto the corpse of someone who had been murdered by an unknown hand. The dead man then came back to life and revealed the name of his murderer. This was miracle number thirteen.

But, did this make an impression in their hearts, moving them and making them more aware of worship and more obedient? No in the least. Rather, to the contrary. Their hearts turned to stone or to something even harder. *(Al-Baqara, 74)*

The Israelites on their journey to Palestine.

Exodus

For forty years they disobeyed God's orders. God then sent the angel of death to Moses, their prophet, for the purpose of making him choose between life and death. He chose death near the holy places. Thus, a stone's throw away from Jerusalem, where a dune of reddish sand had been formed, the angel of death fulfilled his duty and took his soul. Nevertheless, his people did not choose the right path and continued to go astray, incapable of coming out of the desert and the wilderness.

After wandering for forty years, God guided them through the mediation of Moses' disciple, the prophet entrusted to take them to Jordan. The following stories shed light on Moses' torments and worries about his people.

Israelites catching partridge.

"The fact that the Israelites lived for forty years wandering in the wilderness served to end the generation of unfaithful rebels and for another generation to appear, educated under the influence of the prophets."

Israelites gathering maná.

3. The Israelites after Moses

1186 BC

Joshua

At that time Joshua was leading them to the Holy Land. They went to Palestine but not to Jerusalem, according to the most reliable versions. Actually, they went to Jericho, where they fought a battle against the powerful giants mentioned on several occasions in the Koran who were Canaanites. The Israelites conquered Jericho and settled there. History books and hadith stress this fact, as does the Koran. *(Al-Baqara, 58)*

The fall of Jericho to the Israelites after a period of wandering in the desert.

Enter the town

Their prophet ordered them to enter the town and to eat whatever they wanted on condition that they crossed the gate on their knees saying: "Forgive us" (*hettah*), that is to say: "Lord, forgive us our sins". Nevertheless, immersed in their rebelliousness, and out of arrogance and pride, they confused the word by saying *hentah* or "wheat". They deceived Joshua and said they were victorious thanks only to their strength. (*Al-Baqara, 59*)

The conquest of Jericho.

The Temple of Shiloh, where the Israelites kept the Ark of the Covenant, housing the Ten Commandments and other holy utensils deposited by the followers of Moses and Aaron, before they were captured.

The Israelites Go Astray

The Israelites settled in Palestine, where Jericho was their capital until the death of Joshua. After that they became divided and made war among themselves. They had many prophets—more than any other people. At times there were up to three in a single town. "No sooner did one prophet die than another appeared", said the Prophet Muhammad. The Koran even explains how, when the people rejected two prophets sent to them by God, he then sent them a third. *(Yasin, 13-14)* Most of them disobeyed the prophets and even went on to murder them. *(An-Nisaa', 155)*

Infidelity and arrogance became entrenched in their rebellious hearts, and they grew accustomed to associating God with other beings living in sin. They continued to defy the prophets, whom they disobeyed and even murdered. Having slaughtered those who were of their own faith and lineage, they ceased to hold anyone in regard. As a result, they drew the wrath of God on themselves. *(Al-Baqara, 61)*

The children of Israel and their devotion towards the heifer.

Oppression of the Israelites

In Jericho the Israelites were oppressed by the Canaanite giants, who submitted them to all manner of punishment, humiliation and slavery. They deprived them of their sacred possessions and their belongings, including the holiest of all—the Ark of the Covenant—where the tablets of the Law were housed. *(Al-A'raf, 145)*

However, a group of rebellious priests later produced replicas of the tablets, and word spread that only two of the original ten remained in the Ark, together with Moses' staff and the garments of his brother, Aaron. *(Al-Baqara, 248)*

Israelites carrying the Ark.

37

Israelites awestruck as the Ark descends from heaven.

Saul, the new king

This situation endured until the time when the Philistine king Goliath ruled Jerusalem. The Israelites, who had become a defeated, divided, dispirited nation, had no ruler to reunite them. They then called on their prophet to restore their former glory and grandeur, to raise them out of their humiliation and to appoint a king who would lead them to victory. The prophet asked that, with their history of wicked deeds, if God were to grant their petitions, could they be trusted to be obedient and submissive, and not contravene his orders. They replied: "Why shouldn't we obey, when we are now being humiliated? Why should we disobey his orders when it is His wish to restore our former glory and grandeur?"

They were then informed by their prophet that God had appointed a king for them—his name was Saul. They lost no time in voicing their disapproval of this choice, as Saul was not from the customary bloodline of Israelite kings. They regarded others as more entitled to bear the royal title and flatly rejected God's decision. *(Al-Baqara, 247)*

Saul, the new king.

Recovery of the Ark

When the prophet told them about the king's designation, he said that God would give them a sign as proof of it. This was to be the return of the Ark, borne by angels. *(Al-Baqara, 248)* Despite seeing it being transported by angels, they were unwilling to believe their eyes until it was safe in their hands. They then opened it and verified that it was indeed the lost Ark. The people celebrated its return and decided to accept Saul as their new king.

Archaeological finds have revealed the remains of drawings and other images depicting the Ark being transported by winged angels. This episode is documented in Jewish history and books. In fact, they did not actually see the angels. Far from it—they imagined the scene and produced drawings of it. The feat is well known among them, but, did this miracle lead them to show allegiance to their king?

Their disobedience to Saul

Once again they apostatized and objected tenaciously. Nothing more than a limited group of those who had faith and resources went out to fight with their king. The king led the faithful Israelites, who passed by a river on their way. He ordered them not to drink any water from it. He warned them by saying that whoever drank from that river would have nothing more to do with him, and that whoever abstained from drinking its waters would continue with him. It was a way of testing their patience and their will to endure and resist the battle. But the majority satiated themselves, persisting in their disobedience and opposition. *(Al-Baqara, 249)*

The believing minority

In spite of everything, that limited group went into the battle that pitted them against sturdy giants. The majority who refused to take part due to their lack of courage saw how a minority of faithful Israelites were strong enough to defeat the giants who outnumbered them, thanks to God's assistance, and this was because of their patience and prayers. *(Al-Baqara, (249-50)*

The fight between David and Goliath.

"God honoured the Israelites by granting them victory over their enemies, led by their king David. Did they appear to be grateful?"

Historians tell us about a group of seventy Israelite warriors who held out in that battle against the sturdy giants. Goliath went out to challenge them to a duel, but no soldier had the courage to accept the challenge. Only a sixteen-year-old boy dared to go out. It was David. Goliath mocked him and turned him down because of his age, and insisted on encouraging the Israelites to accept the duel. He even promised to give his daughter in marriage to whoever won this combat, so that he would become his successor in the government. Finally, seeing that no one else would take up the offer, he allowed David to confront him.

David placed a stone in his sling and went out to do battle. Goliath lunged at him, but David hurled the stone from his sling and it struck Goliath's head. This is how Goliath died, and his army ended up defeated and expelled. God granted the Israelites a resounding victory under the command of their king, David.

The tomb of David in Jerusalem.

4. The era of David and Solomon

The death of Saul

After this victory, David married Saul's daughter. Saul died in the year 1004 BC and, immediately afterwards, discord and division ensued. Some followed Saul's son. Others preferred David, thus fulfilling their late king's recommendation, who saw his son-in-law to be more entitled to reign that his own son.

1004 BC

King David

David subsequently consolidated his power beyond the kingdom of Judaea. His capital was Galilee. Meanwhile, Saul's son governed Jerusalem and its surroundings.

In the year 1000 there was a battle between David and his adversary, Saul's son, which David won. He entered Jerusalem and made it the capital of the land of the Israelites. His kingdom included a large part of Philistine, since the Canaanites continued to govern on the coast.

1000 BC

The Jews believe David climbed these stairs when going up to the temple in the mountain.

The first kingdom of the Israelites

We should make it clear that the first Jewish kingdom originated in Palestine in 995 BC, but we know that the Canaanites and the Jebusites were the first to settle and govern Palestine for a very long time, going back as far as 2700 BC. Indeed, its origins becomes lost in antiquity and means that those people were the inhabitants of Palestine 1200 years before the Jews arrived. Such evidence denies any entitlement of the Jews to Palestine or any claim to them having roots there, due to the fact that the period of David's rule, followed by that of his son Solomon, did not last more than ninety years. After this time the Jewish community split up and spread around the world.

Jerusalem, the prosperous capital in the time of David.

963 BC

King Solomon

David died that year and was succeeded by his son Solomon as ruler of the Jewish dynasty. Stories about this period are well-known throughout the Koran. God made elements of nature—such as the wind—subject to him, and put geniuses, birds and animals at his service. They would make anything he asked of them, such as altars, statues and palaces. *(Saba', 13)* When king Solomon passed away, his dynasty disintegrated and was divided among his children.

The alleged Temple

According to some sources, it was Solomon who built the first temple, and even today the Jews are proud of its existence. What is for certain, according to the official Islamic sources, is that Solomon had renovated an original place of worship, a "Mosque" of Jerusalem, but he did not build any temple. The word "temple" came from books that were altered by the Israelites, who do not base their claim on any proof or documentation. It is therefore necessary to clarify the following points that are to be found in Jewish books in order to explain this matter of the temple:

1. Many soldiers and bricklayers were said to have built the alleged temple. They were later known as "Masons", in other words, bricklayers. That is where the word "Masonry" comes from, originally taken to mean "builders of the temple".

2. The texts indicate that the Temple was built somewhere close to the Mosque of Jerusalem, but there is no specific date or any evidence to pinpoint its exact location. There is only a meticulous description of its interior and exterior shape in Jewish books.

Building the temple, as imagined by the Jews.

3. The description of its construction in Jewish books is nearer to imagination than reality. It contains much exaggeration and padding, and talks about a fully-fledged golden palace. The Jews boast about the detailed description in their holy books of this construction, with its *mihrab* or sanctum sanctorum (Holy of Holies) that measured 10 metres long, 10 metres wide and 10 metres deep. Before it stood the great altar. All of it was lined with gold, as well as the great chains that spread in front of the sanctum sanctorum, and the statues of angels with wings the size of ten arm-lengths, equally made of gold.

4. The Ark was placed in the sanctum sanctorum, inside the Temple, amid a great feast held for that purpose, and on which an enormous number of cattle and sheep were sacrificed.

5. Historians cast doubt on the veracity of what has been stated about the Temple, because the Holy Scriptures were not written until seven hundred years after the death of Moses. During this time, these writings suffered several alterations

"According to the Talmud, the destruction of the Temple was due to the Israelites' sins."

and modifications that are admitted even by the Jewish priests themselves.

6. Nowadays, the Jews have gone in search of the Temple and excavate in order to find it. Meanwhile, their books and other sources, such as their history books, insist that the Temple was destroyed, burned down and that not even a stone remains.

7. The history books specify that the columns of the Temple were not made of gold, as the Jews assume, but of stone and copper.

These facts are historically documented and corroborated in the Jewish Holy Scriptures, and in the western books, prior even to the Arab ones. In addition, the Koran and the Sunna have already related many details about these events.

The Arab tribes who emigrated from the Arabian Peninsula settled in Palestine 1000 years before the Israelites arrived and, when they did arrive, they stayed for approximately 90 years in Jerusalem, during the time of the reigns of David and his son Solomon.

Salomon's temple, as imagined by the Jews.

PART ONE
Palestine before Islam

CHAPTER THREE
The Assyrians, Persians, Greeks and Romans in Palestine

The Assyrians, Persians, Greeks and Romans in Palestine

1. The Assyrians

The Assyrians

740 BC

In the year 740 BC, the Assyrians, hailing from Mesopotamia, occupied Palestine, where they set up a kingdom under which the Jews were subjugated and forced to pay tax. However, the reign of the Assyrians did not last more than eight years.

The Babylonians

732 BC

Assyrian dominance came to an end when they were defeated by a people called the Chaldeans, who occupied the whole of Mesopotamia and the Assyrian capital, Nineveh. Their dominion spread across the entire former Assyrian sphere of influence, including Palestine.

The Babylonians in Jerusalem

597 BC

The Chaldeans conquered Palestine and Jerusalem. They captured ten thousand Jews, together with their king, and took them captive. Then, they appointed a governor called Zedekiah to rule over those who remained in the Palestinian lands. The Chaldeans obtained promises and commitments from him so that he remained loyal. Zedekiah did not belong to the ruling

Assyrian God.　　Babylon.
　　　　　Assyrian warriors.

house of the Israelites, which made it difficult for him to be accepted by the Jewish population—while he had sworn allegiance to the Babylonians, he did not belong to the bloodline that usually governed.

Fall of the Assyrian strongholds.

Nebuchadnezzar

Zedekiah continued to govern the Jews in Palestine until 586 BC. He then attempted to lead a Jewish coup against the Babylonians. The king of Babylonia intervened—in Arab history, he is known as Naboukhed Nasr, better known as Nebuchadnezzar. He attacked the Jews in Palestine and besieged Jerusalem for one and a half years. Finally, he managed to come out victorious and entered Jerusalem in the year 587 BC, destroying it completely. He then destroyed the Temple built by Solomon, stone by stone. Chapters 24, 25 and 36 of the sacred Jewish scriptures indicate that Nebuchadnezzar left the temple in ruins and took everything he could find to Mesopotamia: pots, precious objects and treasures. They also state that he burned the houses of Yerushalayim or Jerusalem, from where the Jews attempted to flee. Nebuzaradan, commander of the king's guard, was busy burning the priest's house and the king's palace in the sanctuary. Nebuchadnezzar captured 40,000 prisoners and the rest fled to Egypt, so that hardly anyone who was Jewish remained in Palestine. After the surrender of Palestine, he ended up imposing his authority over the remaining provinces of Sham (greater Syria).

There are clear indications in the Talmud that refer to the destruction of that Temple. These texts shed light on the fact that "the destruction of the Temple would not have come about if it had not been for the gravity of the sins committed by the children of Israel and their exacerbation, up to the point that these sins exceeded the limits tolerated by Almighty God". At least this is what the Talmud has to say about the event.

586AH

Gate of Babylon.

562BC

"The destruction of the Temple was due to the sins of the Israelites, according to the Talmud."

Two reasons for Jewish preeminence

We should draw attention here to the mistake committed by some exegates – in my opinion – as to how the word 'God' is interpreted in verse 5 of the koranic sura entitled *Al-Isra'*. According to them, those courageous serfs of God referred to in the verse are Nebuchadnezzar and his soldiers. We disagree with this opinion because God says: 'Our servants are courageous'. Nebuchadnezzar did not profess God's uniqueness and he was actually a disbeliever. How can we reason then that he did this with God's permission and that he was a devout servant of God when in fact he was not?

In my analysis, I find that on two occasions the verses relate the destruction of the children of Israel when they rose up in the land; the fact it happened twice has not materialized until now. All the signs I found after thorough research lead in this direction. The correlation of future events will corroborate this, God willing.

The death of Nebuchadnezzar

Nebuchadnezzar died a year after he destroyed the Jewish kingdom. He had led forty thousand of them to Babylon. The rest fled to Egypt and only a few remained in Palestine, according to the most reliable accounts. This put an end to the true existence of the Jews in Palestine. In the meantime, they lived for generations in Babylon as servants or slaves. They were subjugated and their situation was not to be envied. They therefore considered Nebuchadnezzar to be a curse on them and on their existence in Jerusalem.

Nebuchadnezzar.

Compilation of the Torah

Meanwhile, the Jews started to compile the Torah and the holy books they had not written in the past, approximately 700 years since the time of Moses. The Torah was not recorded in one period. There were several contributions and in no specific order. The Jews wrote different parts, each of their own account, which allowed many of them to speculate and alter whatever they were writing, or to add whatever they fancied, such as gossip, fables, interpretations and exegesis—all of it lacked proper standardisation.

Method of writing the Torah and its reading

The Jews had a specific way of sanctifying and exalting the Torah. They considered it to be their illustrious book and therefore it was not written on consecutive pages. Their scholars wrote it on one single long scroll that they then rolled up completely. It had to be unrolled for it to be read and, once the ritual was over, they had to roll it up again and keep it in a special ark. Even today they continue with this ritual. As for the printed copies of the present-day pages of the Torah, they are nothing more than a glimmer of the Holy Scriptures. It is prohibited even to touch them directly. When reading and unrolling the pages, they use a metal pointing device to manipulate the sheets. So it is not admissible in their creed to touch it in spite of the fact that the Torah was written by human hand and did not escape, as stated earlier, alterations and changes. Besides, it is mentioned in the Old Testament and the Talmud that the Torah is not the result of divine inspiration, nor even the words of Moses. These books were mixed with the Torah, as described in the Koran. *(An-Nisa', 46)*

"Mixing the Torah with other holy scriptures was widespread at the time the Torah was written, so that its authenticity was not preserved."

Torah scrolls, 15th Century.

Alterations to the Holy Scriptures

The alterations introduced by some scholars and notaries deformed canonical laws. Not even Moses or his contemporary disciples authorized this. In this context, we should bear the following factors in mind:

1. Texts in the Talmud suggest the children of Israel are allowed to subjugate, oppress and exploit through usury the whole of humanity, except the Jews.

2. The Jews are considered to be God's chosen people and they distinguish the rest as "the others", who they believe they are entitled to exploit by every possible means.

3. The Jews do not attempt to spread their faith because outsiders can only convert to Judaism on very strict terms. In addition, you are only Jewish if your mother is Jewish. Nevertheless, this subject still raises differences, even among their own kind. There are liberals and those who are extremely conservative. These do not even recognize Yemenite or African Jews as such, because they do not consider them to be the authentic

children of Israel. Today there is an agreement among the Jews that nobody can be converted to their religion. Their religion admits no adherence because it is the one belonging to God's chosen people and hence Paradise is only for them and not for anyone else.

2. Persian dominion

The Persian king Cyrus

The Jews remained enslaved in Babylonia, far from Palestine, until the year 539 BC when Cyrus, king of Persia, conquered Mesopotamia. By taking the kingdom of Babylon, he seized all its properties, including Palestine. This marked the beginning of the colossal Persian Empire.

539 BC

This king allowed the Jews who were in Babylon to return to Jerusalem—they had been forbidden to go back there during the reign of the Babylonians. After having lived for several decades in Babylon they had multiplied, but few returned to Palestine (around 42,000). The majority did not emigrate because at that time Babylon was the capital of fortune and economic well-being, a place of civilization and luxury. So the Jewish community preferred to stay there to look after their interests and fortunes.

The Babylonian Jews refuse to return to Jerusalem

Here we should reflect about the fact that only some of the Jews chose to return to Jerusalem. They claimed to be the chosen people and that the Holy Land was their land, but when they were given the opportunity to return to it, many did not do so.

Nowadays, in spite of what the Zionist entity does by preparing routes and building settlements, in addition to the incentives and facilities given to Jews wishing to emigrate to Israel, the majority of the world's Jews do not live there. Many of them live in America, others in Russia, where their numbers exceed those who live in Palestine.

The Persians conquer Babylon in 539 BC and allow the Jews to return to Palestine.

Construction of the second Temple

The orthodox Jews, who were nostalgic of their ancient history and of the time of Solomon, were immediately employed in a matter of extreme importance to them. It was the question of reconstructing the temple that had been devastated by Nebuchadnezzar. Thus, they re-built it and called it the second Temple as known and stated in universal history and in their holy books.

With their tolerance, the Persians allowed the Jews to build and considerably extend their temple. They recovered the sanctum sanctorum and all the holy things that had been preserved were installed in the Temple.

Self-government of the Jews

Granting them self-government inside Jerusalem portrayed the Persians' tolerance towards the Jews, but, as a limitation, the power that was ceded to them was concentrated in a surface area of 30 km² within Jerusalem. This was the only area in which they could exercise their self-government. A member of the community was responsible for ruling, administering justice and regulating worship. From 515 BC and for 200 years afterwards there was peace and tolerance within this small kingdom, whose inhabitants started multiplying and expanding within the boundaries of Palestine. Nevertheless, their self-government only extended as far as the Persians permitted, to prevent them from imposing their authority and exercising complete control over Palestine.

Model of the Temple as the most orthodox Jews imagined it.

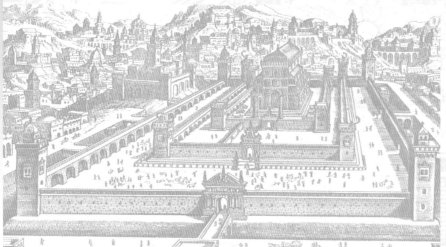

3. The Greek Conquest

Alexander the Great

332 BC

The year 332 BC marked the rise of one of the greatest figures in history—Alexander the Great, who some exegetes refer to as the Bicorn. The truth is that there are many references that indicate the veracity of this issue, in spite of some objections with regard to the existence of some statues of gods at that time. But this does not mean that those gods were precisely theirs. They would more likely be those of the people living there at that time who worshipped those gods. In any case, the existence of statues and sculptures was not prohibited either then or in the time of Solomon. They were only prohibited in the time of the Prophet of Islam.

Alexander the Great was the ruler of the Greeks. (I researched this on the Internet and found 124,000 studies about him. It is well known that his story is very dense. His victories and conquests fill both western and eastern history books). What made him most famous were his three campaigns, one of which interests us particularly. It is the one that took him to Palestine, which he conquered on his way to Persia, Mesopotamia, greater Syria and Egypt.

Alexander the Great, the most famous leader of the Greeks.

Alexander the Great in battle.

53

Nabataean civilisation

Palestine came under Greek rule, and although Greek power became fragmented after Alexander's death in the year 332 BC, the conquered regions continued under its control.

Taking advantage of the power struggle in the Greek empire, the Arab Nabataeans—the ruins of whose capital, Petra, still stand today—attacked southern Palestine, invaded and took possession of it. Their dominion lasted until the year 200 BC; that is, for nearly 100 years.

Petra, the capital of the Nabataeans, is a city carved out of the mountain rock.

The Jews come under Greek oppression

167BC

After the decline of Greek rule, the different groups that emerged to fill the power vacuum included the Seleucids, known for their religious infidelity and perversion. They were able to dominate these regions and began to strongly oppress the Jews, up to the point that their leader was forced to adore Zeus, one of the Olympic Greek gods, instead of Yaveh. The practice of pagan rites led the Jews to separate into two groups. Some followed the Greeks and were called Hellenized Jews, and others stuck to their religion and fled from the oppression of the Seleucids. These were known by the name of Maccabees, a tribute to the main tribe that remained faithful to the Hebrew religion. This tribe, the Maccabees, was headed by Judas Maccabaeus (the "hammer").

Hanukkah—the Festival of Lights

165 BC

Some time later the Greek emperor enacted the decision to stop pursuing the Jews and allowed them to practise their religion. The Hellenized Jews took advantage of this climate of tolerance to re-group. As they were allowed to enter Jerusalem again, on 25 January 164 BC, they did so and illuminated the city. That day was called the "Festival of Lights", known in Jewish history by the name of Hanukkah; it continues to be one of their most holy festivals. This is where the Jewish candelabrum comes from and since then it is one of their main symbols, in addition to the Star of David. This self-determination they were allowed, sometimes extensive, sometimes limited, remained a legacy for the descendants of Judas Maccabaeus. So power was transmitted to their successors, as they were going to be the guardians of religion. The great rabbis directed the process of self-rule, although they were subordinate to the Seleucids when it came to tax-paying.

The reign of Simon

143 BC

The emperor Demetrius II appointed a Jew named Simon as king of Jerusalem, and one of his missions was to collect taxes. After a time these taxes were revoked and permission was given to coin Jewish currency in Jerusalem. They were then granted self-rule over these regions. As a result, Simon's kingdom began to expand.

Trajan's Column.

76 BC

Expansion of the kingdom of Simon

The kingdom of Simon continued to expand until 76 BC, when it reached the sea. However, it was still subordinate to the Greeks officially, legally and politically.

63 BC

4. Roman rule

THE ROMANS IN PALESTINE

The Romans in Jerusalem

The Romans decided to take over the Greek kingdoms one by one until they reached Syria, which they occupied. From there they marched on to Jerusalem, which they occupied in the year 63 BC. There they appointed a Jewish priest named Hyrcanus as governor of Jerusalem, a position he held for 23 years.

43 BC

Herod, the king of the Jews

The Romans appointed Herod as king of the Jews, even though he did not belong to the governing Maccabee family. In his position as governor, he acted as a tyrant towards the Jews. In order to consolidate his position among them and win over more followers from their ranks, he renovated the Temple and enlarged its surface area. However, the territory of his kingdom turned into a battlefield between Romans and Persians, so that sometimes it fell into the hands of the Romans, while on other occasions it was seized by the Persians.

A fortress built near the Dead Sea by king Herod as a palace to protect his people from Cleopatra. Some 960 Jews committed suicide there to avoid being captured by the Romans.

Cleopatra visits Jerusalem

In the year 34 BC, Herod managed to drive out the Persians and consolidate his dominion over these areas. His reign enjoyed great prosperity and safety. Cleopatra's passage through the territory of Herod on her way back from Mesopotamia to Egypt was very important for future relations between Rome and Egypt.

34 BC

MARY AND JESUS

The Birth of Mary

Mary was born in 15 BC and was educated under the protection of Zacharias, who was one of the priests of the children of Israel under the rule of Herod.

15 BC

John The Baptist

Four years before the birth of Christ and John, Herod, the king of the Jews died and the Jewish state was divided among Herod's three children, with no self-government (as previously indicated, the Jews only had an independent government in Palestine with David and Solomon). Four years later Christ was born and, three months before that, John the Baptist was born. He became more famous than Christ among the Jews because he was the son of their prophet Zacharias. He was later known as John the Baptist because he took them to the River Jordan where he baptised them, thus purifying them from their sins. In Arabic this is termed *Al-Basfi Al-mi'madan,* an important Christian sacrament which we will comment on below.

4 BC

The Church of the Nativity in Bethlehem where Christ is thought to have been born.

THE NATIVITY – CHRIST

The birth of Christ

Jesus was born by divine miracle and, in spite of the miracle, the majority of the Jews looked upon it initially with scepticism, accusing his mother of adultery and slandering her. Jesus began his mission by calling the Israelites to turn back to God and showing them the miracles that supported his message.

However, the Jews reacted by accusing him of sorcery due to their un-gratefulness and arrogance.

God sent Jesus to the children of Israel, in addition to Zacharias and John, so that together they could lead the misguided Israelites back to God.

Supremacy of the Romans

AD 6

Power passed from Herod's son to direct rule by the Romans who abol-ished Jewish self-government, although the Jews were allowed to retain control of affairs relating to their judiciary and religion.

The Nativity.

The government of Pontius Pilate

Pontius Pilate assumed power in Judea although he was a non-Jewish Roman. Serious events took place under his rule. Pilate was in power during the era of three prophets (Zacharias, John and Jesus) but the Jews did not recognize Jesus as a prophet and considered Zacharias and John to be high priests.

AD 26

The Roman leaders.

Herod, the governor of Gallilee, wanted to marry his brother's daughter because of her great beauty, but the marriage was illegal under Jewish law. He requested authorization from Zacharias and John to celebrate this marriage. John's response was that he was going to announce it to the people. So Herod assembled them in the Temple and John addressed them there, but, instead of announcing the forthcoming wedding, he flatly declared the prohibition of any such marriage, and that whoever broke this law would be declared unfaithful and sentenced to death. Herod was left disconcerted in view of such a declaration, especially as he boasted about his practice of the Jewish religion, helping the Jews and respecting their holy traditions. In addition he was in favour of what the Jews said about these matters. However, when he heard John's announcement, he was deeply disappointed.

John's murder

Herod's niece wanted to seduce her uncle. She danced before him, made

Unique ancient drawing
of the proposed Temple,
as imagined by the
Jews.

him drink wine until he became drunk and incited him to murder John.
She did not stop until, still under the effects of his drunkenness, he
agreed to his execution. Later on he ordered Zacharias to be murdered, as
related in a well-known story. So, the libertine beheaded two of the Israelites' great prophets before the Jews' passiveness and indifference.

Jesus

So only Jesus was left out of the three prophets. He began to preach, travelling around without a fixed abode. This is why he was called the Messi-
ah. He began to fight against such abominations as selling doves, betting
and auctioning inside the Temple.

In a known report, Jesus entered the Temple by surprise and began to
turn the betting tables over and flog the merchants for profaning that
holy place. Besides, he was one of the known speakers at the Temple. This
is how Jewish religion began to change, by eliminating whatever was un-
desirable.

Jewish religion was a strict religion, full of restriction and punishment
that God had imposed on sinful Israelites because of their injustice, obsti-
nacy and infidelity. In fact, it made them suffer and Jesus came to quash
some of these restrictions and ties. This annoyed the Jewish priests, who

envied the place he had earned in people's hearts. He had diverted toward his own work the attention that the people had paid them. This fact enraged them and they started plotting against him.

Ascension of Christ

Jesus had turned 33 and the Jewish high priests' hatred of him had reached its zenith, so all they could do was to pass a decree by which they presented Jesus before the hearing as a prelude to his death penalty.

Pilate agreed to this. They then asked him to issue an order for his arrest, because, as we have mentioned before, both authority and power were in the hands of the Romans, whereas the judiciary was in Jewish hands. Pilate sent his soldiers to look for him. In this respect the Jews and Romans conspired against Jesus. They began to search everywhere for him and there are plenty of legends and tales in this regard, as well as confusion and alteration.

In short, Jesus ascended up to God after having asked his disciples for one of them to sacrifice himself for Him. A young man stepped forward to accept the sacrifice. He was then transformed by God into the figure of Jesus in front of their very eyes, by way of a miracle of the type they had never seen before. In spite of not being sure that it was the person they were looking for, they captured that young man. Many people knew that he was not Jesus, whereas others claimed the opposite. But, in the end, they seized him and placed a crown of thorns on his head. Then they put him on trial. The priests started to pass sentence on him and, as he had been a disciple of Jesus, he was brilliant in his replies and in quashing their claims. So they could not cope with him, but, in spite of this, sentenced him to death by crucifixion. They made him carry a heavy cross along a route known today by Christians as the Via Crucis. They led him along, but he had to stop fourteen times in different places to rest from so much fatigue. Today these places are known as the Stations of the Cross and are considered to be holy places. A sacred symbol has been erected at each of them.

When they celebrate Easter in April, they repeat the whole scene, and have a person who bears a crown of thorns and carries a cross stopping at those 14 stations to venerate them, until the last station is reached and Jesus' lookalike is crucified.

Scenes of the Crucifixion of Jesus' double.

"The priests of Jerusalem persecuted the early Christians. They were the ones who instigated the crucifixion of Jesus' disciples."

Contrary to the claims that allude to Jesus' crucifixion, the Koran affirms that neither did they kill Jesus nor crucify Him but they thought it was Him. Some of them even disagreed and doubted about it. They had no alternative than to continue with the speculation. God had actually caused Him to ascend into heaven. *(An-Nisa', 157-159)*

Persecution of the Christians

The Jews persecuted the followers of Christ, to such an extent that both his followers and disciples had to hide or flee Jerusalem. Some took refuge in Rome and secretly began the calling to the Christian faith. The Gospel had still not been written, although it was completed within 260 years. In that era, there was more than one version of the Gospel. Some mentioned the actual crucifixion of Jesus. On the other hand, others alluded to events that involved Jesus twenty years after the date of the Crucifixion.

The Jews continued to persecute the Christians, murdering any of them they found. These circumstances contributed to the diffusion of false accounts and legends against the Jews.

Scenes of the Crucifixion of Jesus' double and his followers.

AD 36

DISPERSION OF THE JEWS

The Judaeo-Christian struggle

Three years after the ascension of Christ, Pontius Pilate died. The new Roman emperor allowed the descendants of Herod to return to self-government, providing they paid taxes. So the Jews began to recover under Roman rule but the Jewish kingdom continued to depend on the Romans. Jesus' disciples secretly proceeded with their mission and sometimes even dared to appear in the Temple only to preach and then flee. A fierce struggle began between them and the Jews inside and out of Palestine. The Jews began to drive out of Palestine any Christian detainee. Peter was among those who fled. He went to Rome, where he began to launch secret Christian groups. Peter concentrated his mission on the Jews located in Rome and its surroundings. There was also a man among Christ's disciples called Paul, who urged people to adopt the Christian faith. He directed his efforts both at the Jews and the pagans. Paul introduced numerous philosophical terms in his discourse on Christianity, therefore mixing philosophy with religiousness, and many Christian terms became philosophical ones. This was how the idea arose that consisted of considering Jesus to be God. Afterwards it was said that he is the Son of God.

In this regard many legends appeared that tell how Jesus abandoned his tomb and addressed young people by saying: "I am the son of God".

No version of the Gospel quotes Jesus as having said, "I am the son of God". This sentence was added later. The only reference that exists in the Gospel is, "We are (the family) of God", and there is no objection to this expression, as it can even be found in Islam and means that God is our protector, in the sense of depending on God, and our provider. Therefore "family" does not mean "children", as stated in their translation.

When the emperor Nero discovered the Christians' secret movements, he started searching for them and managed to capture Peter and Paul. He ordered them to be condemned to death, although their followers continued preaching their faith but, admiring amongst other things the beauty of the statues in Rome, they adopted their own icons of Jesus and Mary.

"The Gospel does not contain any text alluding to Christ having said of himself: 'I am the son of God.'"

The Christians practise their religion secretly in Europe.

Revolt of the Jews

66 AD

Finally, the Jews revolted against the Romans in Jerusalem, immediately after which the emperor ordered it to be besieged. The Romans took four years to conquer it. The emperor appointed one of his sons, Vespasian, as the military commander in Palestine. Together with his assistant commanders, he was to put an end to the revolt of the Jews. That was in the year AD 66, but neither did he manage to conquer the city nor suppress the revolt.

Illustrated page from the Old Testament.

The destruction of Jerusalem

70 AD

Four years later Titus the son of Vespasian managed to enter Jerusalem after much difficulty. The long siege of Jerusalem discredited the strength and power of the Roman Empire. In order to reaffirm the greatness of Rome, Titus ordered the Temple to be destroyed and "to leave no stone unturned", according to the Jewish version. Then he took Jews to be sold as slaves in Rome. This was the beginning of the Jewish diaspora in Europe.

Aelia Capitolina and the destruction of the Temple

The Jews who stayed in Palestine were reunified under the command of
Simon bar Kochba, a leading figure in Jewish history, and rose up against
the Roman Empire. Bar Kochba managed to control a fortress and became entrenched there. But, in the course of three years, the Roman emperor Hadrian managed to put down the revolt. He destroyed everything
the Jews had built and erased every Jewish vestige in the area. Then he ordered a new city to be built on top of the rubble of the Jewish sites. The
new citadel was to be called Aelia Capitolina. He also had a stronghold
built on the site of the Bar Kochba fortress known today by the Arabs as
"the Jewish ruin" because the emperor had reduced the place to a heap of
rubble.

Hadrian ordered the construction of Roman temples. This is how a magnificent temple for the Roman god Jupiter was built on the site of the
Jewish Temple. Jerusalem was now known by its new name, Aelia, in
place of the former Yerushalayim. It was known by this name during the
time of the Muslims. And this is how it appears in historical references.

Jerusalem, a city forbidden to Jews

After completely sacking Jerusalem, the Roman emperor issued a decree
prohibiting Jews to enter. This prohibition remained in force for 200
years, that is, up to the arrival of the Roman emperor Aurelian, who went
back to allowing them into the city to worship.

The Diaspora

By that time the Jews were spreading throughout the world, as they were
barred from remaining in Palestine. This region enjoyed tranquillity and
stability for a long time, with the exception of the defeats of Syria and
Egypt by queen Zenobia of Palmyra. This queen became famous, among
other things, for erecting beautiful monuments and other buildings, the
vestiges of which are still standing today. However, her rule in Palestine
lasted only 3 years.

132 AD

"Yom Kippur" or the Day of
Atonement. Festival of
pardon. The Saturday of
Saturdays is the ninth day of
October in the Jewish
calendar. It is a day of
fasting and of penance,
of almsgiving and reading
the Torah.

AD 324

BYZANTINE–CHRISTIAN EMPIRE

Emperor Constantine embraces Christianity

A very important event happened that year in Rome: the Roman emperor Constantine embraced Christianity after having studied philosophy, religion and theology. However Constantine did not break totally with his pagan ideas but adapted them to his new beliefs, incorporating them into Christianity. Many investigators attribute the majority of practices in Christianity to the Constantine era.

Constantine succeeded in dominating the Byzantine dynasty whose capital was Constantinople, present-day Istanbul, uniting it with Rome and also Syria and Palestine. The emperor's mother, who also became a Christian, visited Jerusalem and arranged for the Church of the Holy Sepulchre to be built. This church does not therefore date from the time of Christ, as it was built 324 years later. It was constructed on the site where Christ's double was crucified.

"King Constantine persecuted the Jews and barred their entry into Jerusalem."

Augustine, one of the first preachers of Christianity.

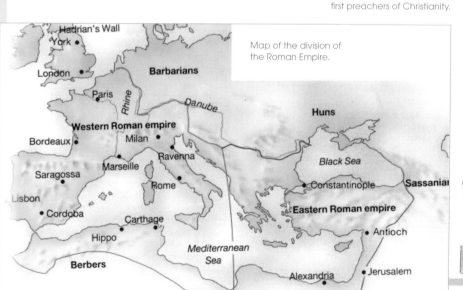

Map of the division of the Roman Empire.

Constantine embraces
Christianity and
incorporates the
cross into his flag.

Among the decisions taken by Constantine, there was one by which the Jews
were again forbidden to enter Jerusalem. They were not well treated by the
new emperor, a trend followed by his successors until the arrival of Julian.
He renounced Christianity and adopted Judaism. As a result, he sought to
restore sacred Jewish property and rebuild the Jewish Temple that had been
twice destroyed, but ended up deciding to turn it into a temple to Jupiter.
Nevertheless, events prevented him from carrying out his design.

Division of the empire and Heraclius' reign
The struggle between Jews and Christians continued until AD 395 when
the Roman Empire was divided into Western and Eastern (Byzantine)
parts, with Rome as capital of the Western empire and Byzantium as capital of the Eastern Empire. Heraclius was the emperor of the Byzantine
empire, which included Palestine and Syria. When the Prophet Muhammad was born, the situation had not changed—Palestine continued under Byzantine rule and there was no prominent presence of Jews in
Jerusalem. The Christians ruled throughout that region.

AD 395

Heraclius' dream
The Byzantine kings inherited the power and all of them adopted the nick-
name of Heraclius. History tells us that Heraclius had a dream which sages
were called on to interpret. It concerned "one of the circumcised kings" seizing his land. Heraclius asked: "Who are the circumcised ones?" and they

replied: "We do not know anybody other than the Israelites who practise circumcision". However, at that time the Jews had no power to take decisions in either Jerusalem or Palestine. They lived in groups scattered across the country and lacked any political or military influence, in spite of the conversion to Judaism of some Roman kings such as Julian, as those who succeeded him returned to Christianity. Islam, as predicated by the Prophet Muhammad, was born within this socio-political climate.

5. The advent of Islam and the era of the prophet Muhammad

The birth of the Prophet

AD 571

In the year AD 571 the Prophet Muhammad was born while Palestine continued under Byzantine rule. At the age of 40, in the year 610-611, he received the prophetic call to Islam. The Jews in Palestine were still under the rule of the Byzantine Romans and lacked both a state and any real entity. They were no more than a debilitated minority.

The Persians drive the Byzantines out of Jerusalem

AD 614

That year the Persians conquered Palestine under the command of their king Chosroes II. They managed to dominate Palestine and to drive the Byzantine Christians out. They took over the city and destroyed the Church of the Holy Sepulchre, stripping it of its treasures. The Jews took part in this battle alongside the Persians, therefore taking revenge for what the Christians had done to them. In this slaughter, nearly 60,000 Byzantine Christians lost their lives. They also took part in the destruction of the Holy Sepulchre and many other churches, not only in Jerusalem but also beyond it. The Jews considered Christianity to be a deviation of Judaism and an apostasy.

Actually the Jews were seeking to obtain favours from the Persians in order to establish a state in Palestine or at least in Jerusalem. Nevertheless, contrary to what they thought, the Persians refused and they even prohibited such a project and imposed severe taxes on them.

The Koran refers to the defeat of the Byzantines in verses 1-5 of sura *Ar-*

"The Palestinian Jews joined the Persians in the slaughter of the Christians in Palestine and destroyed their churches, as they believed Christianity was an apostatical deviation of Judaism."

Rum. In them, the Koran reveals that, after the defeat, the Byzantines were going to conquer the Persians within a few years (between 3 and 9).

This was very strange news since the Persians had colossal power. Their empire was the largest in the world. How could they be defeated by the weak Byzantines? The Arab pagans of Quraysh took advantage of this to mock the Koran, contradicting it as much as they could. So Abu-Bakr placed a bet—before betting was prohibited—for 100 camels that this event was going to happen within 9 years. The bet was accepted.

AD 620

The ascension

This event draws the greatest attention in the history of Islam towards the position of Jerusalem and its spiritual importance for Muslims. The direct ascension of the Prophet Muhammad from Mecca to heaven would have been possible for God but he wanted it to take place from Jerusalem.

Al-Isra', 1 recounts that the Prophet went there by night and then ascended into the heavens. It was the greatest event in his life since the time he had received the message. That miraculous trip drew the attention of Muslims to the specificity of Jerusalem and its extraordinary divine acclaim. God resurrected and assembled the prophets and messengers in the oratory (Mosque) of Jerusalem so that Muhammad could lead the prayer with them.

Because of its purity, nobility, distinction and highest standing, and because it was the source of inspiration and the land of messages, God chose the Mosque of Jerusalem to resurrect that enormous number of prophets and messengers and to assemble them for the first time for the greatest prayer in history.

The Kaaba in Mecca.

Emigration of Muslims from Mecca to Medina

The Hegira took place in the year AD 622. This was when the Prophet fled, together with his coreligionists, to Medina, where the first small state of Islam was born.

AD 622

The Byzantines recover Jerusalem

Five years after the Hegira, or, seven years after the defeat of the Byzantines, Heraclius mustered a great army. They attacked the Persians in Palestine and defeated them. Strangely enough, this time the Jews sided with the Christians in their battle against the Persians after the latter had not fulfilled their promises to give them authority in Palestine. The defeat of the Persians was complete and God's announcement in the Koran was fulfilled in less than nine years.

AH 5
AD 627

The Mosque of the Prophet, Medina.

"The Christians took revenge on the Jews and killed them in Jerusalem. Those who could fled from Palestine."

Byzantine persecution of the Jews

In spite of assurances, the Christian clergy intervened to remind the Byzantines how the Jews had slaughtered them when they had fought alongside the Persians, and taken part in destroying churches and holy places. They prevailed over Heraclius, urging him to kill the Jews instead of granting them pardon.

Heraclius agreed to their wishes and broke the promises he had given the Jews. The Christians embarked on an enormous massacre, killing an endless number of Jews. Many of them fled the land, while some of them hid in Palestine. There was no mention that any of them stayed in the Holy Land.

AH 6
AD 628

The invitation for Heraclius to embrace Islam

Heraclius entered Jerusalem triumphantly and celebrated his victory on a grand scale. That was when he received a missive from the Prophet Muhammad that read: "From Muhammad, messenger of God, to the great Heraclius of Byzantium. Become a Muslim, otherwise you will bear the sin of the Arians".

This message made a tremendous impact on Heraclius.

He was a knowledgeable priest of Christianity, and the signs of this awaited prophet are in the Gospel and Holy Scriptures. What was not expected was that he should appear from among the Arab race in the Arabian Peninsula. He was on the verge of embracing Islam; he even urged priests to the Islamic faith in the course of an essay. Finally they refused and insisted on putting this new religion to an end. Heraclius' position was extremely sensitive—he had found the truth and committed it to his heart. However, he was afraid that, by publicizing his conversion, he would lose his kingdom and thus continued with his Christian faith. He sent a message to the Prophet, the contents of which explained his conversion to Islam, although this was not true.

When the Prophet received the information, he said: "He lied. He is more seduced by power and he clings to it".

AH 7
AD 629

The battle of Khaybar

That year the battle of Khaybar took place in Arabia between Muslims and Jews. It was the result of numerous battles between Muslims and Jews in Medina. Previously, the Prophet had already conquered Bani-Nadhir, Bani-Qaynaqa' and Bani-Quraydha. The reason for all these campaigns was the successive Jewish disloyalties that caused confrontations between Muslims and Jews. They had fled from Yathrib (Medina) to gather in Khaybar. Their conspiracies against the Prophet multiplied, but they were no longer in a position to act treacherously against the Muslims and default on all the agreements and pacts they had established with the Prophet in Medina. Their greatest perfidy was at the battle of the Allies (Al-Ahzab) between pagans and Muslims.

The Prophet waited until after the Al-Hudaybiyyah Treaty, by which he was reconciled with the Quraysh. Having quelled that source of conflict, he could then concentrate on the matter of the Jews. He assembled his companions and decided to attack them in Khaybar. A great battle was fought there and the Jews were defeated. However, they ended up begging the Prophet to let them continue living and farming the land, in exchange for delivering part of their harvest to him. Muhammad agreed and most of them remained under Muslim rule, whereas others emigrated to Palestine.

The situation for these people was soon to change. The era of 'Umar Ibn al-Khattab had hardly begun when they renewed their perfidy and violated their treaties. They deliberately killed a Muslim and, faced with this, 'Umar took the wise and correct decision to throw them out of Medina and drive them out of the Arabian Peninsula forever. They first emigrated to Sinai, but 'Umar also drove them out of there. Then they went to Palestine where they reunited.

Meanwhile, clashes between the Muslims and the Byzantines had broken out, continuing up to the campaign of Mu'tah (Jordan) where the Muslims were unable to gain victory. Instead, they staged a tactical retreat under the command of Khalid Ibn al-Walid and the remant of his forces, in what was considered to be a magnificent manoeuvre.

> **"The Jews of Medina violated their treaties with the Muslims several times until 'Umar Ibn al-Khattab drove them out of the Arabian Peninsula. How, then, can anyone believe in their treaties today?"**

The first Muslim wars, as illustrated by a Persian artist.

The death of the Prophet

AH 11
AD 633

It was in 633 that the Prophet Muhammad died. His death was the pretext for an Arab group that had just converted to Islam to refuse to pay their taxes and apostatize the Islamic creed. Abu Bakr, the Prophet's first successor, managed to control the situation and restore stability to the Arabian Peninsula. He then mobilized his armies and marched on Persia and Byzantium in the course of a single campaign. It was one of the greatest decisions in history—the young state had declared war on the contemporary world's two largest empires.

A page of the Koran.

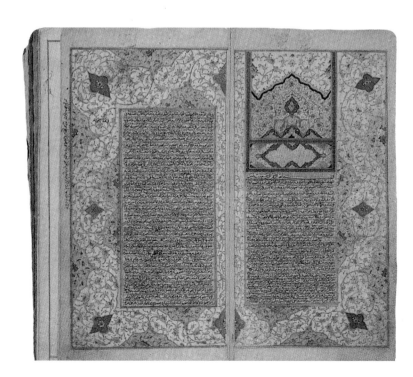

PART TWO
Palestine in the Islamic era

PART TWO
Palestine in the Islamic era

CHAPTER ONE
The period of the Caliphs

1. The Islamic conquest of Syria

2. The conquest of Jerusalem

The period of the Caliphs

1. The Islamic conquest of Syria

AH 13
AD 634

The Battle of Ajnadeen

Abu Bakr ordered Abu 'Ubayda to go to Syria. Then he realized the need for reinforcements so he sent Khalid Ibn al-Walid, who was fighting on the Persian front, to help him.

He carried out an extraordinary 5-day march from Mesopotamia during which he crossed a region of semi-desert in an inimitable and singular military exploit that became famous in Muslim history.

Khalid Ibn al-Walid joins the battle

Khalid Ibn al-Walid ordered the Muslim army to fight four battles, and then he addressed them saying: "This is one of God's days that does not suit either scorn or injustice. Be loyal in your fight and dedicate your prayers to God, as today is the gateway to the future".

Fighting broke out between Muslims and Byzantines which culminated in a battle that took place to the southeast of Jerusalem in the year AD 634, the 13th year of the Hegira. It was the battle of Ajnadeen, the first major battle in the Abu Bakr era. Among those who took part was the sublime companion of the Prophet Mu'adh Ibn Jabal. It was he who addressed the Muslims at the beginning of the battle by saying: "Muslims, bequeath your lives to God because, if you defeat them today, this land will be yours, for Islam, forever!"

Mu'adh was not wrong since the Muslims won a great victory and the conquests took place in Syria.

That same year, in the month of Jumada al-Ula, Abu-Bakr died and was succeeded by 'Umar Ibn al-Khattab who continued directing the campaigns in Syria, Mesopotamia and Persia from Medina.

AH 14
AD 635

The battle of the Yarmuk

Damascus was conquered after a four-month-long battle named after the river Yarmuk, where it took place. This was followed by the fall of Baalbek, in Lebanon, and then Homs, in Syria. The conquests continued until 12 August 636—5 Rajab of the year AH 15—when the great battle of Yarmuk took place. Two hundred thousand Byzantine cavalrymen were mobilized to attack the Muslims. They were aware of the danger. The

> "Khalid proposed that the armies should join together as one and be led in turn each day by one of his commanding officers."

Byzantine army was magnificent and well equipped, but nevertheless the enormous conviction and fervent faith of the Muslims were key in facing that large, well-provisioned army.

Rout of the Byzantines

The battle was fought close to a cliff. Khalid Ibn al-Walid took advantage of the situation and started pushing the Byzantine army towards the abyss, besieging it so that, whenever one member of its army fell, they dragged ten more down. This is how 80,000 of them ended up, falling down the cliff face, besides the 50,000 who died in the fighting. In total, their casualties amounted to 130,000. The Byzantines had never lost so many forces as in the battle of Yarmuk. Meanwhile, on the Muslim side, some 3,000 fell out of a total of 36,000 soldiers. This completed the greatest Muslim victory that had ever taken place—a memorable military miracle.

Then Amr Ibnu-l-As and his army set off towards Jerusalem and en route they seized Gaza, Nablus, Lidda and Jaffa, among others cities. The Byzantines then fortified themselves in Jerusalem.

The battle between the Muslims and Byzantines at Yarmuk.

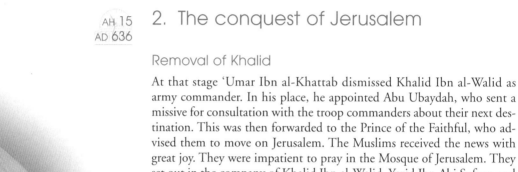

AH 15
AD 636

2. The conquest of Jerusalem

Removal of Khalid

At that stage 'Umar Ibn al-Khattab dismissed Khalid Ibn al-Walid as army commander. In his place, he appointed Abu Ubaydah, who sent a missive for consultation with the troop commanders about their next destination. This was then forwarded to the Prince of the Faithful, who advised them to move on Jerusalem. The Muslims received the news with great joy. They were impatient to pray in the Mosque of Jerusalem. They set out in the company of Khalid Ibn al-Walid, Yazid Ibn Abi Sufyan and Sharjil Ibn Husna, among other great companions of the Prophet. The siege began at the walls of Jerusalem; then the two armies became locked in combat. For ten days, the Byzantines resisted, defying death and defending their last bastion on Syrian soil. Contrary to the Jews, the Byzantines showed courage and firmness in their position, but they were unable to hold out against the might of the Islamic onslaught.

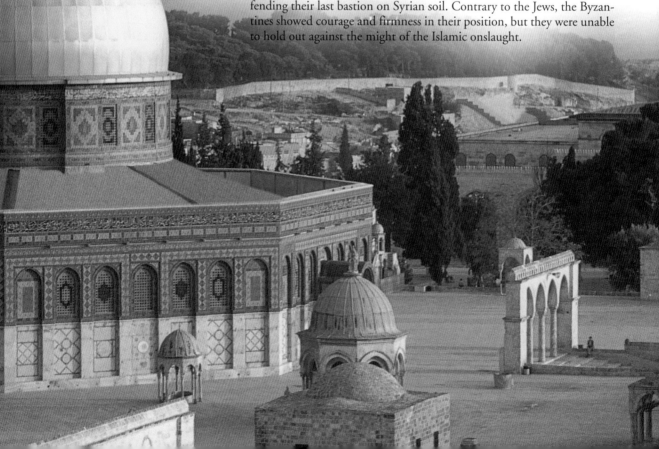

Abu 'Ubaydah reaches Jerusalem

On the eleventh day, Abu 'Ubaydah 'Amir Ibn al-Jarrah arrived. When they saw him, the Muslims were ecstatic and passionately intoned the short prayer: "God is the greatest; he terrifies the hearts of the Byzantines and strikes them with fear". Never before had they heard anything like this. The Byzantines assumed the Prince of the Faithful himself was leading the conquest. They then informed the patriarch about it. He said: "I swear on the Gospel that, if their prince is here, it signals your destruction". On hearing such words, they were surprised and asked: "How can this be?" The patriarch answered: "From the knowledge we have of prophesy, he who conquers the length and breadth of the land, including Palestine, is the dark, tall man, whose eyes have a very black iris and a very white cornea. If he has come, there will no be way to fight him, so surrender yourselves to him".

This is how 'Umar Ibn al-Khattab described it. The patriarch appeared personally before the Muslims to meet the Prince of the Faithful, thinking it was 'Umar. When he realized it was not, he went back to his people and told them to continue fighting.

The period of the Caliphs (the Prophet's successors)
The siege of Jerusalem

The siege took the Muslims a long time and the conquest turned out to be complicated, as it lasted four months. A dreadful shortage forced the patriarch to ask the Muslims by means of messengers for information about their Emir in Medina, and this they complied with. The description coincided with what was written in their Holy Scriptures. He therefore requested to negotiate with the leader of the Islamic army. When he was before him he asked: "Why do you want to conquer this holy land? Whoever aspires to it is exposed to God's imminent rage and to death". Abu 'Ubaydah replied: "It is a blessed land. Our Prophet ascended into heaven from it. It is the origin of the prophets and their tombs are there. We are more entitled to it than you and we will fight for it until God grants it to us as he has done with other lands". The patriarch asked him: "What do you want of us?" "One of three things", replied Abu 'Ubaydah: either Islam (submission), conciliation and tribute, or battle. The patriarch chose conciliation, but he laid down a condition, which was that nobody was to enter Jerusalem before the Prince of the Faithful, 'Umar Ibn al-Khattab.

"God gave victory to the Muslims at Yarmuk. They numbered 36,000, against an enemy of 200,000, of whom 130,000 were killed."

83

'Umar in Jerusalem

Abu 'Ubaydah sent the news to 'Umar and the latter replied: "I'm on my way". He left Medina for Palestine on a journey that would become proverbial in kingly ethics

He rode on camelback and was accompanied by just one servant. They took turns riding it when, owing to his status, he could have been escorted by a sumptuous entourage that would have made the ground tremble under the horses' hooves. However, he wanted to set before the highland kings an example of humility and of giving glory to God alone.

On reaching Jerusalem, it was his servant's turn to ride the camel, but he wanted to give precedence to 'Umar so that the people could see him. 'Umar refused and entered Jerusalem on foot, while the servant rode the camel. When the Muslims saw him, they recited the short prayers that refer to God's absolute greatness and his uniqueness. 'Umar was acclaimed on a mountain that was later called "the Mountain of the Sublime". He approached the army wearing modest, threadbare clothes. From the walls of Jerusalem, the Christians were amazed to see such a strange spectacle—their expressions and gestures belied their amazement that the figure could be the leader of those well equipped armies.

On reaching the ford of a river full of clay, the servant tried to get 'Umar to ride the camel, to prevent the damp clay from touching his clothes, but 'Umar ordered him to ride on. The servant obeyed and took the reins of the animal, leading it into the ford. He took off his shoes, carried them and continued on foot under the astonished gaze of the people. Abu 'Ubaydah could not contain himself at this show of humility and hurried to 'Umar's side saying: "Prince of the Faithful! Today you have performed a magnificent deed before the people, perhaps you might ...?" 'Umar slapped him on the chest and criticized him saying: "I wish someone other than you, Abu 'Ubaydah, had said this. We were a humiliated people and God honoured us with Islam. We were weak, and he gave us strength".

When the patriarch saw the scene, he felt true admiration and Islam grew in stature in his heart. He then said to his people that nobody in the world would ever be able to stand up to these people. He advised them to surrender in order to be saved and he signed a treaty with the Muslims. 'Umar, for his part, offered them safety in Jerusalem and protection for their beliefs, their churches and their holy places, forbidding them to be destroyed or desecrated. Jerusalem was thus exposed to the most merciful and compassionate conqueror, after a long history of conquerors who had completely destroyed the city and slaughtered its inhabitants.

The Omariya Treaty

Muslims and Christians signed a treaty called "The Omariya Treaty", which is still housed in the Church of the Holy Sepulchre in Jerusalem. The contents state:

In the name of God, the merciful, the compassionate. This is the peace that the servant of God, 'Umar Ibn al-Khattab has granted to the people of Aelia for their safety: He grants them safety for themselves, their belongings, their churches and crosses, their sick and healthy and all their co-religionists. Their churches shall not be used as residences and shall not be demolished; nothing shall be damaged in them or their surroundings, nor shall their crosses be removed or any of their property removed. Equally, they shall not be harassed because of their religion, and none of them shall be harmed. No Jew will be allowed to live with them in Aelia.

The people of Aelia shall pay taxes like other city dwellers. They shall also drive Byzantines and thieves out from Aelia.

Those who leave shall have safe passage for themselves and their belongings until they reach a safe destination, and anyone who wants to stay shall be protected and, like the inhabitants of Aelia, shall pay taxes.

Those who prefer to leave with the Byzantines and renounce their churches and crosses, shall leave unharmed, until they reach a place of safety.

Whoever wants to stay, shall pay the same tax as the inhabitants of Aelia and whoever wishes to leave with the Byzantines may do so. Those who want to return to their families can go. No tax shall be collected from them until they gather in their harvest.

As stated in this contract, God's legacy and the protection treaty for his Prophet, his successors and the believers, shall abide as long as the Christians pay their due taxes.

It was witnessed and signed by Khalid Ibn al-Walid, Amr Ibn al-'As, Abd ar-Rahman Ibn 'Auf, and Mu'awiyah Ibn Abi Sufyan.

Jews were forbidden to enter Jerusalem. Actually, they were not there before the conquest. The Christians requested that prohibition and 'Umar accepted it.

After signing the treaty, the gates of Jerusalem were opened to 'Umar and he entered along a promenade that led him up to the Church of the Holy

Sepulchre. There, the muezzin gave the call to prayer when 'Umar was inside. Then the patriarch said to him: "Pray". 'Umar said he wouldn't because, if he were to do so, the Muslims would take the church later on arguing that 'Umar had been praying there.

'Umar gave the world examples of tolerance and generosity when in a position of strength, which he could have used to leave no stone unturned if he had wished. Nobody would have objected, nor would they have reproached him. It was the greatness of Islam that shone in his spirit and was reflected in his ethics, although he was a firm, tenacious man known for his courage and severity.

'Umar cleans the "Mosque" of Jerusalem

'Umar continued walking in search of the second place of worship to God in the whole history of Jerusalem. On not finding it, he asked the patriarch, who showed him the way. When he arrived, he saw how it had been turned into a rubbish dump. 'Umar rolled up his sleeves and started sweeping and cleaning the mosque. As soon as they saw him, the Muslims, the army generals and the soldiers themselves joined him and started cleaning the place. Even his closest companions took part.

Then 'Umar took off his cloak, prayed on it and left it there. It was the first prayer of the Muslims in the mosque of

Jerusalem.

Jerusalem after the Prophet Muhammad. He made two prostrations. During the first one he read the sura *Sad* which talks about David. In the second, he read the sura, *al-Isra'*, in honour of that place. The first person after him to call to prayer was Bilal, the Prophet's muezzin, who had not returned to call to prayer since his death, except on one occasion.

'Umar immediately ordered the mosque to be restored and to pay homage to that place after having fallen derelict. The Muslims worked hard to build it out of wood to ac-

The Umayyad Mosque of Damascus.

commodate a congregation of 3,000 people. They then started praying in this holy place. That was how Jerusalem was conquered and how the great status of its mosque was restored after the affront committed by the Christians.

Mu'awiyah, governor of Syria

AH 18
AD 639

That year the plague of Emmaus spread across Palestine. It was the greatest epidemic to affect the region and caused the death of 18,000 people, including a great number of Muslims. This was the time when Abu 'Ubaydah appointed a young man to be the governor of Syria to replace himself. That young man was one of the wiliest of Arabs. He was called Mu'awiyah Ibn Abi Sufyan and was the first governor of Syria to rule over Palestine, Jordan, the Lebanon and Syria proper. He ruled there for 20 years until he became a caliph and, from then on, he ruled there for another 20 years. That was 40 years without any disorder, whereas in neighbouring countries, unrest was continuous—not even Medina was spared turmoil. When Mu'awiyah was once asked: "How did you manage to keep the people at ease when the whole country was in turmoil?", he answered with his famous phrase: "There is a hair between the people and I; if they stretch it, I slacken it and, if they slacken it, I stretch it". This policy was later known as "the Mu'awiyah hair".

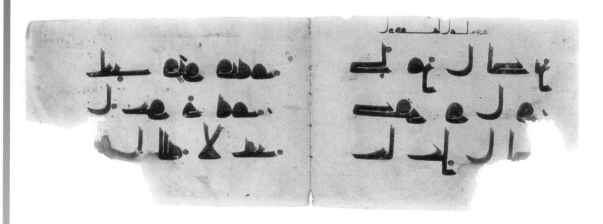

A copy of the Koran that
dates back to the third
century of the Hegira.

AH 20
AD 641

The conquest of Egypt and the prosperity of Jerusalem

Amr Ibn al-'As left Palestine and marched on Egypt. He conquered the country and its inhabitants embraced Islam en masse, as had happened previously in Syria. Islam continued to spread and its territories enjoyed great prosperity. Culture bloomed in Syria and the civilization that flourished was based on the foundations of urbanization, culture, the arts, literature and translation. It became one of the world's centres of knowledge. Some of the Prophet's companions visited Jerusalem and from there the son of 'Umar, for example, entered into a state of consecration to comply with the tenets of pilgrimage to the sacred territory of Mecca. With this gesture he magnified the status of the city and gave credit to its condition. There, civilization reached its zenith and became a centre for culture and learning.

PART TWO
Palestine in the Islamic era

CHAPTER TWO
The Umayyad and Abbasid periods

The Umayyad and Abbasid periods

1. The Umayyad period (AH 40–132, AD 660–750)

AH 65
AD 685

Abdul Malik builds the Mosque of Jerusalem (Al-Aqsa)

'Abdul Malik started the complete reconstruction of the Mosque of Jerusalem adding an enormous building to the Dome of the Rock. He went as far as allocating the tax collection for seven years in Egypt, but he died before seeing it rebuilt. His son, Al-Walid Ibn 'Abdul Malik, took over to give continuity to the ongoing development in the territories of greater Syria (Ash-Sham).

Sulayman Ibn Abdul Malik builds the town of Ramallah

AH 67
AD 687

Later on, Sulayman Ibn 'Abdul Malik assumed power and founded the town of Ramallah, where building work soon got under way. For Muslims, as well as for the rest of the world, Jerusalem and Palestine had reached the pinnacle of civilization and its grandeur warranted ongoing expansion. This was made possible by the efforts of Muslims at the holy places in Syria. Anyone who cares to review the history of the area will see how often Jerusalem and the Jews' sacred properties had previously been desecrated, whereas under Muslim rule no such thing happened in the long passage of time. An unbiased, objective perusal will reveal such

Minaret of the White Mosque at Ramallah.

Umayyad coin.

truths and the facts of life in the Muslim community. These events were written and chronicled in Western records, even before they were documented in the Arabic script. It remains for everyone to open their eyes to the truth.

After all that, what rights do Jews have to Palestine? Where is the proof that they did actually live in the Holy Land, and that they were its first inhabitants? By scrutinizing history, we find no more than some passing emigrations that ended up with expulsion, slaughter or dispersion from everywhere in the land. In addition, they raised no buildings that have endured throughout the course of time and that could be used as a reference and go down in history.

AH 129
AD 747

The Al-Aqsa renovation
That year, an earth tremor damaged columns in the Mosque of Jerusalem. The Muslims hurried to shore up the damaged parts using rudimentary, temporary bracing.

2. The Abbasid era

Advent of the Abbasid dynasty

That year marked the end of the Umayyads and the emergence of the Abbasid dynasty that seized the caliphate. After four years, the second Abbasid caliph ordered the Al-Aqsa mosque to be repaired after sustaining damage in an earth tremor. Nevertheless, the tremors continued to occur until, twenty years later, one of them destroyed most of the building. It was the caliph Almanzor, who commissioned the complete reconstruction and extension of the mosque, which soon regained its prowess and influence.

AH 132
AD 750

The Abbasid period and the rise of expeditions, literature and poetry.

AH 169
AD 786

"The Muslims provided Christians with security and allowed them to build their churches, which they protected. They are certainly closer to them than the Jews, if you stop to think about it."

Tolerance under the rule of Harun ar-Rashid

During that year the caliph Harun Ar-Rashid promulgated a decree that allowed the Holy Roman Emperor, Charlemagne, to commission repair work on the churches of Jerusalem. He was allowed to send bricklayers and the necessary funds for construction work. This he did. He then issued another decree that prescribed protection for every Christian wishing to visit the holy places in Jerusalem. Muslim soldiers were charged with their protection until their visit had come to an end and they had returned to their places of origin. Has history ever seen better conquerors than the Muslim Arabs? Please take note of that tolerance, that chivalry and the ethics involved in treating the Christians. Did the crusaders ever match that benevolence? History shows they did just the opposite.

The Pope crowns Charlemagne

Charlemagne.

The inoperative Abbasid caliphate

A dangerous power vacuum was created that year in Baghdad when Turkish army commanders murdered the caliph, Al-Mutawakkil. The Turks had come from the east in great numbers and the Abbasid caliphs began to depend increasingly on their support, to the detriment of the Arabs, for fear of seeing their sovereignty disappear. However, the Turks had become deeply involved in the state apparatus on all sides and had gradually brought it under their control. It is said that, by the end of the Abbasid dynasty, of the thirty-seven caliphs that had ruled, only three had been born of Arab mothers, while the rest had foreign mothers. The Abbasids entrusted military affairs to the Turks and other foreigners to such an extent that they gave them control of their armies. That was their last mistake, as the Turks imposed their authority over the armies and came to control the destiny of the caliphate. They murdered the caliph and assumed control of the regency. The Abbasid caliphate continued to exist, but only in name.

AH 247
AD 861

The birth of the Tulunid dynasty in Egypt

A serious controversy took place between the governor of Egypt, Ahmad Ibn Tulun, a native of Bukhara of Turkish extraction, and Ahmad al-Muwathaq Talah, the brother of the Abbasid caliph, Al-Mu'tamid. Ahmad Ibn Tulun was a war hero who had studied the Arabic language and Islamic teaching, besides being an expert equestrian. Thanks to these skills, he had mastered the art of warfare, which led him to be appointed the governing caliph of Egypt. As a result of the differences that arose between him and the brother of the Abbasid caliph, Ibn Tulun took over power in Egypt and did not officially communicate its independence. He remained independent from the Abbasid caliph in Baghdad.

AH 254
AD 868

The Tulunids dominate Syria

The rift between the caliphate in Baghdad and the governor of Egypt, Ibn Tulun, grew into open hostility. The Abbasid caliphate was by then informed of his secession. Well aware that the Abbasid state had become debilitated, he mustered an army to invade Syria. This move was taken as a pretext by other regional governors to seek their independence, and the frontier regions of the caliphate were soon occupied.

AH 264
AD 877

Jug given by Harun al-Rashíd to Charlemagne, the Holy Roman Emperor.

Ahmad Ibn Tulun marched north to conquer Antioch, followed by Hama, Aleppo and Homs, and his influence ended up covering Jerusalem and the whole of Palestine. The Tulunids fought several wars against the Abbasid dynasty, which also had other wars to contend with. The Tulunid dynasty was the first movement to split the caliphate through secession, right from its outset, and marked the preamble to many hostilities and rifts.

Reconciliation between the Abbasids and the Tulunids

AH 271
AD 883

When Ahmad Ibn Tulun died, he was succeeded as ruler of Egypt and Syria by his son Khumarawiyya. It was not long before he clashed with the Abbasids in a great battle known as the "Battle of the Mills". Khumarawiyya defeated the Abbasids and strengthened his grip on Egypt and Syria. The war lasted until the death of the caliph Al-Mu'tamid, who was succeeded by Al-Muhtafidh Billah. The latter set out to improve relations with the Tulunids. Khumarawiyya's reaction was to send the corresponding financial tribute to the Abbasid government as proof of his good intentions. In exchange, the caliph recognized him as the leader of Egypt. Continuing along these lines for improving relations, Al-Muhtafidh even went as far as asking for the hand of Qatr Nada, Khumarawiyya's daughter. The governor of Egypt agreed and the wedding took place, burying the differences between the Tulunids and the Abbasids.

The Qarmatians

The reigning calm concealed a dormant volcano of revolution and rifts as a result of the great decadence that had beset Abbasid rule. Some of them, split into Shiite fractions, worked silently in the background. This is how sectarian groups of fanatic Shiites appeared. One of the most dangerous was that of the Qarmatians, a political-religious group founded by Hamdan Qarmat, who had Ismaili convictions. The Ismaili line was one of the most extreme Shiite factions, which have caused the greatest conflicts in the Islamic nation throughout history. The Qarmatian dynasty grew up in the region of Al-Ahsa (Arabia) and had its headquarters on the island of Awal, today known as Bahrain. Their first emir was Al-Hasan Al-Jannabi whose followers were later known as the Jannabids. They were the Abbasids' worst enemies. From the island they started attacking Iraq, Syria and Egypt, creating great upheaval and confusion.

The Ibn Tulun mosque in Cairo.

The astrolabe, an
Arab invention.

Decline of Abbasid power

AH 292
AD 905

At the death of the Abbasid caliph, Al-Mu'tadid, the situation deteriorated. Because of the instability of the caliphate, six caliphs took succession in a short lapse of time. Real power slipped out of their hands and passed to their ministers and military commanders. Under the rule of al-Mustakfi, the person in control was the Turkish military commander, Tuzun. That was when the Qarmatians were spreading their control over the eastern peninsula and Egypt, and had started moving westwards towards Syria. In Ramallah, they founded their mission centre.

3. The Fatimids

The Fatimids dominate The Maghreb

AH 298
AD 911

The Fatimid dynasty then emerged in the Maghreb. It was also a faction of the Shiite Ismailis. Its first caliph, Ubayd Allah Al-Mahdi, imposed his rule across the Maghreb. Sunni Muslim scholars called the dynasty "Al-Ubaydiyah", after the caliph, to avoid associating it with Fatima Az-Zahra', the Prophet's daughter. However, Al-Mahdi declared his caliphate to be Fatimid.

The Ikhshidids dominate Egypt and Syria

AH 321
AD 933

The Fatimids marched towards Egypt under the command of Jawhar As-Saqli. In order to defend it, the Abbasids sent their forces, led by Muhammad Ibn Ikhshid. He managed to drive back the Fatimid assaults in various skirmishes and, as a reward, the Abbasids appointed him governor of Egypt. However it was not long before he gave way to Fatimid incitement and ended up declaring independence from the Abbasids in the year AD 935. Thus began the Ikhshidid dynasty. Its founder lost no time in at-

tacking Syrian territory, defeating its governor, Ibn Ra'iq, who was forced to sign an agreement under which he kept the northern territory, whereas the Ikhshidids ruled over the south. The treaty was adhered to until the death of Ibn Ra'iq, after which Ikhshid again attacked Syria and incorporated the whole of it into his kingdom.

The Ikhshidids who ruled over Jerusalem venerated it so much that they took their kings and leaders to be buried there.

Interior design from the period.

The Buwayhids dominate the Abbasid caliphate

The Abbasid dynasty was severely debilitated by the rise of the Fatimids in the Maghreb, the Qarmatians in the central region and the eastern Arabian Peninsula, and the Ikhshidids in Syria and Egypt. Added to this was an uprising in the north of Syria, instigated by the Shiite Sayf ad-Dawlah al-Hamdani, who founded the Hamdani dynasty. Al-Hamadani conquered Aleppo and made it his capital. Another Shiite faction, the Buyids or Buwayhids, managed to take over Persia and advance west towards Iraq where they were able to conquer the capital, Baghdad.

Caliphal power passed to the Shiite Buyids although they supported the Abbasid caliph as their nominal head of state.

Kafur rules Egypt

AH 334
AD 946

That year, after Ikhshidi died and was buried in Jerusalem, his dynasty soon began to crumble. His son, Unujur, was 14 years old and his tutor was a slave from Eritrea called Kafur. The latter quickly began administering the country's matters in his own style. He faced and won battles against the Ikhshidids and imposed his authority on the government of the country, retaining the child as nominal leader.

The Fatimids conquer Egypt

The Fatimid leader, Jawhar As-Saqli, attacked Egypt once again and this time he was able to conquer it and bring it under Fatimid authority. It marked the end of the Abbasid dynasty in Egypt which had been split into small states. These developments fuelled western European ambitions and prompted the beginning of the crusades in the Near East.

The Egyptian people were faithful to their Sunni convictions and to their community. They therefore rejected the Fatimid Ismaili government for being of mistaken beliefs. Nevertheless, the Fatimid governor managed to calm the Egyptians by promising to uphold their Sunni convictions and doctrine, the judicial system, their rites, their mosques and their schools of religious studies. This being the status quo, peace reigned in Egypt.

Mosque of Muhammad.

97

AH **359**
AD **969**

The Fatimids seize Syria, Palestine and the Arabian province of Hijaz

After stability was achieved in Egypt, the Fatimid ruler set about spreading his influence towards the Abbasid caliphate which had become a puppet regime, with effective power residing in the Seljuk Turks. The Fatimid ruler sent his commander, Ja'far Ibn Salah, to Palestine and Syria, territories he had managed to annex after several battles against the Ikhshidids. They were abetted by the Qarmatians, who ruled the eastern Arabian Peninsula and had established relations with the Fatimids. Both Ismailis, from the most fanatical Shiite factions, the affinity in their reasoning and convictions facilitated their alliance. The Qarmatians were the most radical of the Islamic deviationist groups and the most misguided. The understanding between the Qarmatians and Fatimids led them to mount joint assaults against Syria and Mesopotamia. Damascus fell to Jawhar As-Saqli, while Fatimid authority extended over Egypt and the Maghreb and well into Syria. In the mosques, the imams preached in favour of Mu'iz ad-Din, a Fatimid. Far from being content with that, the Fatimids launched their own raids on Mecca and Medina. From then on, the lands of the Hijaz were annexed by the Fatimids.

Amid the turmoil of these events, the Sulayhids ruled in Yemen, from where they declared their loyalty to the Fatimids. Sermons were then given in their favour. This trend spread to virtually all the Muslim states and was accompanied by the introduction and subsequent hegemony of the Ismaili doctrine.

For various reasons, the close ties between the Fatimids and the Qarmatians began to fray, until they found themselves at war with each other. The Qarmatians launched several campaigns against the Fatimids. Their most famous assault was against Mecca, which they seized, including the Kaaba itself. They desecrated the holy places, took possession of the Black Stone and placed it in another would be Kaaba they had in the Al-Ahsa area. They urged the faithful to make the pilgrimage to the Black Stone at its new site, where it remained for twenty-two years—according to the most reliable sources—in other words, up to the time of the Fatimid Al-'Aziz Billah. He intervened, insisting that the Black Stone should be returned to its original site. The Qarmatians agreed, as they had failed from the outset in their attempt to get people to go to Al-Ahsa. However, be-

Entrance to a Fatimid mosque.

fore returning the Stone, they partially broke it. The Muslims recovered it, restored the Stone with agate paste, and placed it exactly where it stands today.

Al-Hakim Bi-Amr Allah (the Madman)

AH 386
AD 996

The Fatimid Al-Hakim bi-Amr Allah came to the throne that year. Historians nicknamed him "the Madman" because of the endless and extravagant laws he imposed on his people. They were submitted to great pressure and even driven mad by the imposition of his bizarre orders, such as working by night and sleeping in the daytime.

Fatimid Mosque.

During his rule, the Mosque of Jerusalem was damaged in an earthquake. Several parts of the dome on the Dome of the Rock collapsed. Six years later, it was his son who shored it up. However, Al-Hakim bi-Amr Allah destroyed the church of the Holy Sepulchre, which ignited the first spark of hatred between Muslims and Christians after they had enjoyed a long period of conciliation. In the West, this event made a great impression on Christians who were shocked at their holy places having been desecrated. This was one of the factors involved in laying the groundwork for the crusades to follow.

AH 411
AD 1021

The decline of Fatimid power

After the death of Al-Hakim bi-Amr Allah, the power of the Fatimids declined dramatically. The Fatimid caliphs began to entrust their ministers with the state administration and these ministers gradually took over the reigns of power. The caliph's orders were sidelined, although his name was still used. The same thing happened to the caliph Al-Mustansir Billah, who reigned from AH 427 / AD 1036. During his 60 years of reign, he acted mainly as a figurehead. The Fatimid or Ismaili creed considered the caliph to be sacred, and succession had therefore to be hereditary. That is why no attempt was made to change the caliph or oust him, even if he was a weak ruler lacking effective control and authority.

The great Mosque at
Cordova (Al-Andalus).

AH 472
AD 1036

The division of the Fatimid dynasty

Before he died, Al-Mustansir Billah arranged for his successor to be his youngest son, Al-Musta'li Billah, instead of another son, Nizar, who was the eldest and therefore most entitled to become caliph. After his death, differences arose between the two sons. The dynasty split into two factions, the Nizaris and the Musta'lis. A ferocious war broke out between them, producing a rift that further weakened the dynasty. In practice, the Fatimids still ruled Egypt, whereas their authority in Syria had become nominal.

The decline of the Umayyads in Al-Andalus

The Umayyad caliphate in Moorish Spain (Al-Andalus) also collapsed that year. The caliphate ended up being divided into 22 party kingdoms or *taifas*.

4. The Seljuk Turks

Similarly, the Seljuk Turks, under the rule of Alp Arslan, dominated half of present-day Turkey, then known as Asia Minor. Hence, the Seljuks, together with the aforementioned separatist movements, played a crucial role in the disintegration of the Abbasid state.

AH 422
AD 1031

"The Islamic nation, weakened by sectarianism and internal strife, became vulnerable to enemy attacks on all sides."

Seljuk Mosque.

101

Discord in Europe

AH 445
AD 1054

This is the year when political divisions and a great religious schism took place among the Christians in Europe. As a result, the Church was divided into Orthodox and Catholic.

AH 448
AD 1057

After the political-religious split, King Ferdinand I of Castile and León, to the north of Al-Andalus, invaded this Muslim kingdom and announced in Europe a holy war to reconquer it. This invasion of Al-Andalus was a preamble to the Crusades, before they marched on Arab lands in the Near East.

One of the Arab palaces in Al-Andalus—the Alhambra of Granada.

AH 459
AD 1067

The Turks seize Syria and Palestine

That year, the Fatimid vizier Badr Al-Jamali sent a Turkish army to Palestine to put down civil unrest among the nomads. The army successfully quashed it, but they changed their loyalty from the Fatimids to the Seljuks, as they were also Turkish. Consequently, Turkish hegemony covered all Syria and included Jerusalem, at the expense of the Fatimids.

AH 463
AD 1071

The battle of Manzikert and the birth of Turkey

The Seljuks were by then the dominant force. They were known for their Islamic religious fervour. Their dynasty was young and strong, which encouraged them in the year AH 463 / AD 1072 to enter into a fierce war against the Byzantines, led by the sultan Alp Arslan. He routed the Byzantine emperor Romanus IV Diogenes in one of the greatest ever Islamic battles in Asia Minor, known as the battle of Manzikert, located north of Arzanjan. Immediately afterwards, the Turks set out to conquer Asia Minor, thereafter called Turkey. From there, their influence spread as far as Armenia.

5. The religious reform movement

AH 422
AD 1031

The Ulama (learned men) of Islam take the initiative

It is worth pausing here to focus our attention on the sultan's vizier, Nizam al-Mulk, a devout believer and champion of the faith. He respected the ulama and encouraged general education. He was carelessly neglected in Islamic history. Nevertheless, the Muslim people are indebted to him. Apart from encouraging learning, poetry and literature, he built several schools, including the well-known Nizamiyya school. One of the prominent figures closest to him was the Persian poet Omar Khayyam. Another expert in Islamic doctrine who made his mark on that era and led the Islamic movement was the reformist imam, Abu Hamid Al-Ghazali.

His role in the social renaissance was so important that many historians consider him to be the greatest reformer of his time. Many experts, such as At-Tartushi, who were inspired by Nizam al-Mulk, followed his initiative, attempting to awaken people from their intellectual lethargy through stimulating ideas.

"The imam Al-Ghazali is considered to be the greatest reformer of Islamic thought. He pioneered a system in which both political and military leaders were educated and the community was restored to its former glory."

They introduced the concepts of "political sharia" or legal politics of Islam, the "art of public administration", Muslim leadership, and ways of reconciling religious and worldly politics.

Al-Ghazali harangued against the apathy shown by scholars of Islamic doctrine, claiming that they should address the whole community and not only their pupils and followers. He also reproached them for their withdrawal from the people's affairs and criticized them for their ideological fanaticism, while neglecting the basics of religion, and their attention to detail and matters of secondary importance, standing by while the Islamic community was disintegrating into divergent factions that bickered over details but lacked genuine conviction. He also decried the sultans' and politicians' love of luxury and comfortable living and the fact they had turned their backs on affairs concerning the people and religion. By so doing, he set about laying the foundational principles of social justice and solidarity between Muslims.

Under his leadership, a movement of religious renewal took root among the people. A new generation of learned men began to rectify misguided ideas and inspire the people with an extraordinary spirit of revival. As a result, a new breed of students was educated by the reformist movement. The ulama put forward a new methodology and an innovative doctrinal educational study programme based first and foremost on genuine Islamic faith, and on the integration of knowledge from all spheres, in an endeavour to augment learning by the incorporation of a cosmopolitan, empirical approach to science.

This doctrine endured for a hundred years. It became a yardstick for students and experts and yielded leaders of the calibre of Imad ad-Din Zanki, Nur ad-Din Zanki and Salah ad-Din al-Ayyubi (Saladin), as we will see later on.

The Crusades

1. Portents of the Crusades

At that time, Pope Gregory VII, of German extraction, assumed the pontificate of Rome. He was a devout Catholic and a keen, lucid fanatic. He began to urge Catholic monks in France to spread the Catholic faith. France was chosen especially because it was the country with the greatest religious fervour at that time. The Pope centred his efforts on the Normans who influenced large areas within Europe. They were one of the most barbarian, ignorant peoples. In this case the Pope's choice was most successful.

His influence grew to such an extent that even Europe's leaders were afraid of him. The climax of his glory was that he became the supreme religious authority on the continent to whom the Europeans owed total allegiance, and he set about placing the men of his choosing in positions of authority.

In this respect, it is recounted that one such ruler disobeyed Pope Gregory's orders and was promptly faced with a papal bull excommunicating him. The people then declared their disobedience to this ruler, who was forced to walk barefoot from his country to Rome to kiss the hand of the Pope and beg him for pardon. Papal bulls granting pardon multiplied thereafter, as did those of papal indulgence and excommunication. The Pope's strong position enabled him to issue whatever bulls he saw fit, setting himself up as arbiter of whoever he considered worthy of Paradise or else liable to be condemned to hellfire. The fearful European leaders sought to win his affection.

As the Pope's authority spread, the Byzantine emperor asked for his assistance in recovering his empire from the Seljuk Turks. As the Byzantine emperor was Orthodox, by appealing to a Catholic Pope the latter was in a position to seize two great opportunities: on the one hand, to stop the Muslim faith from

A call to the Crusades.

Pope Urban II announces the Crusades in Clermont (France).

spreading into Europe and, on the other hand, to extend his authority and influence over Byzantium, thus unifying Europe as one Christian nation under his authority. It was a good reason for fulfilling the Byzantine emperor's request, and he thus started preparing public opinion and the European leaders for implementing his plan to declare war on the Muslim Turks.

Pope Urban II

Pope Gregory VII died before embarking on any campaign. His successor, Pope Urban II, soon rose to fame, to the extent that portraits of him still hang in many European churches. He furthered his predecessor's mission to declare hostilities against the Muslims and recover the Byzantine territories.

The fall of Toledo

Meanwhile, in Al-Andalus, Toledo fell to Alfonso VI. The loss of that city marked the beginning of the crusades and dealt a severe blow to the Muslims. It was the first major victory of Christians over Muslims, and it caused great enthusiasm in Europe.

The Pope declares the Crusades

Urban II announced his support of Byzantium against the Seljuk army and sparked rumours about Muslims attacking Christian pilgrims on their way to Jerusalem, as well as their hostility towards the Christian holy places and the desecration of Christ's tomb.

He was thereby successful in arousing Christian feeling across Europe, leading to major appeals, from France and Italy, designed to pave the way for a military assault on Jerusalem.

Priests blessing the Christians who took part in the Crusades.

AH 480
AD 1088

107

AH 483
AD 1090

The Sect of the Assassins

In Christian Europe, tension was mounting against the Muslims, while the Arab East had become weak and divided. In the year AH 483 / AD 1091, a man named Hasan Ibn as-Sabah founded the Nizari sect, of Ismaili leanings, known historically as the Assassins, from the Arabic "Hashashin", as the organization allowed the consumption of cannabis (hashish). He was a degenerate who followed a code of conduct that consisted of murdering and eliminating his opponents, sanctioning the shedding of the blood of Muslims who did not agree with his convictions. After the death of Nizar Ibn al-Mustansir, a fierce war broke out between the Fatimids and the Nizaris or Assassins, as Hasan Ibn as-Sabah had decreed that the caliph should be succeeded by his son, Hasan Ibn Nizar, which angered Al-Musta'li and provoked hostilities between them.

The Christians conquer Sicily

Meanwhile, the Christians managed to conquer Sicily, which was then under Islamic rule. It was a great test victory for the Europeans which emboldened them to challenge the Muslims further. They considered it proof that the Islamic nations were vulnerable and that they stood a good chance of mounting successful crusades. However, the Fatimids in the Maghreb realised what dangers such intentions posed, as did the Seljuk Turks, who were about to consolidate their rule in the East, over Turkey and Mesopotamia. The Fatimids then committed a major blunder by seeking an agreement with the crusaders whereby they would allow the latter to invade Syria in place of the Seljuks. Thus, by concentrating their military efforts against the Seljuk Turks, the crusaders were able to drive a wedge between the Seljuks and the Fatimids. Fatimid connivance with the enemy for political purposes thus caused serious disaster, as the crusades gathered momentum, leading to the loss of Palestine and Jerusalem.

A catapult used by the crusaders for launching stones and fire.

2. The Crusades

AH 488
AD 1095

The Crusade "Summit" at Clermont
The Council of Clermont

A lavish meeting was held that year at Clermont (France) under the leadership of Pope Urban II. There, he called for a Christian army to be assembled with the mission of conquering Jerusalem. People came from everywhere to enlist, giving rise to the formation of a volunteer movement for this campaign from most of the European countries.

The reasons for the Crusades

The major reasons for the Crusades can be summarized as follows:
- Religious fanaticism and the call for liberation of the Christian holy places in Jerusalem.
- The existence in Europe of an indigent peasantry for whom the crusades were a means of subsistence through combat in "the rich man's country". The leaders of the First Crusade described the Muslim held Holy Land to their subjects as a rich and unprotected territory.

Byzantine court.

Henry IV of Germany took part in the First Crusade.

• Religious and ideological instruction, carried out by the monks, among the people to incite them to attack those who had taken possession of their holy places.

The army of Peter the Hermit

The Pope ordered a people's crusade to be assembled under the command of a monk named Peter the Hermit, and another led by Walter Sans-Avoir (Walter the Penniless). The first Christian campaign led by Peter the Hermit marched eastwards. It was highly disorganized and lacked any military training. No European leaders intervened. It was a popular, religious campaign with its ranks made up of men, women and children, all commoners, who numbered 80,000.

That crusade reached Byzantium without managing to conquer it. The combatants then devoted themselves to pillaging the surroundings of Constantinople. The emperor of Byzantium, who was an Orthodox, tried to get rid of them by preparing them a fleet to send them to Turkey to attack the Seljuks, who were permanently at war with him.

The Seljuks were well supplied and had a well trained and well organized army. The crusade could not hold out against them and the fight was over from the start—they were overwhelmed by the Turkish forces.

AH 490
AD 1096

The official crusade

The Pope's influence had grown, and his cause made an impression on Europe's leaders, who ended up by heeding his call to arms. He called for a fresh campaign, but this time it was to be better organized. Soldiers enlisted in the European armies that were well disciplined and highly trained in battle. In addition, the armies had at their disposal the latest weapons and equipment available at that time. The official crusade began in France with the Normans, and also in Italy, and they headed for Byzantium. The Byzantine emperor helped them once again on their journey to Asia Minor. After crossing the Bosphorus, they clashed head on with the Seljuk Turks, who were unable to contain the enormous force of the crusaders, supported by troops sent by the Byzantine emperor. Immediately after their defeat, the Seljuk Turks split into five governing families.

The disloyalty of the Fatimids

The Fatimids did not lift a finger in spite of what was happening even though they ruled in Syria. Rather, they congratulated the crusaders on their victories and even organized how the region was to be divided between them as follows:

The Fatimids proposed that Godfrey should keep northern Syria and they would retain the south including Jerusalem. The crusaders accepted on the condition that Jerusalem became theirs because it was obviously their first objective and they considered it to be one of their holy places, which they were ready to take by force. And this is how they failed to reach an agreement. The Fatimids did not give up Jerusalem and their approximation towards the crusaders became more distant until it completely faded away.

After a siege that lasted 6 months, a Christian guard at the fortress of Antioch committed an act of disloyalty against his own people by reaching an agreement with the attacking forces for whom he unexpectedly opened the fortress gates, which allowed them to take Antioch. (That was the decisive result of having soldiers in the army whose loyalty for their countries and their community left much to be desired).

After the crusaders entered Antioch, rumour had it that that a well-equipped Abbasid army under the military control of the Turk Karbougha was approaching. Although they arrived late, it only took them three days to appear, surround the fortress, besiege the crusaders, prevent them from moving out of the enclosure and forcing them to remain locked up inside. There were so many of them and their situation began to be so oppressive that, according to some statements, they ended up by having to eat dog meat. This is how they started to divide.

AH **491**
AD **1097**

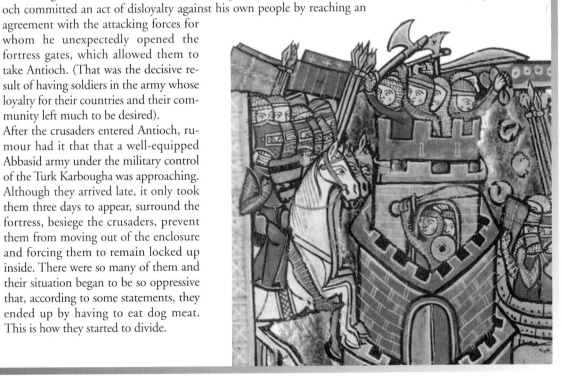

The crusaders
conquer Antioch.

Jesus' spear

The crusader army leader resorted to trickery to raise people's morale. He pretended he had seen Jesus in his dreams and that He directed him towards his spear that was buried in a church in Antioch. The news spread among the people who gathered together around the supposed church to dig in the place he had been told to unearth the spear, just as had been indicated to him. Enthusiasm grew, as the certainty of whoever was to carry Christ's spear would never be defeated, was an act of faith. The people prepared themselves for battle again and they asked the head of the Abbasid army, Karbougha, to allow them to fight against him to resolve the siege. Karbougha gave his approval for a direct combat but one section of his army disagreed with him. This is how the difference started to grow between Arabs and Turks in the Muslim army ranks. Meanwhile, the crusaders had lined up for battle. With profound religious fervour, they were soon to launch a shattering assault that surprised the Abbasid army that was beaten into retreat and dispersed.

A crusader soldier praying during the crusades.

3. The fall of Jerusalem

AH 492
AD 1099

The way towards Jerusalem

With that second defeat, the path lay open for the crusader soldiers. From there a numerous army was led to take Jerusalem. The crusader chief led the campaign by walking barefoot towards the objective with no other resistance that from the governor of Tripoli who rejected the arrival of the crusaders whose ambition it was take over that land too. The governor of Tripoli sent messages and delegations asking for help from the Abbasid Muslims in Mesopotamia and from the small Islamic states in northern Syria. When no response was received, he sent out a last call for help to the Fatimids. A messenger came by sea who, instead of bringing news about the salvation of Tripoli, asked him about a female slave whose beauty had come to the attention of the Fatimid governor and who wanted to buy her. At the same time, he also asked for some sun-dried wood with which to make musical instruments.

The fall of the Islamic cities

Perplexed by the Islamic faint-heartedness, the inhabitants of Tripoli lost their morale and surrendered. It was the third province to be conquered in Muslim territory.

The crusader army advanced towards Jerusalem and conquered Beirut and Saida leaving garrisons in every city. Godfrey of Boullon reached Jerusalem; he surrounded and choked the city forcing the governor to ask everyone for help although he could not find anyone to lend a hand in the middle of that Islamic destruction and so the light of enthusiasm began to go out in the Muslim lands.

New reinforcements came from Europe that brought new equipment and machinery for building special wooden towers for overwhelming fortresses. The garrison at Jerusalem was able to destroy the first tower that the crusaders had lent against the fortress wall. The siege lasted 42 days during which the crusaders erected another tower that again they lent against the fortress wall under an avalanche of flying spears.

The terrible fall of Jerusalem

24th day of Shaaban 492 AH / 15/07/1099

Under an intense throwing of spears and by using catapults, the crusaders managed to get onto the fortress walls by using the second tower. Then there was a battle that finally put an end to the Fatimid garrison. Jerusalem surrendered to the crusaders. Actually it was the Fatimids who were responsible for their surrender. It was they who neither sent help to the Muslims nor aided the garrison, and this is considered to be an act of disloyalty in their history.

The fall of Jerusalem.

"Gustave Lebon relates the following history according to a priest called Raimundo Douglos who was on the battlefield.

He said: Our people went too far in spilling blood in Solomon's temple to the point that corpses were floating in blood, hands and legs were swimming. The soldiers could not bear the stench coming from the corpses."

The slaughter

The crusaders went into Jerusalem with all their brutality. They beheaded people in the streets without distinguishing between young people or old, healthy or disabled persons, women or men. The governing Fatimid Iftikharud-din or Iftiqarud-din took shelter with his soldiers in the citadel whereas the slaughter continued in Jerusalem. Those who could flee did so. Most of the people sought refuge in the mosque of Jerusalem that became filled as well as its courtyard. Some 100,000 young people, the elderly, women and children took refuge there in a tense and phobic wait.

Faced with so many crowds, the crusader governor found no better option than to order them to be beheaded. Slaughtering the crowd began without any distinction on the one hand and without any resistance from the innocent multitude assembled there on the other.

The sack of Jerusalem.

Desecration of the Mosque of Jerusalem

After that enormous massacre, the crusaders divided the Mosque of Al-Aqsa into several parts. A church was made out of the main area. Another part was reserved for accommodating the knights and one was transformed into an ammunitions depot. The porticoes were turned into stables, known by the name of "Solomon's stables".

That was certainly a historical sentence. Just compare that cruelty and violence with the conquest of Jerusalem by 'Umar Ibn al-Khattab, or with the Islamic tolerance shown by Harun Ar-Rashid towards the Christian churches and pilgrims. One may then draw one's conclusions in light of the bare facts.

The people of Jerusalem had already surrendered after having helplessly witnessed how serious the situation was, faced with such barbarity and the faint-heartedness of the Muslim leaders. They were seized by panic and most nearby cities surrendered without any resistance in order to prevent fresh massacres like the one at Jerusalem. An example of a city that surrendered without putting up a fight was Nablus.

The Templars were charged with the mission of protecting Jerusalem.

115

"The crusader kings were fascinated by Arab civilization and ended up imitating the Arabs in their food, clothing and lifestyle."

The Muslims' reaction

Jerusalem fell and the kingdom of the crusaders was established there under the command of Godfrey of Bouillon. Anyone who could fled to Baghdad. The magistrate Al-Harawi was among them, as was a group of members of the religious elite. When they reached the centre of the caliphate, Baghdad, they began to preach in the mosques, calling people to fight for the salvation of Palestine and to recover the occupied Mosque of Jerusalem—Al Aqsa. Their speeches multiplied and the fervour of the Muslims increased. Rallies started to besiege the caliph's palace. At first, the caliph did not respond, but he finally gave in to the enormous pressure he was being subjected to. He then came out to declare the fight for God's cause and sent a missive to the governors to assemble their armies. However, the emissaries returned empty handed. The governors made no effort whatsoever to collaborate in the cause of Jerusalem. The perfidy, division and corruption of the governors doomed any attempt to failure and put to rest any hopes of magnanimity.

The crusaders and Muslim civilization

The presence of the crusaders in the heartland of Syria increased on account of the massive influx of people from Europe. For many, it was a case of being able to live in the lands that they had dreamed so much about. They were fascinated by the way of life of the local civilization and drawn by the refined Arab lifestyle. It was destined to captivate them and to have a profound influence on them.

What they learned in the Arab territories included astronomy, science, mathematics, medicine, translation and Eastern thinking. It became a reason for many Christians to emigrate from Europe. Trade between the East and West intensified. Knowledge and art were conveyed to Europe where they sowed the seeds of progress and science. The crusader kings were fascinated by Arab civilization and ended up imitating the Arabs in their food, clothing and lifestyle.

Aleppo castle.

PART TWO
Palestine in the Islamic era

CHAPTER FOUR
The Islamic liberation movement

1. The first attempts

2. The formidable Zankis

The Islamic liberation movement

1. The first attempts

The first fighter "Moudoud"

Under pressure from the learned scholars in religious sciences and their persevering battle to activate the outburst of enthusiasm in the hearts of the people and their leaders, the first counter-offensive the Muslims started was a fighting movement that was answered by the governor of Musol. Out of all the Muslim territories, he was the only one to react. His name was Moudoud and he was a Turkish Muslim. His reaction attracted many followers, and this allowed him to take a great army to Ur-fa, which they conquered. He was forced to kill some crusaders and capture others. There were Armenians among the prisoners of war, who were caught unaware while helping the crusaders. A glimmer of hope was aroused in the bosom of the Muslim community with that conquest.

Signs of new hope encouraged crowds of Muslims who rushed to Moud-oud. He enlisted them in the army and headed for Jerusalem. The crusaders realized the dangers of that army that was advancing towards them. Nevertheless it was nothing more than a simple muddled army that was going to face a great well-equipped crusader force. The clash was tremendous but neither contender managed to solve it in their favour. Moudoud then thought it would be better to withdraw to Damascus which was still under his influence, so he could reorganize his ranks. In Damascus, he visited the Omeya Mosque one Friday. A Hash-shashin man (from the lost and esoteric gang) waited for him there to murder him.

Maybe it was the utmost limit of disloyalty that someone could be a supporter of Islam and kill a Muslim fighter through which God revived the hopes of an upset community. But this was – and continues to be - the habit of perverted and esoteric groups. They kindle hatred among Muslims and feel hostile towards whoever disagrees with them.

The Islamic liberation movement

The fighting movement was buried in its own cradle without having enjoyed a destiny of success. Because of this, the religious elite stopped encouraging firmness and enthusiasm in another leader. However, the governor of the city of Nardin, after assembling an army, left once again for Urfa. A small battle took place that was known by the name of Qastawan in which the Muslim army managed to defeat and throw the crusaders out, thus spreading renewed hope and optimism among the people thanks to this new leader. Again there were preparations for the battle and the Muslim community was revived.

AH 513
AD 1119

The reaction of the religious elite

AH 529
AD 1135

The Islamic army entered Urfa and stayed there for several years but their dominance over the city weakened and the Abbasid caliph Ar-rashid Billah found out about this. He was an oppressive and corrupt caliph known for his addiction to drink. The learned scholars in religious sciences decided unanimously to fight against the degeneracy in the caliphate and incited the people to kill him by taking advantage of his new bond with the people after so many years of ostracism. Scarcely one year after the Ar-rashid caliphate, the Ulemas declared that honouring loyalty to the Caliph was invalid and that there was the need for him to be removed. On the other hand they declared their loyalty to his uncle. Under pressure from the religious elite and from the people, Ar-rashid stepped down and was succeeded by his uncle who immediately started a global reform movement for the Muslims.

2. The formidable Zankis

Imad ad-Din Zanki

In that year, Imad ad-Din Zanki was appointed governor of Mosul (Mesopotamia). He was a born warrior and faithful follower of the religious and educational reform movement founded by Al-Ghazali and At-Tartushi. This reform was based on the fact that socio-political change was not feasible unless it was preceded by a serene, sincere reform movement, likewise a prerequisite for any attempt to fight for the liberation of territories occupied by the crusaders. After deep reflection, he made two decisions, aware of how weak and divided the Muslim community had become. He proclaimed the following before his people:

- The unity of the Muslim nation, calling for union and concord among the small, nearby states.
- A national struggle (jihad), calling on combatants to meet at Mosul.

These two proclamations made a profound impression on the people. Volunteers flocked from far and wide. However, the leaders were against Zanki's call to arms—they even forbade cooperation with his effort and refused to assist with weapons, funds or men. Zanki continued regardless and assembled his volunteers into an army, which he led towards the city of Aleppo in northern Syria. There he managed to defeat the local garrison and return the city to the sovereign caliphate. He subsequently led his army—by then reinforced and highly motivated—to Urfa (Edessa), which he liberated and restored to Islamic rule after forty-six years of suffering under the crusaders. This victory resonated throughout both the Islamic world and Europe. The Pope and the Europeans concerned realized the danger personified in that one warrior who was highly motivated and backed by the full force of Islam.

High treason

In response, the Pope started to prepare a new crusade against Zanki, at the request of the Muslim governor of Damascus, in alliance with the Christian ruler of Jerusalem. Both sides took up positions for the future confrontation.

Nur ad-Din Zanki

The supporters and detractors of the esoteric groups then reverted to their

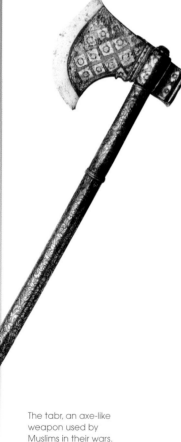

The tabr, an axe-like weapon used by Muslims in their wars.

former, despicable ways and their repeated disloyalty, striking a blow at the heart of the Muslim community. An upshot of this was that the Fatimids murdered Imad ad-Din Zanki, who was succeeded by his son, Nur ad-Din Zanki. He was a man educated in the same commendable religious fighting spirit as his father, which allowed him to become one of the great Muslim leaders at that time. (The curious thing is that many young people are unaware of the biography of this great hero).

His knowledge of life was partly due to the education he received under his father's tutelage, so that it was not long before he made social reform the centrepiece of his leadership. He sent educators to live among the people, put an end to corruption, revived the economy, stimulated trade and reformed the judicial system by appointing the most worthy judges. Morale rose among the people, who came to understand how important their support would be for that new Muslim leader.

He was diligent in defending the Muslim community, for which cause he applied keen political savoir faire and perspicacity. He proclaimed an imminent holy war, which attracted many people to his cause, and for which he mustered his armies. He enjoyed their diligent protection, as they were highly appreciative of his wisdom and sense of justice. To lead his army, he named such commanders as Asad ad-Din Shirku bin Shadi bin Ayub, also known as Shirkuh, and his brother, Najm ad-Din Ayub bin Shadi bin Ayub, the father of Salah ad-Din al-Ayyubi (Saladin), who was born precisely at that time, and was to later receive an excellent education under the tuition of Al-Asbahani.

Lifting the siege of Damascus

The crusaders made preparations to confront the nascent Muslim awakening. In fact, they preempted any such confrontation by breaking their treaty with their Muslim ally, the governor of Damascus, and laying siege to the city. The latter sent an appeal for help to Nur ad-Din Zanki. Far from watching from the sidelines, as other leaders of the time had been content to do, he sought an active response to the passiveness and disloyalty of the governor of Damascus. Moved by Islamic zeal and pride, he decided to defend Muslim Damascus intelligently, with firmness and courage. This enabled him to lift the siege of Damascus and repulse the crusaders' assault. Nevertheless, he allowed the governor to stay on in his post after making promises and commitments to remain as his ally against the crusaders.

AH 541
AD 1146

The liberation of Baalbek and Tripoli

Nur ad-Din, also known as Nureddin, then marched on Baalbek and Tripoli, which he wrested from crusader control. News of his successes spread far and wide and heralded a new lease of life for both the leader and his cause. His reputation grew to such an extent that even the caliph nicknamed him "the Just King", although he himself did nothing to help him. He satisfied himself with lavishing words of praise on Nureddin, and instead focused his attention on remaining in power. But Nureddin did receive much support and encouragement from the people.

The European kings lead the campaigns

During that year another crusade left Europe, under the command of the crusader princes, with the aim of capturing Damascus. The soldiers of this city defended it bravely, fighting with all their might. The governor of Damascus asked Nureddin for help against the crusader forces, and Nureddin provided it in the form of a magnificent army that aborted the siege. He tightened the blockade around the crusaders, depriving them of water. This pressure and the shortage of water forced the crusaders to withdraw and they soon ended up returning defeated to Europe, as they could not leave their estates for long. Realizing that the war against the Muslims was going to take a long time, they opted to retreat.

AH 543
AD 1148

The disloyalty of the governor of Damascus

After the retreat of the crusader armies, Nureddin devoted his efforts to thinking of ways to recover Jerusalem. To this end, he asked the governor of Damascus to provide him with an auxiliary army to lay siege to Ascalon in southern Palestine. The governor turned down his request, alleging that he needed to retain a garrison to protect Damascus. When Nureddin threatened to depose him, the governor sent a secret agent to the crusaders in Jerusalem asking for their help against Nureddin.

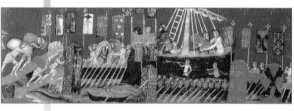

France supplies the crusader ships with provisions.

The crusaders, realizing that this division was a factor in their favour, rushed an army from Jerusalem in support of the governor of Damascus. News of this soon reached Nureddin and he immediately went out to meet the crusaders' army before it arrived at Damascus. He defeated it and scattered it, a feat that was met with great emotion in the Muslim world. In Damascus, the short prayer, "God is great", and the expression, "there is no god but God", were the shouts of joy that were most heard. The children of Damascus sang the praises of Nureddin and created stories and legends about his heroic march.

The conquest of Damascus

The governor of Damascus had no option other than to swear allegiance to Nureddin once he realized that he no longer had either a saviour or an ally in the crusaders. Damascus was handed over to Nureddin, who was received by the people with an uproar of joy and various exclamations. Justice and faith were promulgated under his rule and magnificent buildings, religious trusts and works of public donation were erected that are still standing today. Once Nureddin's rule was established in Damascus, Aleppo and Mosul, he sent a small force to harass the numerous crusader legions that had gathered in Palestine and Jerusalem and to occasionally destroy their abodes. However, he had to concentrate his efforts on extending the nation's territory and on amassing the greatest number of troops and material.

The defeat of Nureddin's army

Fighting continued against the crusaders and, in the year AD 1162, Nur ad-Din Zanki suffered a defeat from which he miraculously survived. He then swore to Almighty God that he would take revenge and avenge his troops for that defeat. He concentrated on preparations for the revenge attack for two whole years. The crusaders grew wary of the enthusiasm shown by Nureddin and resorted to offering reconciliation. Nureddin refused and continued to assemble his troops to confront them. He sent messages and delegations to the emirs, but only a few responded to his call. So he began to organize and train a small army which he imbued with the necessary passion and fighting spirit to confront the crusaders.

The great battle of Harim (Syria)

Having fulfilled his mission of organizing the army, Nureddin marched to the Harim region where he confronted the crusaders in a great battle. Just before the clash, Zanki said a community prayer asking God not to abandon the Muslims, to provide victory for his servants and soldiers and to defeat the crusaders. The battle of Harim took place at dawn the following day. It has been ignored by many historians, in spite of it being one of the greatest battles at that time. Its magnitude warranted the participation of several crusader duchies and principalities, with their princes

AH 546
AD 1152

Centre: world map made by Arab cartographers in AD 1154.

AH 558
AD 1162

AH 560
AD 1164

Lamp from a
Mameluke mosque.

at the forefront. The principalities of Tripoli, Jerusalem and even Antioch took part, and the prince of the last mentioned was present in person that day. At the height of the battle, God answered the prayers of the fighter Nureddin, granting him a great victory. Ten thousand crusaders died and a similar number were captured. The princes of Antioch and Tripoli were among those taken prisoner. It was a resounding defeat for the crusaders, who had never suffered anything like it in Arab lands. The existence of the small crusader states was threatened because of this defeat. The whole of Europe trembled at the news. In the minds of the Europeans Nureddin posed great danger and they started taking stock of their fighting strength and intentions.

The emergence of the Mamelukes

While events were raging in Syria, Egypt continued to be weighed down by Fatimid rule with its Ismaili leanings. However, the Egyptian people were still Sunni Muslims and had avoided being dragged down by esoteric convictions. The Fatimids needed to create new armies capable of defending their dynasty, the foundations of which were crumbling by the hour. To this end, they set about buying foreign slaves, such as Turks and Circasians, and started to train them in the art of combat and the use of weapons. These were subsequently known by the appellative of Mamelukes, men destined to leave their mark on history.

Discord among Fatimid ministers

As was customary in the Fatimid caliphate, power rested in the hands of the ministers. Al-'Abid, the Fatimid caliph, had appointed three ministers— Shawar, Al-'Adid and Dirgham. Because of their rivalry over the post of vizier, they coexisted in great discord. Shawar managed to have Al-'Adid murdered, but was in turn defeated by Dirgham's army. Shawar fled to Syria after being prosecuted in Egypt.

Shawar went to Nureddin to ask him for help in removing Dirgham from office and driving him out of Egypt. To obtain his objective, Shawar emphasized the importance of Egypt as the southern bulwark against the crusaders. Its capture would leave the invaders vulnerable to defeat and annihilation.

Nureddin heads towards Egypt

Nureddin saw this as an ideal opportunity. He realized that a strong Egypt could be of great help in driving the crusaders out of Palestine. Shawar promised to help Nureddin with men and material if he assisted him in regaining power in Egypt and defeating Dirgham. Nureddin was also aware that Egypt was a wealthy land, which would allow him to consolidate his kingdom, reinforce his army and drive the invaders out of Jerusalem.

Nureddin sent an army to Egypt under the command of Shirkuh. Aware of the impending invasion, the Fatimid vizier Dirgham led his army to confront Shirkuh. The clash took place at the Egyptian town of Bilbeis and Shirkuh defeated his Fatimid enemy. He then continued his march to Cairo.

Dirgham unsuccessfully organized another army to defend the city, but it fell to the Syrians. Shirkuh made his triumphal entry into Cairo and reinstated Shawar as vizier.

The agreement was that, having been restored to power, Shawar would provide Nureddin with funds and men to fight the crusaders. However, he began to backtrack on his promise and asked for a postponement. Shawar's irrresponsible attitude and his violation of the agreement prompted Shirkuh to remain in Egypt. He made incursions into the eastern territory and ended up bringing it under his authority. His manoeuvres startled Shawar, who ended up seeking the crusaders' help to rid himself of Shirkuh.

Treachery

Shawar was a vizier of the Fatimid dynasty, part of the esoteric, Ismaili sect that concealed its intentions and pretended to be what it was not. In this respect, too, disloyalty was in the nature of the Fatimid leaders and a clear sign of their religious and moral deviousness.

The crusaders regarded Shawar's call for help as a unique opportunity to take revenge on the Syrian army, which had inflicted numerous defeats on them. Thus, the crusaders sent an army from Jerusalem with the intention of besieging Shirkuh, while, at the same time, the Fatimids moved their army from Cairo to assault the Syrian army on another flank. For Nureddin and his expectations, the situation had taken a radical turn—instead of being able to rely on support from Egypt and its rulers in his struggle against the crusaders, he was forced to see his main army defeated in Egypt itself and seized by the alliance between the Fatimids and the crusaders. His immediate reaction was to give orders for another army to help Shirkuh.

Truce with the crusaders

Nureddin's army was scoring victories on its march towards Egypt, but no news had reached Shirkuh of what was happening. He decided that a conciliatory truce with the crusaders would be the most favourable settlement under the circumstances, as it would spare him from the siege organized by the armies of both the crusaders and the Fatimids. After negotiations, he consequently accepted the truce and agreed to the peaceful withdrawal of both invading forces from Egypt. When Nureddin got wind of the

agreement, he turned back to Syria, realizing that he had advanced too far into Palestine and that his rearguard in Damascus was left with only a small garrison. He also feared that the Christians were setting some sort of trap by taking advantage of his absence. He had not relinquished the idea of dominating Egypt, tempted by the strength of such a front with Syria, and still aimed to sort matters out with Shawar and drive him out of Egypt.

Fresh preparations

When Shirkuh returned to Damascus, Nureddin ordered a fresh army to be organized and to set out once again for Egypt. This is how a subsequent march on Egypt began, commanded by Shirkuh, who by then had acquired considerable knowledge and a vast amount of information about the Egyptian territory and how to conduct a military campaign there. He led his army to Giza where he set up camp. News of his arrival soon reached Shawar, who once again asked for support from the crusaders. They lost no time in responding, hurriedly sending their forces to meet the Syrian army.

The conquest of Alexandria

Shirkuh did not want to relive his previous experience and therefore carried out a wise military manoeuvre—he marched with his soldiers towards Upper Egypt, to avoid being caught in a pincer movement again. This way he could manoeuvre and choose the battlefield against the crusaders. In fact the confrontation took place just as he had wanted and Shirkuh won a great victory over the crusaders. Then, he marched on Cairo to face the army of Shawar, which was joined by the remnant of the defeated crusaders. Between them they still made up a strong army, capable of facing the Syrian army. Again, Shirkuh carried out a tactical manoeuvre by heading towards Alexandria, instead of going to Cairo. Alexandria surrendered and he appointed as governor his young nephew, Salah ad-Din al-Ayyubi (Saladin), who was not yet 25—this was to be the first time he had ever held such a high position. Shirkuh devoted himself to distracting the Fatimid and crusader troops in the suburbs of Cairo to avoiding engaging them in a hand-to-hand fight in one single battle. However both Shawar and the crusaders suddenly marched towards

> "Nothing hurt the Muslims more than the disloyalty of their emirs, who sold everything to retain their power base, which they also lost in the end."

Alexandria to besiege Saladin. Shirkuh was forced to turn back in that direction to support his nephew and managed to waylay the siege. Nevertheless the two armies had become embroiled in a complicated and continuous armed struggle. Shirkuh persisted with such a strategy to avoid confronting the joint might of the Fatimids and crusaders, who made up a formidable fighting force. The deadlock eventually led to a flurry of negotiations by which Shirkuh and Saladin agreed to withdraw from Alexandria in exchange for compensation for the campaign they had undertaken. This amounted to one hundred and fifty thousand dinars. The crusaders' withdrawal from Egypt was also part of the deal.

It was the second time that Shawar was left ruling Egypt without any of the other forces being able to extend their authority over the country. Even this did not put an end to his ongoing rash of disloyalties. He again got in touch with the crusaders, on their return to Jerusalem, and invited them to go back to protect the walls of Cairo, in exchange for a tax which amounted to one hundred thousand dinars in gold. Evidently, the Europeans were not going to let an offer like that go by, and they hurried a military force to Cairo.

Battle shield used by
the Arab soldiers.

The race towards Egypt

AH 564
AD 1169

That bad news reached Nureddin, who realized the danger posed by the permanent presence of crusaders and the formation of a front in Egypt. With their garrison in Cairo, the crusaders took advantage of the situation to start occupying Egypt. They first advanced on and occupied Bilbeis. In view of this attempted occupation and, aware of the disloyalty of his vizier, Shawar, the Fatimid caliph, Al-'Adid, realized that power was slipping out of his control and into the hands of either Shawar or some crusader accomplice. Faced with such a risk, he had no alternative but to send a secret envoy to Nureddin asking for his help to defeat Shawar by breaking his control of the Cairo gates. For Nureddin, this was a new opportunity to prevent the crusaders from taking over Egypt and for him to expand his influence there. He immediately assembled an army and rushed it to Egypt. For the third time, the two armies raced to conquer that territory.

A million dinars for the crusaders

When someone is given to treachery, they are unlikely to change their habits in that respect. No wonder, then, that the vizier, Shawar, contacted the crusaders again to negotiate their intervention in Egypt to repulse Nureddin's army in exchange for one million dinars in gold. It was a fortune that exceeded any of the crusader's ambitions, and it would save them hardship and exhaustion in their occupation of Egypt, which they were not sure they could achieve. They accepted the offer, on which they were given an advance of one hundred thousand dinars in gold.

The march on Cairo

The crusaders started to carry out the ratified agreement. They encamped along the way to prevent Nureddin from entering Egypt. For his part, Shawar started collecting money from the Egyptians, but the amount needed was far in excess of the people's resources. The shortages, hardships and dissatisfaction caused by Shawar's impositions took their toll on the people—several delegations were sent to the caliph, Al-'Adid, to present their complaints. Again, Al-'Adid resorted to asking Nureddin to quickly intervene, in exchange for covering the expenses of the campaign and his men. The offer filled Nureddin with enthusiasm on realizing that Egypt was finally vulnerable. He sent a missive to Shirkuh, who was in Homs, asking for his help with the campaign. Together with Saladin, Shirkuh left with a great military expedition. While, Nureddin was waiting for these reinforcements from Syria, he managed to cut off the crusaders' supply lines between Palestine and Egypt, where their provisions were dwindling. With the approach of a great army and their supply routes cut off, the crusaders realized the dangers they faced and opted to retreat and disperse. They were thus able to avoid confronting Nureddin's army. Shirkuh, for his part, quickly advanced towards Cairo and was able to celebrate a triumphal entry without any resistance.

Shawar, realizing his rule was over, started delaying the handover of Cairo to the Syrian command and hastily sought a solution to overturn the fresh defeat by Nureddin's army. However, Saladin got wind of Shawar's suspicious tactics and requested permission from his uncle, Shirkuh, to execute Shawar. Shirkuh withheld it, saying, "I'm afraid things will turn against us, as we have only been in Egypt for a few days and we should take into account that this land still relies on great support from the Fatimids".

Shawar's execution

When Saladin realized that his uncle did not approve of his plan, he went to the caliph, Al-'Adid, and informed him of his intention to kill Shawar, on condition that he received support and protection from the Fatimids. Al-'Adid agreed, because he wanted to get rid of Shawar at any price. Losing no time, Saladin detained Shawar and executed him. Al-'Adid kept his promise and forbade the Fatimids from exposing Saladin to any danger. Nureddin's rule thus spread throughout Egypt.

Shirkuh, the governor of Egypt

Al-'Adid, having dispensed with the person who managed his affairs, sought a replacement vizier. He could find no one more suited for this purpose than Shirkuh. Although they had arrived as invaders, the caliph considered the Syrians to be more welcome than the crusaders that Shawar had so often called on to face Nureddin's army. Shirkuh was now in control of Egypt and began to conduct its affairs in accordance with his wise politics. Under his rule, justice prospered, scholars and learned religious leaders were honoured, and the people were satisfied. The latter, who were mainly Sunni Muslims, regarded him highly and held him in great esteem. Stability and peace reigned throught the land. However, Shirkuh was in power for only two months before he died. Al-'Adid again had to seek out a minister, and he ended up appointing Saladin as both vizier and army commander. He gave him the title of the king's co-regent. The caliph chose Saladin because of his youth and his skill in handling the country's affairs.

Saladin, the governor of Egypt

Saladin immediately took control of Egypt. He followed the ways of his uncle, acting benevolently with the people and treating them as ethically as possible. This way he soon contented the people and gained their affection. Everything went well for him in Egypt. News of these developments reached Syria and Europe, where upheaval ensued when it became clear that the crusaders in Palestine were caught between two united fronts (Egypt and Syria) under Saladin's command. This prompted Europe to sent crusade campaigns to Egypt.

The hanjar, a curved, double-edged dagger used by Arab soldiers.

129

AH 567
AD 1171   ### A three-pronged assault on Egypt

The crusader armies and fleets moved in from both Europe and Syria. An assault began on Egypt on three fronts: two from the sea, from Europe and Palestine, and one over land from the Sinai. The troops in the First Crusade reached Damietta and surrounded it. There was little Saladin could do to withstand the assault because Egypt was still not completely under his command. The Fatimid forces still threatened his rule as they had started to concentrate in southern Egypt (Sudan) in order to take that country back. He had no alternative other than to write to Nureddin asking for his support. Said and done. A million dinars in gold, weapons and equipment quickly arrived for Saladin, who started attacking crusader defences in Syria and Palestine in manoeuvres of distraction, cutting supply lines and preventing any army from leaving Palestine for Egypt.

The citadel of Krak de Chevaliers

The Krak fortress.

Under pressure from the incessant military moves by Nureddin's army, the crusaders were prompted to withdraw their ground troops and momentarily abandon the idea of attacking Egypt. However, Nureddin continued his assaults and moved towards the citadel of Krak de Chevaliers, one of the crusaders' major fortresses in Syria. For the latter, the situation was critical, so they hurried to rescue the citadel and prevent it from falling into Nureddin's hands. He took advantage of the occupation and the crusaders' hesitation to send a devastating army to Saladin, who met it near Damietta. Together, they liberated the citadel after fifty days of fighting. The crusaders then felt incapable of attacking Egypt and all their armies retreated.

After this victory, Saladin concentrated on consolidating his power over Egypt and achieved total stability. This allowed him to launch campaigns against Palestine from the southern flank, coordinating them with Nureddin, who was attacking from the north. Saladin headed for Gaza and Ascalon, which he conquered. From then on he continued to win victories in the south. Once he controlled the situation in the conquered cities he returned to base. The skirmishes lasted long enough for the crusaders to end up weary and oppressed.

AH 567
AD 1171   ### Death of the caliph, Al-'Adid

That year, the Fatimid caliph, Al-'Adid, died and effective rule was assumed by Saladin. He took advantage of the new status quo to make an extremely bold decision. After having consulted earlier with Nureddin, he formerly announced the abolition of the Fatimid caliphate, which had dominated Egypt and the Maghreb for two whole centuries. In a courageous move, he revoked the discredited Ismaili-based power, banishing it from that land. He preached to the people in the name of the Abbasid caliph in Mesopotamia. Nureddin did likewise, so that, for the first time in centuries, the Muslim community received sermons delivered in the name of one caliph alone. Saladin declared all the Fatimid courts null and void and removed all their judges from office. In their place, he appointed judges from the official Sunni school of law. The situation in Egypt had reached a zenith of perfection in both authority and jurisprudence.

Organization and preparations

Nureddin, buoyed by the removal of the Fatimid dynasty, decided to take advantage of the new momentum by announcing an all-out war against the crusaders in Palestine, on both the northern and southern fronts. However, Saladin asked him to postpone such an initiative because he had not completed the task of stabilizing Egypt. Indeed, a remant of the Fatimids was manoeuvring in the Sudan, which gave cause for concern. In addition, he feared some treacherous move were he to leave Egypt and head for Palestine. He was aware that two hundred years of Fatimid rule would not come to an end quite so quickly. Besides, he considered his priority to be the fortification of Egypt in order to guarantee its stability in view of its new government. Nureddin, however, thought differently. He was in a hurry to crush the crusaders and liberate Jerusalem. To this end, he ordered Saladin to prepare for a full-scale assault as soon as the right moment for it arrived.

AH 569
AD 1173

The Arabian Peninsula under the command of Nureddin

Nureddin commissioned a craftsman to build a mimbar (pulpit), suitably decorated and embellished, to be designed with the maximum expression of beauty and grandeur. Then he promised the people to put it in the Al-Aqsa mosque of Jerusalem with the help of Almighty God. Meanwhile, the preparations and organization of the armies in Syria continued to take their course. In Egypt, Saladin proceeded to send his brother to the Hijaz (in the region of Mecca and Medina), whose people had sworn allegiance to Nureddin and had become part of his domain. The march continued on Yemen, a territory that joined the others. The Islamic front extended in all directions, sending terror into the hearts of the crusaders who were surrounded on every side.

A conspiracy to assassinate Saladin aborted

At that time, the Fatimids were arranging a conspiracy to assassinate Saladin. They had managed to secure the collaboration of some of his palace officials to ensure the success of the plan, but one of Saladin's most faithful followers discovered the plot. He first acted as if he were an accomplice, but kept Saladin informed about developments. He eventually set a trap for them—when the day came, he surprised them and killed everyone he could, while some managed to escape. The first attempt to put an end to Saladin's life had been aborted.

AH 569
AD 1174

Suspicious movements

The Fatimids reunited in southern Egypt (present-day Sudan) after the failure of their assassination attempt on Saladin's life. They then initiated correspondence with members of the Ismaili movement in Syria, who provided assistance by secretly sending troops and other reinforcements. They also contacted the crusaders on the island of Sicily so that, together, they could launch a joint assault against Sal-

adin's forces from both the north and south. The crusaders responded that they would be happy to collaborate, and preparations got under way to carry out the conspiracy. Saladin's original misgivings, when he sought to postpone the assault on the crusaders based in Palestine, turned out to be founded. He realized the danger that lay ahead from those fronts in Egypt as he had sensed suspicious manoeuvres all around.

AH 569
AD 1174

The death of Nureddin. Reflections on a hero's exploits

The day Nureddin passed away, the Muslim community lost one of the greatest leaders in its history. He was greater even than Saladin. History has not accorded him his true place, commensurate with his greatness. He was a profound realist and understood the conflict with Europe well. He fought with authority, command and power, and he fought with conviction. His foresight persuaded him that the struggle should not be between the people of Syria and Egypt but against the invading crusaders. It was a battle by and for Muslims. Nureddin, Imad ad-Din and Saladin were either Kurdish or Turkomen. They were not Arabs. Nevertheless, they were educated and grew up into the authentic Islamic faith, leaving the idea of nationalism and sectarianism to one side. Their one and only concern was to liberate Palestine. One of the strategies that Nureddin always repeated was that the battle was not for a parcel of land in Palestine but for the whole territory, for every span of that territory. One of his most outstanding principles was his insistence that a community could only stand up for itself if it was well prepared, and that a weak and divided people could never win. Preparation had to be made on an intellectual, social, economic and military level. Even during the wars against the crusaders, he never neglected the need for implementing justice and building the country. One of his basic principles consisted in the need to unify the people so they could confront foreign invasion. He even proposed to the governor of Damascus that he remain in office in exchange for supporting him in the war against the crusaders. His ambition was to be able to form a united Islamic community, not a private kingdom. He was sincere and conscious about what he planned and executed.

The testimony of historians

Ibn al-Athir, in his book entitled *The complete history,* says: "I reviewed the history of most of the kings who ruled, from pre-Islamic times up until the present, and found that the most illustrious biographies, after those of the first four caliphs, were the lives of 'Umar Ibn 'Abdul 'Aziz and the just King Nureddin". Ibn al-Athir was speaking with authority, as he lived through those events and chronicled them. He was an eyewitness to Nureddin's battles and defeats.

The pious fighter

Historians describe Nureddin as an intelligent, shrewd and ingenious man. His analysis of affairs was accurate—he was quick to size up a situation—yet he never appeared conceited before anyone. Neither could he be cheated. He was known for his devotion, religious piety and fulfillment of spiritual duties. He kept vigil during his voluntary prayers, and regularly fasted and prayed. In addition, he was educated in the tradition of the reformist movement and in the spirit of religious renewal instituted by the imams At-Tartushi and Al-Ghazali, among others. Nureddin's life and deeds show that he was inspired by the essence of those educational methods.

Nureddin, the legal expert (faqih)

He was a wise legal expert who was knowledgeable about the procedures and quotations of the Prophet and the author of a book on the fight for God's cause. He was never heard to utter anything untoward, even when he was angry. He was discreet, worthy and well mannered. His austerity was such that his wife had to complain on accasion about his thrift. He was totally committed to the prescriptions of Islam. He praised the learned experts in religious sciences whom he encouraged and supported. He was also generous with the preachers, to whom he gave full powers to preach the good and prohibit evil. Moreover, he restored and built religious endowments (pious foundations) and inalienable properties. He started a global social reform and boosted the economy. Tax collection by means of the zakat (fiscal contribution) was plentiful, and trade improved. He gradually eliminated all taxes that were not prescribed under Islamic law. He spent his whole life fighting for God's cause and for unification of the Muslim community. He governed for twenty-eight years, during which he liberated fifty cities and fortifications that had been seized by the crusaders.

After the death of Nureddin

The situation changed, however, after his death. His followers swore allegiance to Isma'il, Nureddin's son, who was hardly eleven years old at the time. The changeover came just when the Islamic community was immersed in the battle against the crusaders, and it came as a setback. The young successor was nicknamed King Isma'il the Kind. Fighting between Saladin and those upholding Nureddin's legacy was soon to break out, as Saladin's purpose was to take over Nureddin's former kingdom. With war between the two parties imminent, the prefects ruling in every city proclaimed themselves governors.

Secession and controversy

The withdrawal was naturally to the crusaders liking and they resumed their assaults to recover the citadels and defences that Nureddin had seized from them. The land of Islam was again in turmoil. In Egypt, Saladin viewed the

"Nureddin, one of the emblems of the Muslim community, deserves his name to be written with a gold quill, and glorified with the most brilliant distinctions."

AH 579
AD 1183

situation with alarm and decided to act—he had no alternative but to proclaim himself governor of Syria, as he considered himself to be its heir, in spite of not belonging to the Zanki family. Being an Ayyubi, the Zankis would not accept him. Under the circumstances, Saladin decided to hand over power in Egypt to his brother, Al-'Adil, and he left for Syria with his best forces. He was accompanied by seven hundred noblemen, including the bravest commanders. They crossed Palestine and started attacking the small states that had emerged since the death of Nureddin. Some of them opened their doors to him and admitted his rule, whereas the majority rejected him. Saladin had to fight both the crusaders and Zanki's followers. The final unification of Syria took him twelve long years.

Several fronts

This was not an easy affair, and it was a misfortune for the Muslims. Saladin was forced to fight the crusaders in Palestine and Zanki's followers, who rejected submission under the unity of the Muslim community. In addition, the crusaders and Fatimids continued to collaborate in a number of operations. Their complicity led them to take advantage of the Muslim secession. A missive from the Fatimids was sufficient for a crusader army to come from Sicily. It reached Alexandria and occupied it, and this forced Saladin to return to Egypt to attack, defeat and drive them out.

That same year, AH 579, the Fatimids assembled fifty thousand troops in the Sudan region, in accordance with a plan they had drawn up in collusion with the crusaders, which consisted of a synchronized assault from the north and the south. Saladin's rapid victory over the crusaders in Alexandria caught them by surprise and they had to change their plans by moving their army, under the command of Kanz al-Dawla al-Fatimi, towards Cairo. Saladin reacted at once and gave orders to Al-'Adil to set off to meet the Fatimids without waiting for him to arrive. Al-'Adil carried out the order and set off with an Egyptian army. A great battle took place between the Sunnis and the Ismailis, which the first-mentioned won brilliantly. The Fatimids were wiped out. Only an insignificant minority managed to escape. After that battle, they never fully recovered again. It was on account of this battle that the most fervent hatred of Saladin grew among the Ismaili—this was the man who had destroyed them and their dynasty after two hundred years of corrupt rule. That hatred is still latent in their souls today.

PART TWO
Palestine in the Islamic era

CHAPTER FIVE
Saladin

Saladin

1. The rule of Saladin

The biography of Saladin

Saladin Al-Ayyubi was born in the year AH 530/AD 1137 in the citadel of Tikrit (Mesopotamia). His father was the governor of the city. Later on, but while still a young man, he held the position of vizier of Egypt. He was educated at the same reformist school as Nureddin and Imad ad-Din Zanki. He had strong convictions, was very devout, took part in communal prayers, and insisted on keeping traditions and supererogatory events. He kept vigils and loved to listen to readings of the Koran. At prayer time, he used to personally choose the imam best suited for his voice and virtues. He was sensitive, easily moved, and full of mercy and tenderness, virtues that were clearly visible to even his enemies. Whenever he listened to the Koran, tears streamed down his face. He loved listening to hadiths (maxims of the Prophet) and praised the divine rites. He had unconditional faith in God and relied on Him alone. He was a good companion—he was just and indulgent with people, compassionate and a defender of the oppressed and the weak. He was generous and extremely chivalrous. His moral conduct was upright, as were his talks, in which he spoke in pleasing tones and only alluded to specific people in the kindest language. He rejected gossip and slander. He was a man who was pure in thought, speech and writing.

An imaginary portrait of Saladin.

The magnanimous

He was equally a brave hero, tenacious in battle and magnanimous. One day, when near Acre, he said: "It occurs to me that if God were to help us recover the rest of the coastal areas, it would clear the country of crusaders". Due to that magnanimity and those supreme intentions, he left to one side his people, his home and his motherland. He spent most of his days on military campaigns. He was known for his affection towards deprived people. When he conquered a city, he inspected the defeated enemies in search of elderly people, women or children who he would treat with affection and indulgence and put himself at their disposal for whatever they needed.

The ascetic king

He lived a devout and simple life in an era in which luxury and squandering abounded, away from the pomposity of kings, distinction and status. He was very indulgent. He never persecuted anybody for his religious beliefs. He let people worship whoever they wanted, without any attempt to prose-lytise them by pressure or coercion. He did not favour killing or spilling the enemy's blood. He would set captives free and sympathize with them. These were his true human qualities, far removed from his enemies' description of a cruel, covetous and bloodthirsty person.

The countdown to Hattin

AH 578
AD 1182

Saladin managed to seize most of Syria, but there were vital regions that es-caped his rule. The situation was more favourable to him in Egypt, the Hijaz and Yemen. He immediately made preparations for the decisive battle, which he carefully planned and which consisted of a simultaneous assault from the north and south. However, he had to reconsider his initial ap-proach and make changes to his plans, as the situation was unlike the earlier Nureddin period, particularly in Syria, where there were attempts at destabi-lization. Saladin decided to unify the armies of Egypt and Syria under a sin-gle command in order to form one crushing force with which to confront the crusaders. This decision was precisely what marked the great Battle of Hattin.

Raynald and the fortress of Krak

AH 578
AD 1182

The crusaders ruled over a large part of Palestine and the whole of its coast-line, where the seaboard afforded access to supplies from Europe. Their largest fortress was that of Krak, located in a very strategic place.

It was a major obstacle along the route that the Islamic armies used between Egypt and Syria. Saladin considered the crusader fortress as an impediment for the unification of his forces. Raynald, the lord of the fort, sensed that Sal-adin had set his sights on the fortress of Krak and he applied a strategy to distract Saladin's attention and prevent him from uniting his the armies. His idea was to lead him away from the region and hold out Mecca and Medina as a coveted prize. His intentions came to the notice of the governor of Damascus, 'Iz ad-Din, whose aim it was to conduct a surprise assault on Krak that would prevent Raynald from fulfilling his aims. His objective was

not to conquer the citadel, as it was impregnable for an army as small as his, but to force him to abort his dangerous plan. In fact he caught Raynald's forces by surprise and caused them heavy losses, destroying the surroundings and burning the land. He then made several tactical retreats followed by fresh assaults until Arnold was forced to move back inside the fortress and abandon his plan or at least postpone it.

Another unsuccessful attempt

Saladin was aware of these developments and concerned himself with protecting Egypt, Mecca and Medina. The solution he hit upon was to assemble a naval fleet in the Red Sea with the aim of protecting the Hijaz in case Raynald tried to implement his plan. Raynald, for his part, was brash enough to carry out his heinous designs. Without his adversary's knowledge, in secret, he had some ships built inside the fortress, dismatled into separate parts and then sent to Aqaba. There the vessels were assembled, his armies embarked and the fleet set sail for the Arabian Peninsula. To complete his plan and, at the same time, disperse the Muslim forces in Syria, he started a series of raids on pilgrim caravans travelling to the holy sites. Saladin, who at the time was besieging one of the fortresses in Palestine, sent a message to his brother, Al-'Adil, for him to intercept Raynald's army before it got to Medina, as it was impossible to intercept it from where he was. Al-'Adil hurried to move the Egyptian fleet used to protect Mecca and Medina. The race between the crusaders' and the Muslim fleets began and the first to reach the region of Rabigh, on the shores of the Red Sea, were the crusaders. Hardly had the crusaders disembarked when they saw the Egyptian fleet arriving. The latter's pursuit of the crusader army, to prevent it from reaching Medina, ended in the Muslims successfully intercepting the crusaders as they arrived on the coast of Hawra'. A great battle took place there that ended in the defeat of the enormous crusader army by the Muslims.

The seige of Krak

AH 579
AD 1183

Saladin was very angry at Raynald's foolhardy expedition. He organised an army the following year and ordered the Egyptian army to join him in besieging Krak. He had catapults brought and used to strike powerful blows on the fortress walls. At this, the crusaders made moves to evacuate the stronghold. Amaury, the king of Jerusalem, sent his army to help them flee but Saladin, who had not yet prepared for a decisive battle against the crusaders, decided to retreat, since his only concern was for Krak. Once in Damascus he restarted preparations and improved the organization of his army. Aleppo was hostile to him and its disloyal governor refused to give him any support. Saladin was forced to change tactics. He momentarily forgot the crusaders and attacked Aleppo, which he conquered in the year AH 579. Then he concentrated on uniting both the cities in Syria and the army under his command. He also carried out raids on Krak, although still without intending to conquer it. The objective was to keep its governor occupied and prevent him from thinking about a new offensive against Medina. Despite their small numbers, his forces managed to breach the walls of the stronghold. Once inside, they were surprised to find that Raynald had built enormous ditches behind them. Forces from the two armies fought across the ditches, which the Muslims vainly tried to fill with earth. The crusaders, who dominated large areas of Palestine, sent reinforcements to break the siege, but Saladin reacted in time by ordering his men to retreat at once towards Damascus.

Saladin again urged other Muslim kingdoms that had remained on the sidelines to help in an all-out assault on the crusaders. He managed to get the Islamic ulamas of Mosul to put pressure on the governor, who eventually gave in to popular demand and pledged support for Saladin. Having achieved his aim, he renewed his battles against the crusaders, and the lord of Krak in particular, for another three years.

The pilgrims' revenge

AH 582
AD 1186

That year Raynald committed a serious error by attacking a large caravan of Muslim pilgrims, looting their possessions and taking everyone prisoner. When they protested that they were simple pilgrims and not soldiers, Arnold mocked them and said: "Tell that to your Muhammad so that he can redeem you". In view of this vile aggression, Saladin swore and promised God he would kill Raynald with his own hands. He started by repealing the truce in force with the kingdom of Jerusalem. He asked the Muslims for help in fighting for the supreme cause and sent security forces to guard the route to the sacred house of God (the Kaaba). He then mounted an assault on the fortress of Krak and destroyed the surrounding areas. He also engaged in several manoeuvres in Palestine to keep the crusaders on the defensive until the great army he was preparing in Egypt was ready. Once it had been assembled, he entrusted its command to his brother Al-'Adil. Saladin continued in the vein of a true strategist by sending forces from Aleppo (in northern Syria) to attack the crusaders' enclave of Antioch. When they were about to enter into combat, the besieged crusaderes proposed a truce, which was accepted, and they laid down their weapons. With that gesture Saladin ensured the neutrality of the kingdom of Antioch so that they would not fight against him or double cross him if they had to fight separately against the crusaders. Some divisions that arose between the crusader commanders in Jerusalem resulted in Saladin sending a secret message to one of them (Raymond) informing him that he was ready to support him. Saladin's offer was well received by Raymond. Saladin then launched a surprise attack on Saffuriyah, a large area where the crusader armies were concentrated. It was a night-time assault in which the majority of the enemy soldiers were killed or taken prisoner.

When they learned what had happened, other crusaders realized the danger they were facing, so they mustered

Palestine in the Islamic era

Saladin, portrayed
by a European artist.

an army of over 63 thousand soldiers under the leadership of Guy de Lusignan, the king of Jerusalem. The various leaders put aside their differences and concentrated their efforts on a joint battle against Saladin. They met at Saffuriyah, which Saladin had abandoned.

Saladin had no intention of engaging the crusaders in a single battle at Saffuriyah, as this was a fertile region surrounded with pastureland and water. To head there would mean arriving with a tired army which would then have to face rested men ready to receive them. Instead, he opted to choose his own battleground. He drew up his battle lines and mounted a series of rapid assaults using light forces that immediately withdrew in order to gradually draw the crusaders out of that area, but this ploy was unsuccessful.

The reconquest of Tiberias

In a change of strategy, Saladin attacked Tiberias, an area of great importance to the crusaders. The route that separated Tiberias from Saffuriyah was difficult to negotiate and the journey fatiguing. Saladin's plan was to progressively push the crusaders towards it. He ended up bursting into the fortress of Tiberias on AD 2/7/1187.

The fall of Tiberias aroused differences of opinion between the crusader princes. Some argued that they could not let Saladin assault their various kingdoms without returning there to put up a fight, while others realized that his strategy was designed to draw them towards a battlefield of his choosing. The latter opinion was upheld by a majority and they opted to march on Tiberias to face Saladin's forces. The march began along that difficult route leading to Tiberias, under the blazing summer sun, with insufficient supplies of water to quench the thirst of the large crusader army. Losing no time, Saladin set up ambushes and sent in light assault groups to harass and wear down the enemy, thus delaying their progress and plunging them into fatigue and desperation. Water was running short, the heat was increasing and Saladin was relentless with his raids and assaults, some of which targeted the crusaders' rearguard, while the rest of the crusader troops were advancing. The rearguard was eventually separated from the vanguard, which had to wait for the rest to arrive, for fear of becoming overstretched and going into battle without their support. Finally, they chose to encamp at the foot of Mount Tiberias, overlooking the valley of Hattin, marking the prelude to the decisive "Battle of Hattin".

2. The great battle of Hattin

AH 583
AD 1187

Saladin had a force of some 12,000 soldiers, whereas the crusader forces to-talled some 63,000 combatants. This disadvantage did not dissuade him from a decisive confrontation. The clash initially took place on the hillside of mount Tiberias, near the Hattin plain. On the morning of Friday, 24 Ra-bi' Al-Akhar AH 583—July AD 1187, the two armies locked in a fierce battle that lasted the whole day, without either side being able to defeat the other. However, thirst, fatigue and the intrinsic difficulties in the mountainous ter-rain led the crusader army to withdraw to the Hittin plain. Saladin then moved his army over night and encircled the cru-saders, leaving them no escape route. On Saturday morning, the fighting resumed. Raymond, the governor of the crusader principality of Tripoli, tried in vain to break the siege by using the main part of the cavalry to violently assault the Muslim army. Saladin, for his part, ordered his soldiers to force their way through, because Raymond had managed to cross to an-other side without realizing he was falling into a trap. A squadron of cavalry was waiting to seal him off from behind. Isolated from the rest of the army, he was struck by fear and fled to Tripoli, galloping non-stop all the way. This is how Sal-adin got rid of one of the most arrogant crusaders.

As soon as the wind started to blow in the direction of the cru-saders, Saladin instructed dry grass to be set alight, so that the smoke started choking the enemy and the blaze burning their faces. This, coupled with the searing heat and the fact that they were growing thirstier all the time, doomed the crusaders to retreat towards the mountain, where they tried to set up camp to recover and get their breath back. It was only an at-tempt, because Saladin's army immediately set upon them when they were just beginning to erect the king's tent.

The battle of Hattin.

Convinced that it was going to boost their morale in battle, the crusaders had brought to the battlefield what they believed to be the cross on which Christ was crucified. It was one of their greatest holy symbols but, after coming under intense pressure on the battlefield, they were forced to aban-don it and flee towards the mountain. The Muslims then picked up the

cross and carried it with them, causing great misfortune to the Christians, as it made them lose their fervour and fighting spirit.

Saladin's victory

Saracen harassment of the crusaders was asphyxiating. In that year alone, 30,000 of a total of 63,000 crusaders lost their lives, while many others gave themselves up. Only about 150 knights remained near the king's tent, on the top of the mountain, defending the sovereign with all their might, managing to repulse three consecutive attacks by the Muslims. It was difficult for the Muslims to overcome them and, in view of this, Saladin realized that they would only surrender if the king's tent were to fall, so he ordered them to focus on bringing that about. The Muslims started slipping behind the knights to bring down the tent and they managed to break the guy ropes, causing it to fall on the king. At this, the crusaders surrendered. On contemplating this spectacle, Saladin fell to his knees before God, crying for joy.

The Muslims collected an enormous booty in money, horses and weapons. Cries of "God is great" and "there is no god but God" rang out. That night, he devoted himself to prayer, reading the Koran and praising Almighty God, in addition to reflecting on how God had awarded victory to a limited Muslim army, numbering less than 12,000 men, compared to the enormous and much better equipped crusader army.

The ethics of war in Islam cannot be compared to the wild attitude of the crusaders. Having won the great victory, Saladin ordered a tent to be erected in Hattin. There, he kept vigil, praying and thanking God for that overwhelming conquest. The following day he ordered the Christian princes to be brought as prisoners. When they were presented to him, he received and honoured them courteously and invited the crusader king Guy de Lusignan to sit next to him on the throne. Next to him was Raynald, from the fortress of Krak, who had so often displayed his perfidious ways against the Muslims, even daring to try to conquer Medina and Mecca. Saladin despised him. Saladin arranged for water to be brought for everyone. Guy drank half a pitcher and offered the rest to Raynald. Saladin's reaction was one of annoyance:

"I have not ordered Raynald to drink. I only offered you the pitcher!" Then he addressed Raynald and said: "Damn you! What a lot of treaties you have violated!" Raynald answered, with all malevolence and arro-

> "Historians, recounting accounts by those who saw the dead, say that it looked as if no one had escaped death, and that, whoever looked at the prisoners could affirm that none of the believers had died."

gance: "It is customary for kings to use disloyalty and deception as a policy to dominate the people".

The execution of Raynald

Saladin was left speechless at Raynald's expression of such despicable ethics and, in view of this, drew his sword and, with a fearful blow, split his shoulder. Raynald fell to the ground, but was still alive. There, the Muslim knights attacked him and finished him off. Thus, Saladin fulfilled his oath to kill Raynald with his own hands. When the crusader king saw this spectacle, he started trembling. Saladin said to him: "We are not in the custom of killing princes, but this one went too far, and he suffered the inevitable".

Crusaders in captivity

Having won that great victory, Saladin went towards Damascus, preceded by the crusader prisoners, who numbered approximately 30,000. Every 30 crusaders, tethered to the same rope, were led by a single Saracen. This way God had exposed the crusaders to humiliation. For a long time they had devastated the lands of Islam until God put them to shame in that fashion.

Saladin breaches the crusader's defences.

The death of Raymond

As for Raymond, who had escaped to Tripoli, he received the news of the outcome of the battle and the humiliation suffered by his coreligionists. Distress and sadness were added to his fury, his heart was torn to pieces and this caused his death. It was another consequence of the battle of Hattin.

The liberation of the cities of Palestine

Saladin then marched on Ascalon, where he settled, and from where he directed his battles. Crusader defeats continued for a period of two months after the battle of Hattin. Acre, Nazareth, Haifa, Nablus, Daynin, Bethsan, Jaffa, Sidon, Beirut, Ramallah, Hebron, Bethlehem and Ascalon were reconquered in that space of time. Thus, the battle of Hattin is recalled in history as one of the greatest importance.

AH 583
AD 1187

3. The liberation of Jerusalem

Fear seizes the crusaders

The crusaders had still not left Palestine and continued receiving provisions from Europe, in spite of the marked Muslim supremacy. But, when the Saracens began preparations for the conquest of Jerusalem, they were seized with fear and sought refuge in the mountain areas and in Jerusalem itself. Clearly, the battle of Hattin had not wiped out the crusader presence in greater Syria. Indeed, their presence in Palestine lasted for almost another one hundred years. Nevertheless, Hattin is considered as the turning point for the Muslims who, previously regarded as the weaker underlings, had grown in strength and begun overwhelming their crusader adversaries.

The march on Jerusalem

The crusaders had occupied Jerusalem for over 91 years, according to the Muslim calendar, and 88 years in the Christian calendar. As mentioned earlier, the crusaders had turned part of the Al-Aqsa mosque into a church, while others had been adapted as accommodation for the knights and an armoury. The rest had been turned into stables, which amounted to desecration of a holy place. Saladin was on the verge of liberating the city. The crusaders still dominated some areas, such as the kingdom of Tripoli, which included part of Lebanon, part of Antioch in southern Turkey and all of northern Syria. The first thing that Saladin did was to distribute the army so that they were able to cut off the supply routes from those kingdoms that were giving support to the kingdom of Jerusalem. It was the prelude to marching on that territory. The crusaders' reaction was to shore up their defences, including the erection of defensive walls. They numbered 20,000 soldiers and saw death as a lesser evil compared to handing over Jerusalem. They were with their families and their Muslim prisoners—men, women and children in their thousands.

Saladin besieges Jerusalem

In the middle of the month of Rajab, in the year AH 583 (AD 1178), that is, immediately after the battle of Hattin, Saladin moved his army towards Jerusalem, which he completely encircled. He started to pound the city walls with catapults, while archers launched their arrows over the top, to the extent that the crusaders did not even dare look over. Saladin gave the order to advance and the Muslims pushed forward. They managed to clear the trenches that had been dug around the walls, but the walls themselves were impregnable. Saladin used his team of lancers to punch holes in the walls. These they then filled with firewood, which was set alight, thus weakening the structure.

Saladin in Jerusalem.

The collapse of the crusaders

The crusaders were demoralized when it became evident that the enemy was about to break through the walls. Women, men, the elderly and children took refuge in the church of the Holy Sepulchre, where they devoted themselves to prayer. The head of the crusaders then sent a delegation to Saladin asking for mercy, promising to hand over the city on the condition that all the crusaders were allowed to leave in peace, with their belongings and weapons. Saladin reminded them that ninety-one years earlier, the crusaders had entered Jerusalem and committed savage acts of slaughter, slashing Muslims to pieces as if they were sheep in the area of Al-Aqsa mosque. He said to them:

"For God's sake! How can I not cut your throats in the same way you did to the Muslims before?" The crusaders were struck with fear and seeing that the Muslims were longing to avenge their forefathers, they realized that their death was inevitable.

"Saladin's generosity was unheard of in the world at that time; only the prophets, messengers and companions of the prophet Muhammad had displayed such values."

A dangerous threat

Faced with the magnitude of the misfortune they were about to live through, the crusaders could find no better solution than to send a new delegation to Saladin with a dangerous message. In it they threatened to kill the Muslim prisoners detained in Jerusalem, to destroy all the mosques and holy places, to break the rock of Al-Aqsa, to burn the entire city and to commit suicide.

The reconciliation

Confronted with this threat, after some deliberation, Saladin assembled his staff to consult them about the delicate situation. They all agreed the threat was serious, as they realized the crusaders had nothing to lose, knowing that they were going to die just the same. Agreement was reached and they began negotiations for the surrender of Jerusalem, on condition that the crusaders left the city without their weapons, although they were allowed to take their belongings and money. Before leaving, everyone had to pay one gold dinar. Some elderly and handicapped people asked Saladin to exonerate them from paying this tax, to which Saladin replied: "Go in peace".

Unusual generosity

To what extent may we compare the conquest of Jerusalem by the crusaders and the reconquest of it by the Muslims? For instance, Al-'Adil went to his brother, Saladin, and said: "Let me be responsible for paying the taxes of one thousand civilian crusaders". Saladin granted this to him and Al-'Adil set them free. Other Muslim princes followed his example and liberated a great number of Christian civilians. In spite of this, many were left who could not find anybody to pay for their release because, as previously indicated, they numbered almost 70,000 in Jerusalem. The poor crusaders started to ask the rich ones for just one gold dinar, but they refused to help the poor members of their community, who ended up as prisoners. Some women went before Saladin complaining that their husbands had been killed at Hattin and that they had no money with which to settle the tax. Saladin allowed them to leave without paying. And he gave his own money to those women who had no sponsor to pay the ransom for them, so that they could leave. Even Raynald's wife asked him to set her son free, as she was afraid the Muslims would kill him because of who he was. Saladin said: "I shall give him every protection", and freed him.

Historians took note of this episode. Those men he had set free were soldiers who later reunited to fight against him. It would therefore have been more practical to either imprison or kill them, but he was a man with the highest degree of Islamic ethics.

Triumphal entry

On the eve of the twenty-seventh day of Rajab, in the year AH 583—the second of October, AD 1187—coinciding with the celebration of the Prophet's overnight journey from Mecca to Jerusalem, and his ascension into heaven from there, after 91 lunar years and 88 Gregorian years of crusader occupation, the Muslims were able to enter Jerusalem and, after so many decades, they were once again able to hear the voice of the muezzin from the Al-Asqa mosque calling them to prayer. Enormous joy was expressed by short prayers about God's uniqueness and greatness which could be heard in different parts of Jerusalem and its surroundings. The Muslims hurried to the Dome of The Rock mosque, where they clambered up to remove and destroy the cross that the crusaders had placed on the top, and, as they did so, they broke into prayer under the resigned, humiliated gaze of the crusaders.

Reinforcing the mosques of Al-Aqsa and the Dome of The Rock

Saladin immediately ordered the Dome of The Rock to be reinforced, and the Al-Aqsa mosque enlarged. The bricklayers started work at once to recover the engravings, inscriptions, xylographs and commemorative sculptures embellishing the mosque in gold-coloured marble.

Nureddin's pulpit installed in Al-Aqsa mosque

Saladin ordered the great wooden mimbar (pulpit) to be brought. This was the pulpit Nureddin had commissioned 20 years earlier for the Al-Asqa mosque, but which he had not been able to see in Jerusalem before his death. Once in place, it became a yardstick for other mimbars built thereafter. Especially for us, it is a lesson in patient perseverance in our efforts to set Jerusalem free.

The mimbar remained in the Al-Asqa mosque until it was destroyed in a fire, started by a Jew, Mike Rohan, which engulfed the mosque on 21 August 1969. Only a few small planks and some pictures remain of what

Nureddin's mimbar as it was before being burned by a Jew in 1969.

"In the name of God, the merciful, the compassionate. The renovation of this sacred mihrab and the reconstruction of the Al-Asqa mosque are the works of the fearful and faithful servant of God, Yusuf Ibn Ayyub Abu-l-Mudhaffar.*"

*"Victorious King", Saladin's epithet

was considered to be a unique work of art—they are today preserved in the Islamic museum adjoining the mosque. The mimbar was a model of precise workmanship and contained a plethora of Islamic motifs.

The immunity of the Christian holy places

Some Muslims went to Saladin demanding that the church of the Holy Sepulchre be demolished in revenge for what the crusaders had done to the Al-Aqsa mosque. Saladin said to them in disapproval: "Omar safeguarded it and you want me to destroy it". That was the maximum expression of respect for other religions and the consolidation of the greatness of Islam.

Jubilation invades Muslim lands

News of the recovery of Jerusalem and Al-Aqsa, when hope had been all but lost, spread to Muslim countries, and joy was expressed everywhere in public celebrations. Events marking the reconquest were held for a whole month. Its liberation was one of the greatest real-life events in which Muslims regained their dignity.

Lessons to be learned

If the crusaders' occupation of Jerusalem lasted 91 years and, despite that, Saladin and his forces never lost hope of reconquering it, today's community should likewise not be dispirited at their chances of recovering it, however long that may take.

The reconquest continues

Saladin lost no time in sending his forces to besiege Acre, followed by an assault on the principality of Tripoli. The crusades had floundered in Jerusalem, which sent aftershocks throughout Europe. The Pope then called for a Third Crusade to liberate Jerusalem. Meanwhile, Saladin continued with his campaign of reconquest.

The first sermon in liberated Jerusalem

On Friday, AH 5/8/583 (AD 10/10/1178), orators met to decide who would have the honour of preaching the sermon at the Friday community prayer held in the Al-Aqsa mosque, but it was Saladin who chose the well-known

The Dome
of the Rock.

speaker, Muhyid Din ibn Zaky ad-Din, who began his brilliant speech: "Praised be God, to whom we owe Glory and Victory, Who humiliated those who deny the Faith. He is The One who has bestowed his talent upon us and has sanctified Al-Aqsa. I bear witness that there is no god but God, and that Muhammad is His Servant and Messenger. He is The One who at night took the Messenger of the mosque of Mecca to Al-Aqsa, and from there to the remotest place in Heaven. Blessed are the disciples and companions of the Prophet and everyone who follows in his footsteps. Al-Aqsa is the place where your father Abraham worshipped God and from where your Prophet Muhammad ascended into Heaven. It is where you directed your worship to God before doing so towards Mecca. Al-Aqsa is your first qibla, the second place of worship on Earth and the third mosque worthy of being an object of pilgrimage. God has dignified you by making you instrumental in its recovery. Today you are an object of praise by the angels and men of good faith.

The conquest continues

Saladin continued his conquest of citadels, and such cities as Lattakia and Safed. He even managed to destroy the fortress of Krak which for so long had proved impregnable to all Saracen assaults. However, he had given instructions to keep free all the routes used by crusaders who were crossing through the territory and had no intention of taking part in battles. Those who fled before him took refuge in Tyre. The fact that he had allowed this to happen earned him criticism from historians, who considered it to be his most serious mistake.

The siege of Tyre

Saladin's extraordinarily tolerant nature led him to set king Guy de Lusignan free after the latter had sworn never to attack the Muslims again. Once liberated, however, he hastened to break his promise, reunite with his people and start preparing his forces, taking advantage of the reinforcements that were arriving from Europe. The enormous European support made Saladin realize the mistake he had made. His reaction was to mount a siege on Tyre. The winter cold was setting in and the stream of powerful crusader fleets were met with snow. This state of affairs prompted Saladin to withdraw from the fighting, lift the two-year siege and move out of Tyre with the intention of better organizing his forces in the spring.

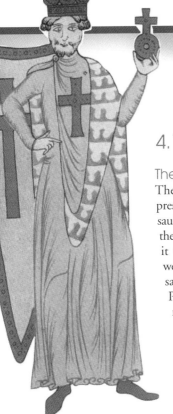

4. The major battle of Acre

AH 585
AD 1189

The European kings besiege Acre

The crusader forces, having consolidated their presence in Tyre, used this base to mount an assault on Acre, chosen on account of its location in the middle of the coast, and owing to the fact that it was a key trading centre, a source of great wealth and a strategic point from which the crusaders could move to dominate the whole of Palestine. With burning enthusiasm from Europe to restart the war, the crusaders from Tyre managed to surround Acre. In fact, the European kings had started to head towards Syria but had stopped in Sicily, which they conquered, and later on reached Palestine. Their campaign was called the Kings Crusade, in contrast to the earlier ones known as the Princes' Crusades. One episode in the events leading up to the arrival of the crusader reinforcements relates to Frederick I, king of Germany. He was leading an expeditionary body overland which was heading towards Acre when he stopped to swim in a river and drowned. Historians state that if the German expedition had reached its destination as planned, Acre would not have resisted. In effect, the Germans had split into two groups. One group returned to their country, whereas the other continued the long journey to Acre.

Top left:
Frederick I, king
of Germany.

Bottom right:
Richard the Lionheart, as he
appeared in Western books
at the time.

Richard the Lionheart leads the crusaders

At the head of the fleet, Richard the Lionheart set sail towards Acre. In the Mediterranean, his ships took the wrong course and were attacked by the Christian governor of Sicily, who seized some vessels. After a second assault Richard managed to occupy the island, from where he organized his forces. This episode postponed his arrival in Acre. Between him and the king of France, who had also sailed to Acre, their troops numbered two hundred and fifty thousand soldiers.

Saladin's call to arms (jihad)

News of the Christian reinforcements coming from Europe prompted Saladin to organize his army. He then called on the Muslims to fight for the supreme cause in their territories. Volunteers started joining him and the army that had massed at Hattin, which numbered approximately twelve thousand soldiers. On learning that Acre was surrounded both by land and sea, he marched on the city with his available forces and called for support from the Muslims living in lands at peace. He sent messages to the Abbasid caliph and to all Muslim forces in the East—his call even reached the king of the Maghreb.

The crusaders that Saladin had originally allowed to go free from Jerusalem had joined the Christian forces in Tyre. From that staging point they marched on Acre and besieged it just as the European kings were sailing towards the area.

Saladin's situation became critical, faced with the enormous number of crusader soldiers. As a united force, they numbered approximately two hundred and fifty thousand, whereas Saladin's army, at best, was hardly twelve thousand strong.

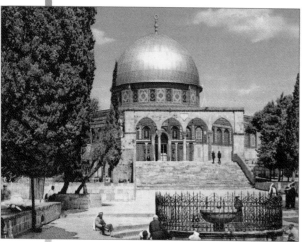

The Al-Aqsa mosque, Jerusalem.

The attitude of the Abbasid caliph

Facing overwhelming odds, Saladin made a call to arms and asked the Abbasid caliph to send his forces from Baghdad. In exchange, he was prepared to hand over all his possessions, including his own kingdom. The only response he received was criticism for having earned himself the epithet "The Victorious King". As it was also applied to the caliph, the latter was jealous of it being used for anyone else. Faced with the probability of losing Palestine, and possible defeat at the hands of the crusaders, the caliph's response left much to be desired. It forced Saladin's hand, leading him to attack Acre with the aim of breaking the blockade, in order to provide supplies to the besieged city. At the same time, he continued to renew his calls for assistance, warning that it would be impossible to hold out if the European army arrived. The danger would then threaten not only Palestine but all the Muslim territories as well.

Saladin awaits reinforcements

Saladin then maneouvred his army away from Acre. They moved to a hill called al-Jerbah to wait for the arrival of his brother Al-'Adil, the governor of Egypt, with relief forces. Fighting then broke out on the outskirts of Acre, which was completely encircled by crusaders. There was only one breach that Saladin had managed to make in the enemy lines. Despite his fierce resistance, many of his men had fallen, so Saladin was forced to make a tactical retreat. The crusaders took advantage of this to seal the breach in their lines and dig trenches in the areas where they expected Saladin to attack later. He defended his position, waiting for the Egyptian troops to arrive. The Egyptian fleet was the first to appear. Egypt was still under his control, as were Syria, the Hijaz and Yemen. Only Tyre, Acre, Tripoli and Antioch remained in enemy hands.

The arrival of the Egyptian fleet

A small crusader flotilla forestalled the Egyptian navy, although the latter soon destroyed it and continued its voyage, laden with munitions and provisions for the Muslims besieged in Acre. Fighting between Saladin and the crusaders resumed, leaving the battlefield strewn with rotting corpses that gave off a sickening stench. Saladin fell ill because of this, but he did not stop fighting. The doctors urged him not to fight in that condition, but he answered them with his famous phrase: "When I go into battle, the pain eases and ends up disappearing".

The arrival of reinforcements from Aleppo and Mosul

After some time, the expected reinforcements began to arrive. An army sent by Saladin's own son, Imad ad-Din Zanki, arrived from Aleppo. His father had named him after the great hero of the same name. 'Ala' ad-Din ibn Mas'ud Zanki, the governor of Mosul, and one of the heroes of the Zanki family, also answered Saladin's call and arrived escorted by some well-known commanders. Forces gradually trickled in from various places, including those driven by self-esteem and the will to defend the Muslim holy places. However, Saladin was still indignant over the passivity of the caliph in Baghdad, and that of the other governors and leaders. None of them made the slightest gesture to help the Muslim army in its decisive battle against the crusaders. In spite of everything, Saladin managed to attack and engage in

battle, thanks to the limited reinforcements that had joined his army. He delivered some severe blows and caused many losses in the crusader ranks, which continued to resist united. As Acre had very high walls that protected it perfectly, the crusaders built even higher towers which they readied to push against the walls, forcing the city's defences to gain entry. The people of Acre were terrified and convinced that the crusaders would end up seizing the city.

The creativity of a young man of faith

Saladin tried to come up with a way to destroy the towers and he consulted with those who were experienced in the art of warfare, as his attempts to launch stones from catapults was more wishful thinking than an effective measure. That was when a young man appeared, the son of a coppersmith, aged about sixteen, who said: "I will burn them for you". Bemused by his self-confidence, the soldiers mocked him, saying: "You are going to burn them, when our heroes and specialists have failed to do so?" The boy insisted: "Yes, I will burn them for you". When Saladin heard this, he said to them: "Let him try". So the boy took a little malt oil and mixed it with chemicals to produce an inflammable and long-lasting torch which he launched at the towers—they caught fire and were destroyed.

Malt oil was known at that time, but it had only been used to light fires that were quickly extinguished. However, it was more effective with the chemical mixture and could be used as a projectile. In view of its success, Saladin said: "Bring that young boy to me so I can reward him. He has saved Acre." When he came before Saladin he refused what he was offered, saying: "What I have done is for Almighty God and I will not accept any reward that does not come from Him". The souls of heroes are like that—souls with faith, faithful to the Almighty.

This is what the young people educated in the true religion are like and it is with them that Muslims can fight and achieve victory.

The attitude of the king of the Maghreb

Thanks to that "invention", Saladin was able to carry out a fierce assault on the crusaders, causing heavy losses, although they stood firm thanks to their large numbers, far in excess of Saladin's forces. Heavily outnumbered, Saladin asked the king of the Maghreb for help but, because of the distance, there was no time to send land forces. Saladin had a message delivered to him that said: "Come with anything".

The battle of Al-Adiliya

The king of the Maghreb sent his fleets to harass the crusader fleet. The manoeuvre was successful as it somewhat delayed reinforcements from Europe, allowing Saladin to continue his raids on the crusaders, who still resisted. Indeed, they built more trenches and secured specific areas that allowed them to come and go as they pleased. Thus, in a surprise manoeuvre, they emerged from their trenches and caught Al-'Adil's forces unawares, just as they were arriving from Egypt. A great battle took place between the two sides and Saladin ordered an attack that caused irreparable losses to the enemy on the battlefield, on the outskirts of Acre. It was named the battle of al-'Adiliya, after his brother, Al-'Adil. After that setback, the crusaders decided to refrain from confronting Saladin and concentrated on their seige of Acre. Day and night they launched catapult attacks on the city, inflicting terrible injuries on its inhabitants.

The inhabitants of Acre attack

The people of Acre decided to act. Without warning, they opened the city gates and charged out in a surprise attack on the enemy. They broke through their lines and reached their tents, which they set alight. The crusaders eventually rallied, repulsed the attack and recaptured their initial positions, before continuing with the siege.

A coastal battle

The crusaders then decided to attack Acre from the sea. However, a huge tower located on high rocks jutting out of the water at the mouth of the harbour stood in the way of their assault on Acre. The tower occupants were on the lookout to repel any attack with fire and arrows. The crusaders then planned to set the tower on fire to destroy it, so that they could get past it and reach their objective. Three ships had to be sacrificed to assault the tower.

They built a turret on the first ship from which to set fire to their objective. The second one, which carried naphtha oil, was to be torched after manoeuvring it alongside the Muslim vessels so that the fire could spread across the whole port of Acre. The third ship was fitted out with a huge hold laden with soldiers. Safe inside the ship's hold, they would be out of range of all arrows shot at the vessel.

The three ships set out on their incendiary mission and, in an extremely dangerous manoeuvre, they set the tower alight and ignited the ship earmarked to burn down the Saracen vessels. However, that day God whipped up the wind, preventing the ships from reaching the Muslim fleet, so that it was the crusaders' vessels that were burned down at sea. The Muslims took advantage of this development to attack the third vessel with its cargo of soldiers, and not one was left alive. They also extinguished the fire at the tower. Thus, the whole assault, which posed a serious threat to the Saracens, ended as a disastrous failure.

An iron battering ram

Far from giving up, the crusaders decided to attack the tower again. To this end they built a huge battering ram attached to a long piece of timber which they assembled on a warship. They gradually sailed towards the tower with the aim of ramming it. They also gave orders to launch a simultaneous assault by land. The inhabitants of Acre were aware of the imminent danger of the coordinated land and sea attack, and they realized that the battering ram was capacble of destroying the harbour tower. To avert such a disaster, they sailed out in small vessels to approach the ship carrying the battering ram, and this allowed several Muslims to climb aboard the enemy ship and set it on fire before it reached the tower.

The assault with the armoured vehicle

The crusaders, far from losing heart, decided to make an armoured vehicle—a crawling device made of wood, but armoured with three layers of metal to prevent the Muslims from burning it. The vehicle began to approach Acre. The Muslims attacked it continuously, day and night, with burning naphtha oil. In spite of its armour plating, the incendiary oil filtered through until it reached the wood, setting the invention on fire and burning it out completely.

Crusaders training in the art of combat.

The crusader kings arrive on the scene

For six months the manoeuvres ran their course, as did the siege of Acre. Meanwhile, the European forces arrived, led by their kings. King Philip II was in command of the French army. With less fortune, the German king, Frederick I, known in Islamic and western history as Barbarossa, had led his army by sea, but drowned on the way, leaving a broken army, of which the majority chose to return home, while the rest carried on in the direction of Acre. Another king, the Englishman Richard the Lionheart, also took part in the expedition.

The journey lasted six months, in spite of the delay suffered by the English and the French, who were held up first by the fleet from the Maghreb and subsequently when Sicily seized some of their vessels. Richard stopped to punish Sicily and bring the land under European rule, which also prevailed in Cyprus. Indeed this island provided the crusaders with an additional 10,000 troops, who brought the total number of crusader forces to 250,000 men. All of them took part in a continuous siege by land and by sea.

Saladin continued trying to break the crusaders' land siege by fierce fighting, day and night, bombarding the enemy with catapults and mounting continuous assaults on crusader lines for two days at a time, except for a two or three hour break for the soldiers to get their breath back. Nevertheless, the crusader forces continued putting up staunch resistance, which Saladin was unable to break.

Inside Acre, the situation was going from bad to worse. Nobody could either enter or leave the city. The only correspondence with Saladin was via carrier pigeon.

The walls of Acre weaken

The crusaders approached the walls of Acre and destroyed part of them. Danger threatened the Muslims and from the inside they tried to seal the breach, where fighting had become hand-to-hand. Saladin continued attacking the crusaders on the outskirts, but Acre was showing signs of flagging after a large stretch of the city walls had crumbled. The Muslim governor was aware of the danger that lay ahead—if the crusaders entered the city, and they were on the verge of doing so, they would most likely slaughter the Muslims, as they had done in Jerusalem. To avert this, he decided to begin negotiations with the Christians, without consulting Saladin, for the surrender of Acre, on condition that they showed mercy to his people and did not kill any of them.

Richard the Lionheart and Philip Augustus were vehement in their response, retorting that he could not possibly hand over what was already in their grasp, and that they had no intention of sparing anybody. Faced with such an attitude, the governor of Acre appealed to the Muslims saying: "We will die rather than surrender" and, to the crusaders he said: "None of us one will die until we have killed fifty of your nobles". Then he resumed the battle, having been on the verge of surrender.

Failure of the negotiations

At this stage the crusaders started deliberating about the fact that they would not conquer Acre without sustaining some losses. The price they would have to pay seemed high to them, as defeating the city was not a simple matter. They considered resorting to negotiations and sent two delegations, the first one to Saladin and the second to the governor of Acre. The condition for Saladin was that they would release all the inhabitants of Acre, while, in return, he would do likewise with the crusader prisoners he held. The crusaders took the opportunity of this lull in the fighting to gain time, so as to rearrange most of their battle positions. As Saladin expected this to happen, he organized attacks during the talks so that he could negotiate from a stronger position. However, the negotiations ended in failure, as did Saladin's assaults. The situation of the inhabitants of Acre was by then critical. Shortages had reached such a point that starvation was wreaking havoc. The inhabitants of Acre met and resolved to fight and die with dignity, rather than succumb to the invading crusaders, while Saladin continued attacking the huge crusader army with his meagre forces, and sent messages of encouragement to the people of Acre.

Two years of siege

The battle of Acre lasted two whole years, during which the starving people were forced to eat dog meat. To save Muslim lives, the governor of Acre requested fresh negotiations and made some tempting proposals to the crusaders. He sent them a message saying: "I will surrender Acre to you, and hand over 500 crusader prisoners and 200,000 gold dinars, on condition that you allow the Muslims to leave with their belongings". When Saladin got wind of this, he sent a missive to the governor informing him that he did not approve of such an offer.

The crusaders, who had 250,000 men and had spent nearly two years using all available means to besiege Acre, were by now becoming demoralized about their chances of success. Thus, they thought the governor's terms of surrender were worth accepting. After much deliberation, they reached agreement and informed the governor of their decision.

AH 18 JUMADA AL ÁKHIRAH 587
AD 12 JULY 1191

The massacre of Acre

Can the governor of Acre be criticized, after such a long siege and faced with such an enormous army, for having opened the gates of Acre to the crusaders without Saladin's permission? That day the crusaders entered Acre and, in violation of the terms of capitulation, took everyone prisoner. What is the point, then, of a protection and immunity agreement? The crusaders then announced that they would not let anybody leave without handing over all their money, besides demanding that Saladin should pay 200,000 dinars.

It was a flagrant breach of the the agreement they had accepted, as well as being treacherous. Nevertheless, Saladin arranged for the money to be collected, being concerned about the welfare of the Muslims, and informed the crusaders he was ready to pay if they were allowed to leave. He said:

"Release the Muslims and we will pay the ransom". They answered: "Give us the mon-

Muslim soldier.

ey and we will release them", to which Saladin replied: "How can we trust you when you violated the initial agreement?"

Then he called on the priests and religious leaders to guarantee the Muslims' release in exchange for paying the ransom. The clergy warned him that they could show mercy but that they could not guarantee the promises of their kings, who were capable of going back on their word again. Saladin stood firm in his position.

When Saladin failed to deliver the ransom, the commander-in-chief of all the crusader forces and king of England, Richard the Lionheart, ordered Muslim prisoners to be beheaded. He led 3,000 men out of Acre and sat them down on a hillside in front of Saladin who cried out:

"Release them and you will get the money". Richard ordered them to all be killed. It was a bloodbath, an implausible act of barbarity and a spectacle that would disgust even the most hard-hearted. It was an example of how the crusaders used to violate treaties and a foretaste of how the inhabitants of Acre were to be subsequently butchered. The magnitude of the crime even met with the disapproval of European historians.

Saladin then warned Muslims everywhere that the crusaders only intended to slaughter them and that Palestine was going to fall, city by city, if he did not receive any help. His messengers travelled across the Muslim territories to spread the news, but received no response whatsoever. Only the Turkoman governor promised to send support.

The fall of Haifa

After having subjugated Acre, where he left a garrison, Richard ordered his army to march on Haifa. Saladin attempted to waylay him, but could not hold out for long. As the city was not fortified, Haifa was easy prey—it was also a stepping stone towards Caesarea. The Muslims meanwhile kept up

"According to Ibn ash-Shaddad, one of the historians who witnessed the battles and chronicled the event, seven out of the original twelve thousand Muslim soldiers perished. 'I saw Saladin on his own, and also with some children and young people, just as I had seen Al-Adil alone with a group of youths'."

159

their harassment of the crusaders using guerrilla tactics, as their marked numerical inferiority precluded any conventional assault. Besides, the crusaders avoided direct engagement, preferring to march on cities. However, in view of Saladin's raids, during one of which Richard himself was injured, they dispatched part of the army to counterattack while the bulk continued on to Caesarea, which fell to the crusaders.

Realizing that his progress was slow and that Saladin and his army were still engaged in a war of attrition, Richard contacted Saladin to propose negotiations. In order to gain time for the Turkomen and other Muslim forces to arrive, Saladin agreed to negotiate, delegating the mission to his brother, Al-'Adil.

The battle of Arsuf

The crusaders had the three main cities under their control. Saladin was struggling to survive. The Christian forces continued advancing, this time towards Arsuf. Aware of their intentions, Saladin hurried to preempt the crusaders by sending his troops to Arsuf where they shored up the defences. He then surrounded the enemy, as he had done at Hattin. Richard urged his men to take revenge and Saladin called on his men to fight for the supreme cause and a repeat of the glory achieved at Hattin. The battle of Arsuf, one of the major encounters between the two forces, got under way. The crusaders routed Saladin's forces, which ended up fleeing before the European legions.

The fall of Arsuf and Jaffa

Having crushed the Muslim army, Richard the Lionheart took Arsuf and continued his march on Jaffa, which he also conquered. Richard then announced his intention of advancing on Jerusalem. Saladin had conquered all those cities after Hattin. They had fallen one by one, while Muslims across the region had looked on as mere spectators, without lifting a finger to support Saladin, even after the heroic feats of Hattin and Jerusalem.

The fall of Lydda and Ramla

The Christian forces in Syria numbered 250,000 strong and were joined by another 250,000 from Europe. Together they began their march towards Jerusalem. Saladin had no alternative but to order all the Muslim forces to leave whatever cities they were in and head for Jerusalem. This is how he was

The wall of Jerusalem.

able to get ahead of the crusaders and build up strong defences. When Richard reached Ramla, he found it in ruins. Saladin had ordered its inhabitants to destroy the city walls before leaving, to deprive the crusaders of all possible booty. Richard took it without any resistance, just as he had done at Lydda, whose walls were equally destroyed and whose surrender posed no major problem.

5. Back to Jerusalem

AH 588
AD 1192

Aware that the crusaders' main objective was Jerusalem, Saladin concentrated all his forces in the vicinity and launched raids relentlessly against Richard's troops, who grew increasingly more disorientated. He also mobilized the local nomadic tribes, who played an important role in fighting the crusader army on their way to Jerusalem. The result was the depletion of their forces. In the end, Richard arrived in a fury, due to the delay caused by those assaults, only to find that the city's defences had been powerfully reinforced and that Saladin had entrenched himself and his forces inside the city. He started to gather information about Jerusalem, its structure, its walls and its supply sources. He realized he was facing an extremely well prepared city and he only had two options:

1. To attack from only one side, in which case he would encounter staunch resistance from Saladin.
2. To distribute his forces around Jerusalem and therefore risk Saladin attacking from any given side.

The advantage of attacking from only one side would allow his forces to remain in a compact block, but this would also enable Saladin to boost his defence with reinforcements from other entrances.

Richard studied the situation carefully. He inquired about Saladin, his way of fighting and his tactics. In the end, he reached a conclusion, which he announced to his troops: "This city is impossible to take while Saladin remains alive inside. He has resisted for all these years due to his fighting spirit, and there is little hope of conquering the city. As long as he remains within the city, it cannot be besieged because, if we attack on one side, he can bring reinforcements from other sides and, if we distribute our forces around the city, he could at-

Saladin, as portrayed in European tracts of the time.

161

Richard the
Lionheart withdraws.

tack us from one side and defeat us. What's more, we are far from our overseas supply sources and he is closer to his land in Syria". Richard's final decision was to order the retreat from Jerusalem.

The crusader retreat

Discrepancies arose among the crusaders. Some of them complained that their very mission for leaving Europe was to conquer Jerusalem. Richard replied that he had ample experience of warfare and that Jerusalem could not be taken. These divisions came increasingly to the fore. Many insisted on mounting the siege, but Richard was able to enforce his decision to withdraw and return to Ramla. In spite of this, the divide between them grew.

The governor of Tyre, Conrad, the Marquis of Monferrat, who took part in the expedition and was the first commander to besiege Acre before Richard's arrival, realized the risk involved in retreating. He understood that Jerusalem was the objective and to retreat from there was equivalent to withdrawing from the whole of Palestine, leaving him to face Saladin alone. He feared the most terrible revenge. He lost no time in sending Saladin a message, before Richard had withdrawn, proposing negotiations. "I am ready to hand over Sidon and Beirut, on condition I can keep Tyre and you show us mercy". Saladin agreed but added another condition, which was that all Muslim prisoners in Tyre were to be released.

The Assassins reappear

In spite of the secrecy surrounding these negotiations, news of the developments reached Richard the Lionheart and tensions between himself and Conrad increased. This was precisely what Saladin had hoped for, as he had long attempted to foster a situation that would end up dividing the various crusader forces. However, an unexpected turn of events was due to scuttle those plans. The Assassins reappeared on the scene—they tried, unsuccessfully, to assassinate Saladin, but did manage to eliminate Conrad, creating a golden opportunity to divide the crusaders. The way was again open to Richard to take control of the situation. Once more, these events clearly show the danger to Islam and the Muslim community posed by esoteric sects.

Richard's perplexity

Saladin continued to send troops to protect different cities, and his forces won all the minor battles. Meanwhile, Richard was going through a moment of confusion. He did not know what to do. To withdraw and return to Europe would mean having failed in his mission, and, to stay on without conquering Jerusalem would be an even bigger failure.

Conquering Jerusalem was an impossible task, so he decided to draw Saladin's forces out, engage them in battle and play any future decision by ear. He had subjugated the whole of Palestine except for Jerusalem. As fate would have it, he then fell ill and was on the verge of succumbing. Saladin sent him physicians, fruit and ice. At this, the people were surprised and criticized Saladin for helping his enemy to recover. However, from his viewpoint of deep reflection, he saw things in a different light. Saladin was a man of great wisdom and perspicacity. Some historians have interpreted it to mean that Richard's survival suited Saladin, as he had taken the decision to withdraw from Jerusalem, while another commander would have attacked the city. Other historians consider this simply as further proof of Saladin's great magnanimity.

Negotiations between Richard and Saladin

In any event, Richard recovered and agreed to negotiate with Saladin and seek reconciliation for two reasons:

First: The unlikelihood of being able to meet his objective of conquering Jerusalem.

Second: Saladin's extraordinarily generous treatment of him. An endless amount of legends fill the history books about this. Some tell how Richard challenged Saladin to a duel. Others recount how Saladin disguised himself as a doctor and went to look after Richard personally. All of them are imaginary and have no foundation. The fact is that Richard requested a meeting with Saladin, but the latter declined to meet him personally and delegated the task to his brother, Al-'Adil. The main condition laid down by the crusaders was to have Jerusalem handed over to them, in return for allowing its Muslims freedom to worship and preserving their mosque. Curiously, these are the same conversations that are taking place at present. That is, the Israelis would officially retain

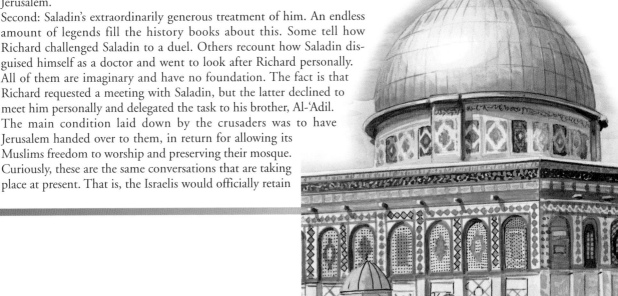

"Saladin's name became so dreaded in Europe and instilled such fear in its people that, when a woman wanted to scare her children, she would say: 'Saladin is coming!'"

AH **588**
AD **1192**

Jerusalem, but the Muslims would have administrative control of the Al-Aqsa mosque.

Richard presented this proposal to Al-'Adil, who then consulted with his brother. Saladin replied: "Jerusalem is ours as much as it is yours, and it is more important to us than to you. It was the destination of our Prophet after his night journey and it is impossible to imagine us relinquishing it. No Muslim, whoever he might be, can make such a decision. As for the lands that comprise Palestine, they are only in your hands temporarily because of the weakness of the Muslims who live there. Negotiations with you at this moment cannot turn into lasting peace. It will be a temporary peace. This is why we are unable to hand Jerusalem over to you".

The negotiations took a long time. The crusaders were determined to gain control of Jerusalem, while Saladin remained firm in his attitude. His insistence led Saladin to cut the conversations short and announce a fresh battle. It was clear that any other city could be the object of negotiation, even including a truce, but, in the case of Jerusalem, it could only be taken with blood. Once again fate intervened when Richard received news from England that his brother had taken over the rule of England and declared himself king. Richard was seized with awe and realized that, by wanting to gain Jerusalem, he was going to lose England. He immediately headed for his country, as preserving his kingdom was far more important to him.

In these circumstances, Saladin moved his forces towards Jaffa and, although it was strongly defended, managed to conquer it. As for Richard, he clearly saw that he could not continue fighting and called for a resumption of talks, agreeing to withdraw his claims to Jerusalem. Saladin accepted the conditions and again sent Al-'Adil.

Richard withdraws claims to Jerusalem

Richard accepted the Muslims' conditions but he differed with Saladin over some cities. In the end, both parties agreed that the coastal cities, from Tyre to Jaffa, should stay in Richard's hands, providing he recognized Jerusalem as an Islamic city. Although Saladin wished to reach an agreement with Richard, he did not approve ceding control of the coastal towns to the crusaders. Under pressure from his forces, his close friends and his counsellors, he felt obliged to accept the agreement with Richard.

By that stage, Saladin's army was weary after four long years of war. His soldiers were exhausted. His commanders, however, regarded Richard's withdrawal from Jerusalem and his return to England as an auspicious moment to be taken advantage of. Conditions were ideal for Saladin to sign a truce and simultaneously prepare for war. Agreement was finally reached and was known as the Ramla Treaty. The crusaders retained the coast, and the Muslims the rest of the Palestinian cities. The truce lasted 3 years and 3 months.

The end of the Third Crusade

The crusaders demanded a lasting peace, but this was regarded as an illegitimate claim by the Muslim 'ulama' because it meant forfeiting rights to their own land. How can we recognize their tutelage over a land that does not belong to them? A temporary truce was not detrimental in terms of the Muslim weakness or the crusader strength. It gave the Muslims time to take stock of the situation and readjust their position. As decreed by their jurisconsults, Saladin had limited the truce to 3 years and 3 months. The contents of the agreement allowed the crusaders to visit their holy places, as long as they did so in small groups. The situation stabilized and Richard asked for permission to go on a pilgrimage to Jerusalem, which Saladin agreed to. After the visit he at once returned to the coast where he boarded a ship bound for England.

His history in England is extensive, but does not concern us here. What is relevant is to remember that the purpose of the Third Crusade, in which 500,000 crusaders participated and 120,000 were killed at the battle of Hattin and later clashes, caused a huge number of casualties, even in terms of modern warfare.

Trade expansion, an inherent part of Islamic culture.

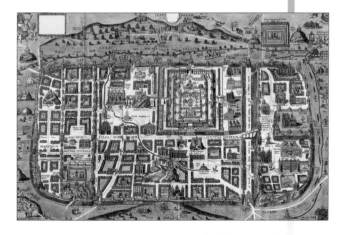

A unique map of old Jerusalem.

Saladin on his
deathbed.

Truce and safety

The truce brought stability to Palestine and safety to its people. Muslims went into cities occupied by crusaders, who in turn moved freely from one town to another and traded with the Muslims. Security and peace reigned in these areas, just as it had during the agreement of Al-Hudaybiyyah between the Prophet and the pagans of Quraysh. They were free to enter Medina, while the Muslims could enter Mecca. This was a complete truce, a complete peace. Saladin settled in Jerusalem after Richard had departed and he prepared for a pilgrimage to Mecca, as he felt his time was coming.

6. Farewell Saladin

According to Ibn ash-Shaddad, a historian close to Saladin, who was also a legal expert and a judge, Saladin asked him: "What is the noblest death?" To which ash-Shaddad replied: "Death for a supreme cause". Saladin added: "My greatest desire is to meet a noble death, and for years I have wanted it for the supreme cause".

Saladin cancels his pilgrimage

AH 589
AD 1193

While preparing his pilgrimage, correspondence arrived from the qadi (judge) of Egypt saying: "Attend to the Muslim people. Postpone your pilgrimage. The country is in ruins, the economy has weakened and disorder is spreading. Do not worry about the pilgrimage; do not leave the country, as this is far more urgent and of greater importance than the pilgrimage". Being a responsible leader, Saladin responded by cancelling his pilgrimage and concerning himself with the plight of the people. He commissioned renovations in the municipality of Jerusalem, including reconstruction of the Al-Aqsa mosque, and paid official visits to the Syrian cities.

The greatness of Saladin

In the month of Shawal, AH 588 (AD October 1192), Saladin visited Beirut, where he was received as a hero amid great celebrations. In the eleventh month of the same year he returned to his capital, Damascus, after having been away for 4 years. His reception was tremendous.

Saladin had governed Egypt for 24 years and Syria for 19 years, of which 16 had been spent on horseback, fighting to free the area from the crusaders. He managed to change the political geography of the region and the political situation in Palestine. He put an end to the Third Crusade and besieged the enemy on the coastal strip. This is how he brought peace and safety to the area, in addition to rebuilding it. He also guaranteed safety along pilgrim routes.

Thrift with public funds

Al-'Adil asked his brother for a plot of land in Aleppo. Saladin answered him in a letter, saying: "Do you think the country is up for sale? Have you still not realized that the country belongs to the people who inhabit it and that we are the treasury of the Muslims and those who guard its properties?" Clearly, Saladin was thrifty with public funds and Muslim property, as he was tolerant and merciful with the growing number of soldiers taken captive. He had 17 sons, whom he took with him to the battlefield, including the youngest of them, aged from 10 to 12. At one of the battles, some of his young children asked him to let them kill a prisoner. Saladin became angry with them, scolded and reprimanded them. His troops were surprised at his reaction, as the prisoner had been condemned to death. They could not understand why he would not let them kill the prisoner. Saladin said to them: "It is so that they do not get used to spilling blood. We only kill if we are obliged to, and we do not educate our children like this".

Consultation and ethics

Saladin did not move a finger without consulting the learned scholars of Islam, the princes, military commanders, etc. If they disagreed with him but were in agreement among themselves about something, he would support their decision and carry it out, as with the Ramla Treaty. He was virtuous in word and upright in company, forbearing and patient. He sympathized with the poor and humble, was tolerant of others, but also courageous in battle, as well as decisive and ambitious. He sought to conquer the whole of Syria and wrest it from the crusaders. His life was full of passion, chivalry, nobility and generosity. This is why he earned the love and affection of the people.

The world map
of Al-Idrisi
Al-Maghribi,
AD 1154.

167

AH 589
AD 1193

The ethics of a sick king

After a reception held for some pilgrims, he felt exhausted, and had a temperature and a headache. According to Ibn ash-Shaddad: "I went to see him in the company of his Excellency, the Qadi and, when we came out, the latter said to me: 'Be content with his behaviour'. I said to him: 'What do you mean?' He answered: 'I have just seen Saladin asking for lukewarm water, for he cannot drink either cold or hot water because of his illness. They brought him water that was too hot for him to swallow, and the same thing happened when they gave him cold water. All he did was to again ask for lukewarm water, without making any further comment. For God's sake, if it had been another king that had asked twice for the same thing, without getting what he wanted, he would have shouted and meeted out punishment. Spread these ethics, since Muslims are beginning to distance themselves from them'".

The death of the great hero

In the year AH 589 (AD 1193), Saladin passed away after being ill for only ten days. The qadi went down to his tomb and, placing a sword next to Saladin's body, said: "This is the sword that will allow you to rest in paradise, the sword that will bear witness to your 16 years of battle for the supreme cause, in which you won magnificent victories and shook the foundations of Europe". A state of melancholy settled over the Muslim countries, and the news reached Europe. Even the crusaders were sad about his death and said: "We saw no one with the moral conduct of Saladin among the Muslims and Christians who fought against us". There are various works written by Europeans about him and they still remember his ethics and his upright conduct.

Saladin's banner

Before dying, Saladin called the standard bearer who he used to take to all his battles and said to him: "You who have carried my banner in war, shall carry it after my death. Set it at the top of a long lance and walk with it into the territory of greater Syria; call the people, so that they see it and tell them: 'This banner belongs to the king who has died, the one who has only taken with him a small piece of fabric, used as his shroud, which is as old as this one I have in my hand.' Tell them that, with all the vast possessions and fabulous treasures he had within his reach, Saladin could only make his own these three linen shields in which he is wrapped."

THE
LAND OF
MORIAH
OR
JERUSALEM
and the
ADJACENT COUNTRY.

Jewish Cubits.

Roman Miles.

English Miles.

A Temple on Mount Moriah
B Zion, or city of David
C Acra, or the Lower Town
D Bezeta, or the New Town

a Fountain Gate
b Dung Gate
c Valley Gate
d Genter Gate
e Ephraim Gate
f Fish Gate
g Fish Market
h Benjamin Gate
i Wood Market
j Sheep Gate
k Horse Gate
l Pool of Bethesda
m Ophel, Dwellings of the Nethinim

n Horse Gate
o Water Gate
p Queens House
q Solomons House
r Upper Market
s House or the Mighty
t Davids House
u Herods House
v Hippodrome
w Millo
x Fort of Anthony
y Theatre
z Helene House
& Fort of Antiochus

A unique, idealized
drawing of old Palestinian.

169

The banner was a cloth that Saladin had not changed in all his battles. It had survived 16 years of battle, and had been knocked down and flown on high. Saladin left the world with a winding sheet as his only possession, leaving behind him his battle flag. He himself was one of the greatest banners of Islam. He personified devout ideals, reliance on God and a love of fighting. He pledged to safeguard the unity of the Muslim community and was a scholar in jurisprudence and an expert in command skills. His aspiration was to purify society, to spread justice and to live an austere and simple life.

People's love of Saladin

It is said that one of the ulamas, who had preached a sermon in the sanctuary of Mecca before the battle of Hattin, and had prayed for the Abbasid caliph and for the governor of Mecca, also prayed for Saladin. The people had great faith in his prayers. When he prayed for Saladin, the walls of the mosque trembled with the roar of the people's response. While the people's love for him before Hattin was patent, it has grown steadily ever since.

The legacy of Saladin to his son

In the will that Saladin left his son, king Al-Afdal, it said: "I bequeath to you a fear of God, which is the culmination of all good, and I order you the same as what God has ordered you, as it is the reason for your success. I forewarn you against blood, as well as becoming involved in it. Do not kill because of a simple suspicion. Do not kill without reason. Do not kill if there is no need to do so, as blood does not sleep. Protect the hearts of your subjects. Bear their needs in mind and always interest yourself in them, since you are my guarantor and the guarantor of God before them. Calm the heart of the princes, the dignitaries of the dynasty, and the social representatives, since I did not get to where I have come except by conciliation with the people. Do not bear hatred against anybody, because death does not spare anyone. Be cautious in your relations with people, as God only pardons with their indulgence. Do not oppress anybody because, if you do not treat people fairly, God will not spare you unless you have been pardoned by whoever you maltreated. As for what there is between you and God, be aware that God is generous, he gives pardon and does not abandon penitents".

PART TWO
Palestine in the Islamic era

CHAPTER SIX
After Saladin

1. A rift in the Ayyubid dynasty

2. The second fall of Jerusalem

3. The third fall of Jerusalem

4. The Mameluke dinasty

After Saladin

1. A rift in the Ayyubid dynasty

A fresh crusade

While differences were becoming more pronounced, crusaders in the kingdoms of Acre, Tyre, Tripoli and Antioch had started cooperating among themselves and with Europe to clear the way for the recovery of Jerusalem. The Germans assembled a formidable army which sailed to Syria. From there they advanced on Beirut, which they took without much resistance. However, disputes arose between the Germans and the crusader kingdoms which ended with the Germans retracing their steps and returning home without achieving their aim to conquer Jerusalem. It was divine mercy, as it helped cushion the effect of the divisions at the heart of the Ayyubid dynasty.

Internecine fighting between the Ayyubids

After the departure of the German forces, the governor of Beirut and its environs realized that his kingdom had been left in a position of weakness and he feared for its safety, prompting him to seek reconciliation with Al-'Adil, who did not hesitate to reach agreement, aware of the consequences of the division in his dynasty. The pact remained in force for three years. That year, AH 595, 'Abd al-'Aziz, the governor of Egypt and southern Palestine, died. His son, Al-Mansur, who was only 10 years old, succeeded him on the throne, but without any *de facto* authority. Differences between the Egyptian Ayyubids multiplied. The military commanders asked members of the Ayyubid family in Syria to send a regent for Al-Mansur in a bid to shore up the unity of Egypt. Al-Afdal, the governor of Horan, who had been removed from office in Damascus, offered to take charge of the regency and was accepted. He presented himself and took possession of his new post. However, he was soon to return to his old ways. His method of exercising the regency was harmful to the people's interests. In addition, he abused his position by conniving with some Ayyubid rulers of certain small kingdoms to take over power in Damascus. To this end, two armies left Egypt and Aleppo, under the command of Al-Afdal and Adh-Dhahir, respectively. They surrounded Damascus, from within which Al-'Adil put up fierce resistance. Six long months of siege ended in stalemate, with Adh-Dhahir returning to Aleppo, and Al-'Afdal to Egypt. The attempt had failed.

Al-Adil imposes his authority

Al-'Adil was aware of the dangers posed by Al-Afdal's conspiracies and disloyalty, and he immediately mustered his troops in pursuit of Al-Af-dal's retreating forces. After overtaking and defeating them, he continued on to Egypt, which was again brought under his command. Al-Afdal himself fled to Horan. Most of the Ayyubid kingdom was then reunited under the rule of Al-'Adil, except for such autonomous kingdoms as the Yemen, the Hijaz and Mosul. Al-'Adil adopted Saladin's style of governance and appointed his sons to head up the different kingdoms. He entrusted Egypt to his son, Al-Kamil Muhammad Ibn al-'Adil. As governor of Damascus, he appointed another son, Mu'adham 'Isa Ibn al-'Adil. He subsequently conquered Horan, who his third son, Al-Ashraf Musa Ibn al-'Adil, was appointed to rule. Once al-'Adil had imposed his authority, and the lands under his command were stable, the Hijaz renewed its allegiance to him. Indeed, for his subjects, the rule of al-'Adil was reminiscent of the glorious reign of his brother, Saladin.

A new truce

Such consolidated Muslim rule over such widespread territories again gave the crusaders cause for concern, as they were afraid that Al-'Adil's influence would spread to their dominions. To mitigate this state of affairs, they asked him to extend the truce. Al-'Adil accepted without hesitation, as he still needed to further consolidate his power and stabilize the region. The six-year truce contained in the agreement reached in the year AD 1205 gave Al-'Adil the necessary breathing space to build up his kingdom, expand it and bring its affairs under control.

AH 601
AD 1205

The truce extended

Six years later, the crusaders came back to request a further extension of the truce, owing to their fear of Al-'Adil's power. He again accepted, having reckoned that he still needed to impose a greater degree of stability. The renewal of the truce meant seven more years of peace, which lasted until the year AH 615, when Al-'Adil died.

AH 607
AD 1210

2. The second fall of Jerusalem

The crusaders in Egypt

Immediately after Al-'Adil's death, his kingdom was divided among his three sons, Al-Kamil, Al-Mu'adham and Al-Ashraf. The Pope took advantage of this division to call for a fresh crusade to recover Jerusalem. An army was put together, led by John of Brienne, whom he called "The future king of Jerusalem". The army left Europe and headed towards Cyprus and from there it proceeded to Egypt. John of Brienne chose to enter Egypt via Damietta, enabling his fleet to sail up the Nile as far as Cairo. The Muslims, aware of this stratagem and the dangers it involved, hurried to find a way of averting the assault. They placed an enormous chain across the Damietta branch of the Nile to prevent ships from entering. The chain was permanently monitored from a fortress that overlooked the town.

Inside the walls of Old Jerusalem.

However, the crusaders besieged Damietta, but were unable to get to Cairo. They then warned Al-Kamil that they would occupy Egypt and declared their willingness to evacuate it in exchange for the surrender of Jerusalem. Al Mu'adham, the governor of Damascus, sent a small army to help his brother, Al-Kamil, and wrote to the Muslims to ask for their assistance.

Negotiations over Jerusalem

At that time the Mongolian Tartars were sweeping across the world from the east. They swiftly brought eastern Asia and India under their rule and, driving westwards, reached the frontier of Mesopotamia, threatening the Abbasid caliphate himself. This was one reason why Al-Kamil could no longer count on the arrival of relief forces from other rulers—he realized it was futile to ask for help in such circumstances. He felt that the only dignified way out was to surrender Jerusalem, thus avoiding the presence of the crusaders in Egypt.

When the Pope was consulted on the outcome of the negotiations, he ordered the crusaders at Damietta not to renounce Egypt, as it had become vulnerable owing to the lack of outside support. His orders were first to occupy Egypt and then to head towards Jerusalem. Meanwhile, Damietta continued under a fierce 17-month siege that had caused terrible famine, after which it is said that a single egg cost as much as a gold dinar.

The crusaders head towards Cairo

AH 616
AD 1219

Damietta finally fell to the crusaders and they lost no time in preparing for the occupation of Cairo. They wrote to the Pope, asking for reinforcements. These arrived en masse from Europe, by sea and by land. The objective was Cairo. The people of Egypt did not remain impassive when they realized what was coming. Defying death, people plucked up the courage to harass the advancing army by breaking the dams storing water upstream of the Nile delta. The delta then flooded, making it difficult for the crusaders to press on towards Cairo. They repeated the operation and staged ambushes whenever the crusaders tried to mass for the journey to the capital. This state of affairs lasted three long years. The crusaders grew so weary that they finally decided to withdraw to Damietta, where they also encountered ambushes, assaults and all kinds of difficulties created

by its inhabitants. Relentless guerrilla warfare eventually forced them to move back to Acre, averting the threat that had hung over Egypt.

The Mongols on the move

The Mongol threat to Mesopotamia was still latent, even though the death of Genghis Khan temporarily led the conquest of Mesopotamia to be postponed so that internal affairs could be put in order. After a time, the Mongols changed direction and headed north. They conquered Moscow and made similar attempts in other European countries. Subsequently, they conquered India, Afghanistan and Persia. The threat once again loomed over Mesopotamia and there was fear about the savage ways of these uncivilized, nihilistic people when they took the cities, destroying whatever they found, setting everything on fire and murdering everyone.

AH 624
AD 1227

Frederick, the future "king of Jerusalem"

This period saw the rise of Frederick II, emperor of Germany, known as the "*church fugitive*", as Pope Gregory IX twice excommunicated him and denied him the right to Paradise, declaring him a major heretic for having refused to take part in a campaign on Jerusalem that he had arranged.

At that time, John of Brienne died after returning from Egypt and imposing his rule on the crusader kingdoms. It was his daughter, Isabella, who inherited the throne of the kingdom of Jerusalem, as it was called, despite the fact that Jerusalem was not then under crusader rule. Frederick proposed marriage to Isabella. She accepted, as it would have been any woman's ambition for this man to take her to the altar. After the marriage was consummated, he declared himself King of Jerusalem. Al Mu'adham Ibn Al-'Adil died that same year. Al-'Adil's

Genghis Khan.

Hulagu Khan, the Mongol.

176

sons succeeded him in the kingdoms of Syria and Jerusalem. Al-Kamil, who ruled in Egypt, annexed Jerusalem and Al-Ashraf, who governed what is now Jordan, did likewise with Damascus.

AH 625
AD 1228

Further dissent among the Ayyubids

Frederick moved north towards Acre with only 500 horsemen at the beginning of his campaign. In fact, his arrival was motivated by a previous call from Al-Kamil, who had asked for help against his brothers in exchange for handing over Jerusalem. Frederick was late in arriving, which he did just in time for Al-Kamil to take control of Jerusalem after the death of his brother. Without intending to surrender it, he began negotiations with Frederick.

AH 627
AD 1229

Frederick II, emperor of Germany.

The Jerusalem compromise

Circumstances did not favour Al-Kamil. He realized that matters were becoming complicated, what with the campaign led by Frederick, and he did not have the means to confront the crusaders. This is why he asked for negotiations. Both parties reached a fresh agreement by which the crusaders promised not to attack Egypt or any territory ruled by Al-Kamil. In exchange, he would hand over Jerusalem, Nazareth, Bethlehem, Lydda and Sidon. As previously indicated, Frederick's army only amounted to 500 men, but Al-Kamil wanted to secure the crusader front to enable him to concentrate on attacking his brothers, thus compromising his loyalty to his community and his religion.

Frederick's success in leading a small force, without fighting a single battle and yet securing Jerusalem, was quite incredible. His journey to that city ended anecdotally—he was met by priests throwing rubbish. After all, the Pope rejected him. Frederick's response was to ask the crusaders to thank God for the miracle of having acquired Jerusalem so easily—with just 500 horsemen, when Richard had been unable to do this with 500,000! Of course it was not really like that. It was Al-Kamil's disloyalty and his weakness that brought it about. The Muslim world was up in arms about it—Muslims everywhere deplored Al Kamil's attitude and condemned his action as abominable.

AH 628
AD 1230

The Mongols threaten Mesopotamia

Frederick's success made the Pope revoke the excommunication and privation of Paradise that his predecessor had imposed on him, in consideration of his heroic deed. Jerusalem had been in crusader hands for 10 years, which was the length of the truce with Al-Kamil. The crusaders wanted to take advantage of that time to send reinforcements to Jerusalem and thus reassert their control there, but serious conflicts had broken out in Europe due to differences between its kings. There were more pressing matters to be attended to before thinking of sending aid to Frederick, so he was forced to return to Germany. This left Jerusalem under crusader rule but without a king to govern it.

Mongol soldiers.

Meanwhile, the Ayyubids had allied themselves with the Seljuks against the Khwarismian Turks, who had started threatening the Abbasid caliphate, also under threat from the Mongols. The Ayyubids were afraid the Khwarismians would take over Mesopotamia and extend their rule throughout Syria. This is why they asked the Seljuks to help. All this activity diverted their attention from the crusaders, who were placidly governing Jerusalem. At the same time, the Mongols started to compete against the Khwarismians to invade Mesopotamia. Armed battles between them ended in the defeat of the Khwarismians, who scattered across Arabia, and into Syria, where they regrouped in isolated guerrilla parties. With Mesopotamia surrounded, the Khwarismian threat had disappeared and the alliance with the Seljuks was no longer necessary. Indeed, differences arose between them and the Ayyubids, eventually erupting into armed conflict.

AH 633
AD 1236

A split in the Muslim nation

Weakness in the Muslim community and internecine strife spread as far as Al-Andalus (Moorish Spain), where the Arabs could not prevent the

The Mongol army.

Christians from using all their potential to occupy the cities. That was the year Cordova fell and the ailment affecting the whole community was confirmed.

Al-Ashraf also died that year. Differences immediately arose between his sons, Al-'Adil As-Saghir and As-Salih Ayyub, causing a rift throughout the Ayyubid dynasty that ended in fighting. The various factions even resorted to using Khwarizm gangs to fight each other.

Biographic sketch of As-Salih Ayyub

He was solemn, dignified, quiet and solitary, in as much as his rank would allow. He was known for his skill, training and magnanimity. However, he imposed his authority on his companions and on the princes in his dynasty, whom he managed to impress. Some historians consider him to be the greatest ruler of the Ayyubid dynasty after Saladin. As-Salih Ayyub was the first to assimilate the Turks into his regime and turn them into princes, high-ranking army officials and personal bodyguards and advisers. To this end he built the citadel of Roda for them on the Nile, the location of which inspired the name by which they were later to be known—Bahri Mamelukes or "Mamelukes of the sea". They would subsequently found their own dynasty after the assassination of As-Salih Ayyub's son.

Historians emphasize his penchant for commissioning buildings and urban complexes such as the military city of As-Salihiya, erected on the desert boundary separating Egypt from greater Syria where troops used to be concentrated. Practically nothing is left of the numerous palaces he built. Nonetheless, a large part of his As-Salihiya school—the first to unite the four Sunni doctrines—is still standing. That is where his tomb lies.

The crusaders violate the agreement

AH 635
AD 1238

A year after the death of Al-Ashraf, the sultan Al-Kamil passed away, leaving behind him division and increasing strife. One of the terms of the

179

agreement with the crusaders, reached when Jerusalem was handed over to them, was that no fortress was to be built, maintaining its status as a religious open city. However, the crusaders took advantage of the lack of Ayyubid unity to violate the agreement and built the fortress of the Tower of David. The Ayyubid sultan of Damascus, An-Nasir Dawud, considered this to be a violation of what had been stipulated and prepared to attack Jerusalem.

AH 636
AD 1239

The recovery of Jerusalem by force

Around the same time, when the truce with Al-Kamil had come to an end, the Pope started to make preparations for a major campaign to protect Jerusalem. Forces headed towards fortified Acre, still in crusader hands. The dangerous situation prompted Dawud to recruit a mainly volunteer contingent of approximately 10,000 Khwarismians. Together they carried out a major assault on Jerusalem and managed to take control of it in AH 637, ten years after Al-Kamil had handed it over to Frederick II, in AH 627. An-Nasir Dawud went to the places that Al-Kamil had handed over to the enemy and defeated them in several battles, resulting in the death of 1,500 soldiers and the capture of as many prisoners, who were taken to Egypt, then under the rule of Al-'Adil II.

Arab world map, 1154.

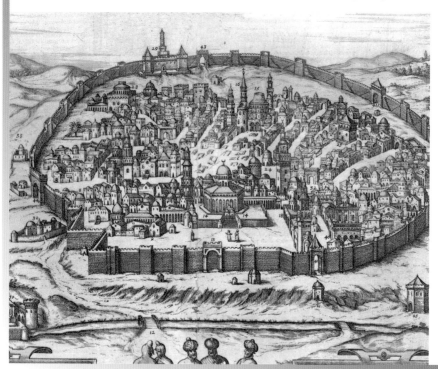

180

3. The third fall of Jerusalem

New disloyalties

AH 637
AD 1240

A conspiracy took place that year against Al-'Adil II. He was removed from office and replaced by the sultan As-Salih Najm ad-Din Ayyub, subsequently to become the protagonist of a paramount event in Islamic history. He had a Mameluke maid who he was madly in love with and whom he freed in order to marry her. He called her Shajarat ad-Durr (tree of gems).

Meanwhile, in Syria, internal strife between the Ayyubids worsened—conflict arose between An-Nasir Dawud, the sultan of Jerusalem, and As-Salih Isma'il, the sultan of Damascus, on the one hand, and, on the other, As-Salih Najm ad-Din Ayyub, sultan of Egypt. They saw the latter as a threat to their survival. Their fear led them to seek help from the crusaders. The crusaders viewed such internal quarrelling among the Ayyubids as the ideal opportunity to stake their claims and they agreed to support the sultans, providing Jerusalem was handed over to them in return. An-Nasir Dawud and As-Salih Isma'il agreed to the deal and handed Jerusalem over to the crusaders.

The handover of Jerusalem

AH 641
AD 1243

For the third time, Jerusalem, together with other cities, passed into crusader hands. It was actually As-Salih Isma'il, the governor of Damascus, that brokered the deal. His disloyalty and the surrender of Jerusalem to the crusaders aroused anger among his subjects. One of the major religious authorities at the time was the Damascene ulama, Al-'Izz ibn 'Abd as-Salam, who ruled that people were no longer bound by loyalty to the sultan, As-Salih Isma'il. He ordered sermons in the mosques not to be preached in his name. The government foundations started to crack.

The sultan then ordered Al-'Izz ibn 'Abd as-Salam to be deported from Syria and banished to Egypt. However, he was facing growing unrest, both for having handed over Jerusalem and for having driven out religious leaders. He resorted to force to quell the unrest. One of the insurgent garrisons that had entrenched itself in the fortress of ash-Shuqiq looked on in amazement as the sultan conquered the fortress and then

proceeded to hand it over to the crusader enemy. The whole Islamic world witnessed this treachery.

Naturally, the crusaders entered Jerusalem without any resistance. They immediately made it their own by profaning the holy Islamic places and celebrating a feast on the Sacred Rock, on which wine was served. It was one of the blackest episodes in the history of the Islamic community.

AH 642
AD 1244

The second Hattin

New treachery materialized when a joint army was assembled between the crusaders of Palestine, a Muslim army from Arabia and one from Damascus. It went to Egypt to attack sultan As-Salih Ayyub. He personally led his troops to Gaza, where the battle took place. What nobody anticipated was the surprise move of members of the Syrian army who, just before entering into combat, withdrew their allegiance from As-Salih Ism'ail and joined forces with the Egyptian army. The crusaders, initially at a numerical advantage, were suddenly outnumbered by the Muslims, who routed the enemy. Some 30,000 crusaders died in the battle, which was then dubbed "the second Hattin". Some died, others fled and the rest were taken prisoner and sent to Egypt. Sultan as-Salih Najm ad-Din Ayyub, not satisfied with that victory, pursued the retreating forces as far as Acre. He went on to take Syria and Palestine, besieged Jerusalem and defeated the sultan As-Salih Ism'ail at Damascus, after his flight from Gaza. The latter vowed to leave the city, on condition that he was allowed to take his treasures with him. The people of Damascus accepted, not wanting to go to war with his supporters. By recovering the city, As-Salih Najm ad-Din Ayyub was able to reunite the Ayyubid dynasty.

Arab scimitar.

Jerusalem liberated again

As-Salih Najm ad-Din Ayyub asked the Khwarismians, who had conquered Jerusalem once before, for their help in reconquering it. In effect, they joined forces with him and were easily able to enter Jerusalem and take 6,000 crusader prisoners, just one year after it had been occupied.

However, sultan An-Nasir Dawud took advantage of the influence he still had among the Khwarismians to free the 2,000 crusader prisoners they held. The Khwarismians yielded to his request, but were relentless with Dawud. When the crusaders had left the city, the Khwarismians realized the mistake they had made, setting them free by paying attention to a traitor king. At once they pursued and overtook them before they reached Acre. Thus, Jerusalem returned to Muslim hands time after time, and finally remained under their rule until its occupation by the English in 1917.

4. The Mameluke dynasty

Louis IX's campaign in Egypt

AH **646**
AD **1248**

In response to the call for a fresh crusade by the Pope, King Louis IX of France, nicknamed "the saint" because of his devotion, once again headed a great army to occupy Egypt and recover Jerusalem. When they arrived, they had to fight hard against the people of Damietta before it fell. In view of the crusader threat, the sultan As-Salih Najm ad-Din Ayyub hurried to offer Jerusalem in exchange for Egypt, as if history was repeating itself. Louis refused the offer, as his predecessors had done, because he felt that Cairo was within his reach, having conquered Damietta. He aimed to avoid making the same mistakes as his predecessors and have his soldiers drown in the marshes that the Egyptians were about to flood. He chose a roundabout route to Mansura, but Egyptian guerrilla forces forestalled his advance by raids everywhere, as they had done in the past. Guerrilla warfare so exhausted him that, when he arrived at a settlement near Mansura, he had already been stretched to the limit. That is where the armies of Louis IX and ad-Din Ayyub met. The battle had hardly begun when death befell the sultan As-Salih in his tent. His wife, Sha-

Crusader cannons.

jarat ad-Durr, known for her strength of character, took a momentous decision—she ordered the doctors to keep the sultan's death a secret and began to organize the battle herself from the tent, without the troops being aware of it.

She then summoned her husband's son, Turan Shah, heir to the throne of Egypt, who was in Mosul, and set him on the throne left by his father. Under the command of Shajarat ad-Durr, the Egyptians won a great victory. Louis was defeated and suffered heavy losses, besides himself falling prisoner to the Egyptians. He was brought before Shajarat ad-Durr, who ordered him to be imprisoned in Mansura jail, from where Louis initiated negotiations for his liberation. He went as far as offering exorbitant sums of money that could be counted in millions. Shajarat ad-Durr finally decided to set him free, on condition that half the amount was given to her before he was set free, and the other half afterwards. Once the money was paid, she released him. Louis gave Shajarat ad-Durr his word never to return to Egypt. Hardly had he reached Acre than he broke his promise and began to organize another army to attack Jerusalem.

Louis IX sought help everywhere, and won the support of the Assassins, the Ismaili enemies of the Abbasid caliphate, as well as from crusaders in Syria and Mesopotamia. Those who could not respond to his call were the Mongols, who were busy with their internal differences, and the Pope, who was involved in a campaign against the Holy Roman Emperor. Louis' preparations lasted for 4 years.

Shajarat ad-Durr

AH **648**
AD **1250**

When Turan Shah took over, the first thing he wanted to do was to put an end to Mameluke influence. The Mamelukes were Turks whom the Ayyubids had brought en masse to make up the army front lines in battle. In time they rose in the military ranks and their influence grew. That worried Turan Shah. One night, while he was drunk and his tongue had loosened, he used his sword to strike out at some candles that were in front of him, saying: "This is what I will do to the Mamelukes". He actually did this in front of some Mamelukes, while they were watching. They then plotted with Shajarat ad-Durr to kill Turan Shah and to proclaim her as sultana in his place. Turan Shah had only lasted 70 days on the throne when he was assassinated by a Mameluke commander named Akey, and Shajarat ad-Durr took over the reins of power. The Mamelukes and the princes of Egypt pledged allegiance to her and she then became the first woman to rule in the Islamic world.

At that time Syria was dependent on Egypt but refused to swear loyalty to her, saying: "We do not give our loyalty to a woman". The Abbasid caliph in Baghdad sent a letter to Egypt in mocking tones: "If Egypt does not have any men to give orders, we can provide you with some". Shajarat ad-Durr felt she would never be accepted as governor of Egypt and that things were slipping out of her control. Skilfully, she embarked on a devious strategy. She chose one of the weaker Mameluke commanders and proposed marrying him. He was called 'Izz ad-Din Aybek. Once the marriage was consummated, she abdicated in his favour, after ensuring she would still wield effective power in the country. Syria would not recognize him either. Aybek, the new sultan, proclaimed the Mameluke dynasty in Egypt and declared the end of the Ayyubid dynasty, which was also brought to an end in Syria one year later. Shajarat ad-Durr, who held effective power, made changes in Egypt, as well as organizing an enormous military force and founding a great maritime fleet.

Reconciliation between the Mamelukes and the Ayyubids

At about that time, differences between the Syrian Ayyubids flared up again, while their rejection of Mameluke authority in Egypt was absolute. Meanwhile, Louis IX continued planning to recover Jerusalem. Aware of the danger posed by Louis IX, the Abbasid caliphate intervened to settle the differences between Ayyubids and Mamelukes. The initiative was designed to prevent internecine struggles distracting Muslims from the crusader danger in the area and, with Abbasid mediation, matters calmed down and reconciliation between the Ayyubids and Mamelukes was achieved through an agreement stipulating that Jerusalem, Gaza and Nablus were to remain under the command of the Mamelukes, whereas Syria and the remaining areas were to continue under Ayyubid control.

AH 649
AD 1251

The end of Louis IX

Louis IX was still trying to assemble armies from everywhere except Europe, which could offer him no support because of internal conflicts and wars of its own. When he realized he could not put together an army capable of ensuring the recovery of Jerusalem, he was forced to withdraw and return to Europe, in AD 1254. However, he left Acre in crusader hands. The greatest crusade of that era, destined to occupy Jerusalem, was over. Afterwards there would be only one other similar attempt, in the year 1270, when Louis IX went to Tunisia, where his forces were repulsed by the Hafsids, in league with other powerful tribes. He lost his life there and his body was taken back to France. Indeed, with the withdrawal of Louis IX, the crusades to Palestine came to an end, even though the coastal region remained in crusader hands.

AH 652
AD 1254

Louis IX discusses plans for Egypt.

AH 655
AD 1257

"Once again, at a critical moment, the erudite ulamas were decisive in bringing about social reform and preserving Muslim dignity. Without them, the community would remain dormant and indolent."

A picture from the era of Mongol rule.

AH 656
AD 1258

The end of Shajarat ad-Durr

That year, the sultan Aybek tried to wrest effective power from Shajarat ad-Durr. He wrote to the Emir of Mosul, asking for his daughter's hand. By so doing, he was trying to create an alliance that would help him take over power in Egypt. However Shajarat ad-Durr discovered the plot and incited some Mamelukes against her husband, who was arrested and murdered. Thus, she again took over the reins of power and offered herself in marriage to the Mamelukes of Egypt. Nobody accepted the offer, for fear of her cruelty, as they all remembered what had happened to Aybek.

Realizing her plan had failed, she resorted to appointing Al-Mansur, her stepson and Aybek's son, sultan of Egypt. The fact is that Al-Mansur was not even 10 years old, and this suited her, as she could then continue to rule. However, an army commander, Sayf ad-Din Qutuz, came on the scene and declared himself regent of the new sultan, in opposition to Shajarat ad-Durr. The Mamelukes then declared their allegiance to Sayf ad-Din Qutuz, which left Shajarat ad-Durr powerless and led to her imprisonment. She appealed to her followers, but they could do nothing for her. When she was about to be arrested, she gave orders for all her jewellery and adornments to be brought to her; she then picked up a mortar and smashed them to pieces. Once arrested, the mother of sultan Al-Mansur asked Qutuz if she could take charge of Shajarat ad-Durr, after which she ordered her servants to club her to death with clogs and throw her body over the palace balcony into a ditch. She remained there for several days until the guards found and buried her.

The Mongols and the fall of the Abbasid caliphate

This was the year the Mongols invaded Baghdad and killed the last Abbasid caliph al-Musta'sim and all his family. They engaged in a massacre unprecedented in history. For the most optimistic historians, the number of victims amounted to approximately 800,000 Muslims in the course of 40 days. Afterwards, they dealt with the Baghdad library, the most important library in the world at the time, throwing the books into the River Tigris. It was said that there were so many books that they used them as a bridge to cross the river on horseback. The Mongol commander at the time was Hulagu Khan, and his military commander, who sacked Baghdad, was a ruthless man named Ket Buqa, nicknamed "the drinker of blood". In view of the violence of the attack, the Muslims in Syria and Egypt were struck with fear. The reaction came from the supreme religious leader, al-'Izz ibn 'Abd as-Salam, who announced the dismissal of the sultan of Egypt, Al-Mansur, still aged 10, and, in his place, he appointed Qutuz, on condition that he announced his intention of fighting for the supreme cause. Qutuz obeyed and al-'Izz ibn 'Abd as-Salam decreed that taking part in the battle was the religious duty of every Muslim man and woman.

Meanwhile, the Mongols marched on Syria. Damascus surrendered without a fight. They then headed straight to Aleppo, where the people resisted, but ended up succumbing to the force and cruelty of the Mongols, who left 100,000 Muslims dead on the battlefield. The Mongols then turned their sights on Egypt. Through his army commander, Ket Buqa, Hulagu Khan sent a letter to the sultan, Sayf ad-Din Qutuz, saying: "Learn from your fellow beings. Give yourselves up and submit yourselves to our orders, as we do not feel sorry for whoever weeps; nor are we moved by whoever complains. There is no land that will shelter you, no road that will save you and no country that will protect you. You cannot escape from our swords and you cannot avoid being afraid of us. Fortresses are vulnerable to us, troops are useless in the fight against us and your entreaty to God is pointless".

The Mongols occupy Baghdad. The picture shows a pillar made out of skulls.

When Qutuz had read Hulagu Khan's letter, he sent for the Mongol emissaries, killed them, quartered and beheaded them and hung their heads on a gate in the city centre. Commending himself to Almighty God and trusting in Him, he gave orders to learned men and preachers throughout Egypt to announce a general mobilization (Jihad), and asked people everywhere to prepare for war. In effect, people came from everywhere and began to march on Palestine under Qutuz's command. The Mongols had installed their forces there and imposed their authority throughout its territories. On reaching Gaza, Qutuz encountered a small Mongolian garrison which he quickly seized. The next day he headed towards Ain Jalut (Goliath's fountain).

AH 658
AD 1260

The battle of Ain Jalut

On Friday, 25 Ramadan AH 658 (AD 6 September 1260), in a place called Ain Jalut in north-east Palestine, the armies of Qutuz and the Mongols met. The Mongol army was greater in number, more experienced and better equipped. Its bases were strategically placed, with easily accessible supply routes nearby. In addition, their morale was extremely high, since until then they had never lost one single battle. On the contrary, Qutuz was far from his supply routes, having penetrated deep into Palestinian territory. He had a medium-sized Muslim army, which included ulamas and preachers who had come along to maintain the morale. Qutuz was known for his modesty, his profound faith and his great efficacy in battle. When confronting the Mongol army, Qutuz chose to delay combat until after Friday prayers. As the people found this strange, he explained that he preferred to wait for the beneficial effect of the Muslims' prayers throughout the world, as everywhere they were praying for the Muslim army.

The battle got off to a fierce start. The Mongols charged the Muslim forces until they reached Qutuz's tent, where they struck his wife, Jullanar Hab ar-Ruman, but the Muslims were able to force them back. Qutuz flew towards his wife and, seeing her on the verge of death, said to her: "My beloved!" She replied:

"Do not say my beloved! Say instead, beloved Islam!"

May God make Muslim women follow her example and teach boys and girls to say: "Beloved Islam!" instead of "My beloved!"

Qutuz stood up at once and fought fiercely, until his horse was injured and fell, but this did not prevent him from continuing the fight on foot. One of the Mamelukes offered him his horse but Qutuz refused and asked him to bring another horse. The horseman insisted, reminding him that, if he were to be killed, the soldiers' morale would fail. Qutuz then answered him: "If they kill me, my destiny will be Paradise. As for Islam, God will be its protector".

With faith and valour, Qutuz continued fighting until victory was won. The Muslims killed the Mongol commander, Ket Buqa. When Qutuz found out about his death, he dismounted and fell to his knees, praising God for the victory. Then he pursued the Mongols into Syria. Panic took hold of the Mongols, whereas the Muslims were confident, thanks to their enthusiasm and faith in battle against the invaders. In their flight, the Mongols left all their belongings, their money, prisoners and everything they possessed. They were only worried about saving their lives. In just one month, Qutuz had managed to drive the Mongols completely out of Syria.

Victory filled Qutuz with strength and he started preparing to liberate the crusader kingdoms on the coast—Acre, Beirut, Tripoli and Antioch. His objective was cut short, however, because he was murdered on his way back from Syria. It has been claimed that his second-in-command, Baybars, committed the homicide, but evidence shows he was not involved. Nothing further is known about who committed this crime.

The Mamelukes liberate crusader-held cities

AH 662
AD 1264

It was Baybars who succeeded Qutuz. The first thing he did was to go directly into Palestine. In the year AH 663 he was able to liberate Caesarea and Haifa. The following year he besieged the crusader capital of Acre, but he met with strong resistance from its occupants, assisted by its solid fortifications. After several thwarted attempts, he decided to leave and to head for Safed, which he conquered. He then took Jaffa, in the year 666, before going on to Syria.

Baybars' objective was to destabilize the crusader kingdom of Syria. To do this he left the Christian kingdoms behind and went to Antioch in the north. It fell to him after only five days' battle. This was such a blow to the crusaders that its effect resounded as far as Palestine and Europe. Antioch was one of the most important crusader kingdoms in Syria and its fall drove the crusaders to ask for reinforcements from Europe, and help from the Mongols. The Mongols, beset with internal problems and still smarting from their defeat, could not send more that a few light forces.

In Europe, a decision was made to send reinforcements. Nevertheless, Baybars continued to exploit his run of conquests—he was able to liberate the solid, impregnable fortress of Tripoli. After a short time, reinforcements arrived from Europe and joined the Mongol forces. Together they formed a fearsome adversary for the Muslims.

AH 670
AD 1272

Another truce with the crusaders

The situation facing Baybars left him no alternative but to negotiate with the crusaders, and so the parties established a 10-year truce during which they agreed to content themselves with the territories already under their rule. War stopped and stability reigned once more. Six years later, Baybars died, leaving an extensive kingdom that spread from the Black Sea to the Indian Ocean and from the Euphrates to Tunis. He was succeeded by a Mameluke named Qala'un. In the year AH 682, the truce with the crusaders came to an end. Qala'un requested its renewal, because the Mongols had again attacked parts of Muslim territory, and he feared they would again seek an alliance with the crusaders.

AH 688
AD 1289

A new alliance between crusaders, Mongols and traitors

Qala'un's forecasts were not mistaken. In AH 688, the crusaders and the Mongols reached a secret agreement with the governor of Damascus, who had been newly appointed by the Mamelukes. This resulted in the assembly of an enormous army, consisting of 80,000 soldiers, which went to meet Qala'un, but the clash ended in favour of the Muslims, thus severing the alliance. Qala'un pursued the defeated army and conquered Tripoli, but he was unable to enter Acre because of its impregnable fortresses. Its occupants, aware of the strength of Qala'un's army and the danger it posed, adopted the strategy of making sorties from the fortresses, attacking the Muslims and returning swiftly to entrench themselves in Acre. On seeing this, Qala'un resolved to conquer Acre, as he realized that the source of the crusader threat resided there.

AH 689
AD 1290

The liberation of Acre and the end of the crusades

Qala'un declared war in God's name to conquer Acre, while the crusaders declared a holy war against the Muslims. At the head of a great army, Qala'un marched on the city, where crusader forces from other kingdoms had also rallied to protect it. However, Qala'un died before reaching Palestine. His son, Al-Ashraf Khalil, whom his father called Khalil Salah ad-Din, in honour of Saladin, succeeded him.

Facing the danger that laid ahead, the crusaders tried to initiate negotiations for a truce, but the sultan refused and continued marching on the city. For reinforcements he called on the people of Syria, who came to his aid in the year AH 690 (AD 18 May 1291), and the siege of Acre began. It ended up being conquered by Al-Ashraf Khalil Salah ad-Din, who continued to set the rest of Palestine free, putting an end to the crusaders' presence there 200 years after they had arrived. After that, Palestine remained under the rule of the Qala'un family.

AH 690
AD 1290

Persecution of the Jews in Europe

That year, King Edward I ordered the Jews (the infidels) to be driven out of England. This is a reminder that, while the Jews only ruled Palestine for 99 years, Muslims did so for over 1,200. Besides, the periods in which the holy places were under Muslim rule were always times of prosperity, flowering culture and the stimulus to develop the spirit of scientific investigation. We should also add that the years when the Jews lived under the protection of Islam, in conjunction with Muslims and Christians, were periods of great religious tolerance, whereas in Europe they were oppressed, tormented and humiliated.

A unique map, drawn by European artists using quill pens.

191

Palestine in the Islamic era

"Qala'un's forecasts were not mistaken. In AH 688, the crusaders and the Mongols reached a secret agreement with the governor of Damascus, who had been newly appointed by the Mamelukes. This resulted in the assembly of an enormous army, consisting of 80,000 soldiers, which went to meet Qala'un."

Birth of the Ottoman dynasty

After its remarkable expansion, the Mameluke dynasty then started showing signs of weakness. Their influence had spread to Hijaz, Egypt, Syria and the lands of the Maghreb. Coinciding with this, the Byzantine Christians also embarked on a period of decline. This was when a new dynasty appeared for the first time, headed by its founder, Osman I, in Asia Minor, the area known today as Turkey and its surroundings. He was soon to impose his authority over the whole region.

Expressionist map showing the crusades, as imagined by a Greek artist.

PART THREE
From the Ottoman era to the British mandate

CHAPTER ONE
Palestine in the Ottoman era

1. The first Ottoman period

2. The French Revolution and the Napoleonic era

3. Khedive Mohammed Ali Pasha

Palestine in the Ottoman era

1. The first Ottoman period

AH **700**
AD **1300**

The early years of the Ottomans

That year the Ottoman Turks managed to occupy the lands of the Seljuk Turks who ruled over Asia Minor, at a time when the Mameluke dynasty ruled in Egypt, greater Syria and Palestine.

AH **706**
AD **1306**

France and the Jews

Persecution of the Jews was the predominant affair in Europe during a large part of the Middle Ages. In 1306, King Philip of France drove the Jews out of the country after forcing them to choose between adopting the Christian faith, being imprisoned, or facing death or expulsion. The rabbi of France ordered the expulsion of Jews for feigning the Christian faith, which had a marked effect on the life of Jews in Europe. Due to their apparent Christianity, they started moving up in Christian social circles and filtered among the Catholics. Many occupied important Christian positions. The rabbi ordered them to abandon agriculture and industry and to devote themselves basically to trading. He knew that money was the dominant force and a guarantee of their permanency in Europe.

Since then, the Jews began to become active in currency trading, while they also traded in other goods in the countries where they lived, aware of the strength that money provides and the possibilities that would offer them in exerting their authority.

Meanwhile, Mameluke rule continued unabated in Palestine, where they commissioned such major works as gold-plating the Dome of the Rock mosque. This was in the era of the sultan, An-Nasir Muhammad Qala'un, when the Mameluke dynasty reached its peak, just as the Ottoman dynasty was about to conquer Asia Minor.

Ottoman mosque, Istanbul.

Mehmed II "Fatih"

After coming to the throne in AD 1451, the Ottoman sultan Mehmed II "Fatih" ("Conqueror") attacked Byzantium. In 1454 he was able to conquer Constantinople, a feat which had taken the Muslims more than six hundred years to achieve—this was thereafter considered to be one of the greatest ever Muslim victories. It was the beginning of the Ottoman expansion in Europe, which reached as far as Greece, Bulgaria, Bosnia and Herzegovina.

AH 855
AD 1451

Sultan
Mehmed II
"Fatih".

Islamic justice

AH 878
AD 1473

In that period, the Mameluke sultan Qaitbay ruled most of the Middle East. Muslims and Jews disputed the ownership of a building located between a mosque and a synagogue in a Jewish district. The matter was taken before an Islamic court. The verdict was that the house belonged to the Jews, was recorded as such in the register of welfare and religious property and was classified as a religious bequest. This is an example of the integrity that characterized the Islamic justice system.

The Jews were witnesses of Islamic equity, of the justice and clemency established throughout the Muslim territories, while they were suffering oppression and persecution in Europe. Despite the test of time, they were unable to accord it the due value and importance.

Mamelukes and Ottomans grow apart

AH 886
AD 1481

That year, Sultan Mehmed II "Fatih" died. He was succeeded by Bayezid, who had his differences with the Mameluke sultan Qaitbay. Mediation to settle the differences between both parties was doomed to fail. The upshot was that Qaitbay organized a campaign against the Ottomans. In AH 890 (AD 1485), he armed the people in the Palestinian cities, but they then had their money and saddlery confiscated, much to the indignation of the Palestinians. That was not all. In AH 989, the Mameluke Sultan demanded privileges to be given to the Jews, at the expense of the Muslims, not only in Palestine, but everywhere else, which increased the indignation of the inhabitants of Palestine. Their acceptance of the Mameluke rule began to falter.

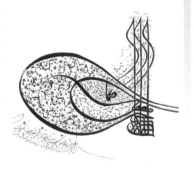

Krak Castle

Turkish helmet.

AH 920
AD 1514

The Ottomans defeat the Safavids and Mamelukes

Another battle took place at the time between the Ottomans and the Safavids, who lived in Mesopotamia and Persia, and the latter were finally defeated. Thus, the Ottomans had effectively encircled Mameluke territory. In AD 1516, the Ottoman sultan Selim I defeated the Muslims at the famous battle of Marj Dabik. Not only did he manage to defeat and conquer Syria and Palestine, but he was also able to extend his rule over most of Mesopotamia. Mameluke rule was then limited to Egypt.

After that victory, Selim I turned to the worrying issue of the mass movement of Jewish immigrants in Palestine, and in AD 1516, a law was passed that prohibited them to emigrate to Sinai and Palestine, as it was thought that they actually intended to dominate the Holy Land. Except for Sinai and Palestine, they were allowed to live wherever they chose in Ottoman territories.

AH 923
AD 1517

The end of the Mameluke dynasty

That year, the sultan Selim I attacked the Mamelukes, penetrating into Egyptian territory, and defeated them at the battle of Ridenieh. He announced the fall and the end of the Mameluke dynasty. Then he entered Cairo and joined the territory of the Mamelukes to those of the Ottoman dynasty, which by then had reached its peak and become the most powerful empire in that era.

Suleyman II the Magnificent

That year the sultan Suleyman II rose to power. He is known in the history books as Suleyman the Magnificent. It was he who built the walls of Jerusalem and shored up the Dome of the Rock mosque. His policy was to continue prohibiting the Jews from living in Palestine and Sinai. It was clear to the Ottoman rulers that the Jews had their sights set on colonizing Palestine, which is why they were so committed to enforcing this prohibition.

In spite of being driven out of Spain and suffering oppression when living in Europe, Jews were allowed to reside wherever they liked throughout the Ottoman territories, with the exception of the Holy Lands. It was an attitude of maximum tolerance and justice towards them, well aware that in ancient times the Jews had sought to occupy

Suleyman II the Magnificent conquers Europe.

Jerusalem. We should recall the way non-Jewish Palestinians are now treated by the Israelis, in spite of their being well treated in Muslim lands in the past, as opposed to the persecution they suffered in the West.

AH 943
AD 1537

Ottomans
conquering Europe.

The Turkish Sephardis

However, one group of Jews was not in favour of the status imposed on them by the Ottomans. In view of their condition, in 1665, the Turkish Sephardis, led by a Turkish Jew named Shabtai Tsvi, founded an organization whose specific ideological orientation was based on demanding the return of the Jews to Palestine. He even dared to head that organization at some spectacular rallies in opposition to the Ottomans' state policies. The sultan gave the order to put an end to his following. Shabtai Tsvi's reaction as its leader was to order the Turkish Jews to do the same as their coreligionists in the rest of Europe, that is, to outwardly practise as Muslims. This is how a new, secret, messianic Jewish movement was born, known variously as the Donmeh, Sabbateans or Frankists, as Ottoman Jews were called Franks. With the help of businessmen and wealthy people, the followers of that organization gradually acceded to important positions within the Ottoman state apparatus.

AH 1075
AD 1665

Ottomans in full battle.

Ottoman Sultan.

AH 1203
AD 1789

2. The French Revolution and the Napoleonic era

Protestants and the Reformation

At this time in history, Europe was experiencing a wave of religious reform, during which a new Christian doctrine called Protestantism was about to emerge. This doctrine now dominates America and many European countries. Its founder was the famous pastor, Martin Luther. However, the Jews were behind this movement. They were the ones who organized it and worked to spread and divulge it. In essence, it was based on reviving belief in the Old Testament. Everyone knows the Bible consists of the Old and the New Testaments. Among other things, the first mentioned includes the teachings of Moses, while the New Testament contains the teachings of Christ as transmitted by the Evangelists. The purpose of the Reformation was to recreate the idea that true religion was found in the Old Testament, rather than in the New, which is greatly modified. The followers of the movement spread the news that they were awaiting Jesus' return. The Jews who outwardly professed to being Christians were the leaders of the new movement and preached the return to the Torah, as it concerned the Old Testament. Besides, they promoted the idea that the true population of Palestine was Jewish, while the role of the Christians was to help them return. That reformist movement soon spread to Great Britain, Germany and Holland and subsequently to the United States. A new group, called Christian Zionists, came to light. They were Protestants who preached adherence to the Old Testament and the return of the Jews to Palestine. They considered the latter to be a fundamental issue of Christian religion. This, however, was not the case. The Jews who were outwardly Christians, and who infiltrated among the latter, were responsible for spreading that idea. The issue culminated in the events that came to a head during the French Revolution, in 1789, and led to the downfall of the monarchy in France.

The ideologies of the French Revolution had a great impact on the rest of Europe. Some believe it to mark the beginning of modern Europe, of nationalism, of laity claiming the separation between religion and state. The Industrial Revolution then emerged under the umbrella of the newfound laicism.

Martin Luther, the Christian reformer, who first sympathized with the return of the Jews, but later opposed them and called for their places of worship to be destroyed. He wrote a book entitled, "The Jews and their Lies".

The reconciliation between Judaism and Christianity

AH 1205
AD 1791

Curiously, one the most noteworthy contributions of the French Revolution was the fact that its leaders advocated the introduction of laws granting Jews equal rights with other European citizens, especially in western Europe. From then on, the Jews began to play a prominent role in politics, economics and the media. One of them even became Prime Minister of France. The strategy of outwardly professing Christianity allowed them to infiltrate hierarchies and successfully reach top office. This is how the Jews recovered their position in Europe after many years of oppression, war and suffering, compared to their lot in Muslim countries, where they enjoyed tolerance, freedom to worship and life under the protection of the Ottoman dynasty.

Napoleon near Cairo.

AH 1213
AD 1798

Napoleon marches to Egypt

By July 1897, Napoleon Bonaparte had conquered much of Europe. His objective then became Egypt, which was under Ottoman rule. In a short space of time and without encountering any resistance, his troops occupied the country, leaving the Ottomans at a loss to respond and showing up their weakness, which also allowed Napoleon to decide on the occupation of Palestine. He marched on the country and met with virtually no resistance.

However, by that time the British had taken their empire across the globe and had the most powerful fleet. Wary of the spread of French influence and French ambitions, they set course for Palestine, leading to the outbreak of war on three fronts—between the Ottomans, who ruled Palestine, Napoleon, who had left Egypt with the intention of taking it over, and Great Britain, which was heading to Palestine in an effort to halt the spread of French influence in the region, bearing in mind the danger it represented to their own ambitions and interests in that part of the world.

AH 1214
AD 1799

Napoleon in Palestine

When Napoleon realized the race toward the region was on, he redoubled his efforts and was able to occupy the towns of Palestine one by one until he reached Acre, which he besieged on 18 March 1799. That was when the British arrived. On seeing the conflict had begun between the Ottomans and the French, they decided to let them get on with it and watch them closely. When the scales tipped against the Ottomans, the British fleet backed them against the French. Their aim was to weaken both sides. The aid the British gave to the ruler in Acre, Ahmed Pasha al-Jezzar, allowed him to hold out against Napoleon who, after a siege lasting three months, lost only five of his generals and 2,200 soldiers, besides 250 wounded and unfit to fight. Napoleon resorted to diabolical shrewdness. That same year, on 4 April, during the siege of Acre, he issued a communiqué in which he invited the Jews throughout the world to settle in Palestine. By so doing, he hoped to gain Jewish support, which indeed he did, from both Europe and the rest of the world. Napoleon was the first person to promise to secure Palestine for the Jews, long before the Balfour declaration of 2 November 1917. Jewish support arrived from all over the world, but especially from Turkey, and was both moral and material. Thanks to this, Napoleon was able to occupy Nablus and Ramla, and to travel long distances in Palestine. However, did not dare go too deeply into the territory, as he had left Acre behind to the British, whose fleet had anchored near the city walls. Napoleon then started calling on Jews to join his army in Egypt because he intended to advance eastward, beyond Egypt and Palestine. The Jews were not long in responding but, when the situation seemed to be set, an epidemic wiped out a large number of French soldiers. With Acre still to be conquered, the English positioned on one side, and the Ottomans on the other, they had no alternative but to withdraw from Palestine and head back to Egypt, on 17 May 1799. In addition, Napoleon was burdened with 3,000 Ottoman prisoners and did not know what to do with them. In the end, as if it were the simplest thing in the world, with no

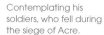

Napoleon
Bonaparte

Contemplating his soldiers, who fell during the siege of Acre.

laws governing their deeds, no agreements and absolutely no ethics, Napoleon ordered them to be shot. In a single day, he ended all their lives.

The French presence in Palestine had reached its end with Napoleon's return to Egypt, where he planned to stay. However, the uprising led by the ulamas, learned religious scholars from the Al-Azhar University, made him desist. On the other hand, upheavals and other dangerous events in France were hastening his withdrawal from Egypt.

The French campaign in the East was the first intimation of a promise to the Jews for their return to Palestine. They then numbered just under five thousand, living on Palestinian soil. The support Napoleon gave them revived the hopes and ambitions they had long harboured with regard to the Holy Land.

Napoleon seizes power.

Napoleon Bonaparte confronting his government over differences about his Egyptian campaign.

A rifle used in the
Ottoman era.

3. Khedive Mohammed Ali Pasha

Once the French had left, the Ottomans returned to Palestine. The Turk of Albanian extraction, Mohammed Ali Pasha, was named viceroy of Egypt or "khedive", a title the Ottomans gave to rulers of Egypt. Naturally, the khedive had to be a Turk. Once Mohammed Ali Pasha had imposed his authority in Egypt, the weakness of the Ottoman dynasty became evident. His personal ambition to extend his rule, and to be independent from the Ottomans, took Palestine into account, too. He quickly headed there, wielding some untenable arguments.

The Ottomans reacted by sending an army to confront Mohammed Ali Pasha both in Egypt and Palestine. But he was able to defeat the Ottomans, conquer Palestine and annex it to Egypt. Despite having taken it over, he declared it to be under Ottoman rule, wary of precipitating direct confrontation with the latter. His dependence was merely nominal, even though sermons had to be delivered in the name of the caliph, and prayers addressed to the Ottoman sultan. Actually, Mohammed Ali Pasha enjoyed true independence in both Egypt and Palestine.

Mohammed Ali Pasha's ambitions did not stop there, as he imposed compulsory military service on all the inhabitants of Egypt and Palestine and levied taxes. He resorted to asking the Jews for help, as they had huge fortunes, as well as to the Christians. Both communities gave their support and took advantage of the opportunity to become involved with the structure of that particular Muslim dynasty.

Nevertheless the Muslims of Palestine and Egypt reacted to the khedive's bias with a huge revolt, which was implacably quashed. The khedive extended his authority and his kingdom up to the borders of Syria.

Great Britain, the Khedive and the Jews

Khedive Mohammed
Ali governs Egypt and
quells revolts.

AH 1219
AD 1804

Great Britain was planning to topple the Ottoman dynasty and was aware of the emerging strength in the regions of Syria and Egypt. However, it did not want a switch to a new Ottoman dynasty, nor one with khedives. Thus, Britain intervened to protect the Ottomans under the khedive Mohammed Ali Pasha in Syria, to put pressure on the Egyptians and to check any further expansion. This was a classical British strategy—to support the weak and the strong, in order to bring them both down.

Highly important events were taking place in Great Britain, where an officer at the palace of Queen Victoria, Sir Moses Montefiore, established a friendly relationship with a Jewish businessman named Rothschild, whose financial power in Britain is still a major force today. Through the marriage of convenience between Rothschild's daughter and Montefiore, an alliance was forged between government and capital. From then on, Moses Montefiore supported the first effective campaign for the return of the Jews to Palestine.

Montefiore's project

AH 1243
AD 1828

That year, the so-called Moses Montefiore project came to light. With the aid of the Government and the French Republic, the British officer managed to put pressure on the Ottomans, until they passed a law allowing Jews to settle and set up workshops in Palestine.

The Zionist plan for settling in Palestine

AH 1244
AD 1829

Moses Montefiore reached an agreement with the Zionist leaders in England, Italy, Romania, Morocco and Russia to collaborate in drawing up a Zionist project that consisted of converting Palestine into the Jewish homeland.

At the same time, the khedive dynasty was growing in strength. A battle between the latter and the followers of Muhammad Ibn 'Abd al-Wahhab took place in the Arabian peninsula. Mohammed Ali Pasha's chief military commander was his son, Ibrahim.

The Khedive broadens his kingdom

AH 1247
AD 1831

Ibrahim Mohammed Ali Pasha took charge of further extending his fathers' kingdom by conquering Syria, the Hijaz and part of the Arabian Peninsula. The spread of the khedive dynasty was achieved to the detriment of the Ottoman empire.

At the same time, the influence of the Zionists, who were contributing money and support to the khedive, was also growing, while pressure on the Muslims in Syria and Palestine was stepped up, with increased taxes and compulsory military service.

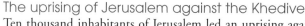

AH 1250
AD 1834

The uprising of Jerusalem against the Khedive

Ten thousand inhabitants of Jerusalem led an uprising against Ibrahim Pasha, who was governing in his father's name. One of the khedive's regiments in Jerusalem set about quelling the unrest, but this only complicated matters, leading to an escalation in hostilities, until Ibrahim himself ended up being encircled. He appealed to his father in Egypt. Mohammed Ali Pasha sent three infantry regiments and a squadron of cavalry, which he himself led to Palestine. He also had the support of the Jews and the Christians. With coordinated tactics between the khedive regiment inside Jerusalem, and the Egyptian army on its outskirts, the revolt was eventually put down, but it left a legacy of serious upheaval in the Khedive regime in Palestine.

At that moment Great Britain submitted a request to the Ottoman dynasty. It concerned opening one of their consulates in Jerusalem. In order to achieve their objective, they used their political influence to convince the khedive to give his consent. Once the diplomatic headquarters were open, the first letter received from the British government contained an order to give protection to the Zionists of Jerusalem.

Moses Hess,
whose influence
foreshadowed the
Zionist state. 1862

AH 1261
AD 1845

Great Britain and France back the Zionist movement

Immediately afterwards, Great Britain became encouraged by its diplomatic progress and started to demand that the Ottoman dynasty should use its influence over the khedive, persuading him to drive out the inhabitants of Palestine and openly let the Jewish immigrants settle there. However, the khedive was closely watching the British and Zionist manoeuvres and made the firm resolution not to allow the Zionist expansion to grow any further in Palestine.

Meanwhile, in Europe, Zionists continued to occupy high-profile positions in society and government. They also founded the Universal Israelite Alliance, which was widely promoted throughout France. Then the World Zionist Organization was created. Two years later, Moses Hess, a well-known German Jew in Zionist history, published a book entitled "Rome and Jerusalem". In it he referred to so-called Jewish nationalism although, up until then, Judaism had been nothing other than a religion. Now it had suddenly been transformed into a doctrine with nationalistic tendencies.

Shot from a film entitled "Roots in Poland", about a Jewish gathering in that country, which admitted half a million extremely poor Jews in the 19th century.

The reign of sultan Abdülhamid II

AH 1291
AD 1874

1. The Sultan confronts the Jews

The growth of Zionism spread from France to other countries. By 1874, the Jews had obtained constitutional laws in their favour in most of Europe, most of them dating from the time of the French Revolution. That year, Sultan Abdülhamid II acceded to the Ottoman throne and his influence had reached Palestine. The khedive's rule had declined and was now limited to Egypt. Abdülhamid II began to organize the state by proclaiming the Ottoman constitution—he established a parliament and introduced the consultative assembly. He had the Arabs take part in government, although royal prerogatives remained in the hands of the Turks. He held the first session of parliament in the year 1867 (AH 1270). It was the first time the Arabs had effectively participated. They were represented by two members of parliament for Jerusalem, chosen to represent their interests in the Turkish parliament.

Sultan Abdülhamíd II
refused to sell Palestine.

AH 1293
AD 1876

Anti-semitism emerges in Russia

Having taken over the reins of power, the Ottoman sultan started to closely watch Zionist movements in Palestine. By then, their presence had grown to 14,000 people. Two years later (in 1878), they founded their first settlement in Petach Tikvah.

Meanwhile, in Russia, the Jews were accused of taking part in conspiracies against the Czar, Alexander II, who they allegedly intended to assassinate. After escaping the foolhardy attempt, he reacted violently by persecuting Jews and exerted pressure on them to emigrate from Russia. Then the so-called anti-Semitic appeared—hatred of anything Semitic. The origin of the Jews is Semitic, as it is also that of the Arabs, but the Jews in Russia were better known as having such origins. Based on this, the anti-Semitic movement started to become a talking point.

Russia was sheltering millions of Jews, a figure exceeded only in Europe, which posed a huge problem when it came to finding a place for them to settle. As a result of this, a movement called the "Friends of Zion" appeared whose efforts convinced the French and British states to request the Ottomans, as neighbours of the Russians, to allow the Jews to immigrate to the Ot-

toman Empire. It was under the flag of that demand and Islamic tolerance that Sultan Abdülhamid II permitted Jews to settle in Ottoman territories, with the exception of Palestine.

The United States appears on the scene

During one of the first appearances by the United States on the international political scene, their ambassador intervened before Sultan Abdülhamid to voice his disapproval of the decision to prevent Jews from residing in Palestine. Up until then, the USA was no more than an isolated
country, with no military or political activities in the rest of the world.
Curiously, their first intervention at world level was in favour of the
Zionists. Sultan Abdülhamid's response took the shape of a sentence that
went down in history: "I shall not allow immigrant Jews to settle in Palestine while the Ottoman dynasty still exists."

Prohibition for immigrant Jews to settle in Palestine

AH 1298
AD 1881

In accordance with that decision, the Ottoman dynasty received the Jews
on its soil, without allowing them to go as far as Palestine, from 1881 until 1914, when the Jewish problem arose in Russia. In that space of time,
nearly 2.5 million Jews emigrated from Russia and the rest of Europe and
settled in Ottoman territories, specifically in Turkey.
Only 155,000 (that is, 2%) of all the Jews who emigrated were able to
infiltrate into Palestine. In this respect, the demographic policy of Sultan
Abdülhamid could be considered a wise one, although the following year
he allowed Jews to visit the holy places without permitting them to actually settle there. Due to the persecution they suffered in some European
countries, a few Jewish groups managed to emigrate to the north of
Palestine, where they founded their first settlement in the most absolute
secrecy.

Growth of the Zionist movement

AH 1299
AD 1882

That year, the British occupied Egypt, then under the rule of the khedive
and officially dependent on the Ottoman dynasty.
At the same time, the Franco-Jewish millionaire Edmond Rothschild
founded a movement that provided financial support for the establishment in Palestine.

It was also in that year that another Jew, Leon Pinsker, published a book entitled "Auto-Emancipation" in which he invited Jews to reject the idea of becoming rooted to their current abode—his writings bore fruit in the minds of many. He made it clear in his book that true emancipation for Jews resided in the creation of a national Jewish centre that would serve as a state and motherland. This is where the idea of the creation of a Jewish state was born.

This helped to increase the number of Jews that infiltrated Palestine and built settlements discreetly hidden from view, although the inhabitants of Palestine realized what was happening and started a resistance movement from inside the country.

AH 1303
AD 1886

The Sultan administers Palestine personally

The first armed incident was soon to take place between Palestinian farmers and Zionist settlers. Meanwhile, Arab newspapers started issuing warnings about the danger that Zionists posed to Palestine, insisting that they intended to settle in the country. Sultan Abdülhamid was also aware of the danger involved and issued a decree to isolate the Sanjak district of Palestine so as to bring it directly under his rule. Palestine thus came under the patronage of the Ottoman Turkish government, which was known as "the High Gate". By being directly in touch with the administration of Palestine, the Sultan could, through meticulous surveillance, monitor the developments in those settlements and establish whether they continued to grow.

While the Sultan exerted pressure on the immigrant Jews, to urge them to move out of Palestine, some European countries did the opposite—they pressured him to allow the Jews to settle individually on Palestinian soil, although without building settlements.

Prohibition of Jewish immigration

It was in these circumstances that Sultan Abdülhamid II passed a decree that prohibited mass Jewish immigration to Ottoman lands, while even individual visitors were prevented from staying for longer than three months in Palestine.

The German Emperor, Wilhelm II, at the Dome of the Rock mosque, during his visit to Jerusalem in 1898.

Ban on the sale of real estate to Jewish immigrants

AH 1305
AD 1888

AH 1308
AD 1891

As a result of the success of this policy and the consequent stability achieved in Palestine, the sultan arranged for khedive Abbas Hilmi of Egypt to take over administration of the coast of Palestine because he had to devote himself to other important matters.

In Europe, there were several different reactions to the Sultan's decision. In Germany, Baron Maurice de Hirsch founded the Jewish Colonization Association and declared the beginning of Zionist immigration to Palestine. German Jews took advantage of the khedive's weakness in controlling the coastline and pressed ahead with their immigration, building Zionist settlements on Palestinian soil.

When the sultan found out about the Zionist movements he again assumed direct rule of Palestine and its coast, and sent troops from Turkey to drive out the new German Jewish immigrants from the Palestinian coast. This was followed in 1892 (AH 1286) by a decree prohibiting the sale of land to Jews, even if they were resident in Palestine.

However, the European countries once again started to put heavy pressure on the Sultan to allow the Jews to buy land, on condition that they did not crowd together in settlements. The sultan's response was negative. He did not give way to this pressure and remained firm in his attitude. He understood the ulterior motives involved—they had to settle Palestine in order to dominate it.

Theodore Hertzl, the leader of the Zionist Movement.

2. Hertzl and the Zionist movement

Hertzl, author of "The Jewish State"

AH 1314
AD 1896

Hungarian born Theodore Hertzl, founder of the Zionist movement, emerged on the international political scene with his book entitled *Die Judem Stat* (The Jewish State), published in 1896, which called for the creation of a Jewish state in Palestine and, failing that, in Argentina.

Our attention is called here to two facts regarding Palestine or Argentina as the preferred place in which to create a Jewish State:

– Palestine did not have as much spiritual and nostalgic value for Zionists as they now claim.

– Sultan Abdel Hamid II's determination made Zionists question their capacity to carry out their plans.

Hertzl proposes buying Palestine

AH 1315
AD 1897

That year war broke out between Greece and the Ottoman State, which was suffering from a severe economic crisis. Hertzl, taking advantage of the situation, offered the sultan, through the Ottoman ambassador in Vienna, several million pounds in gold in exchange for breaking the boycott on the immigration of Jews into Palestine, but the sultan's response was: "It is not in my hands to surrender even an inch of Palestinian land, simply because it is not personal property, but belongs to the people. My people have fought for many years and have spilt a lot of blood to preserve it". This missive disappointed Hertzl and those who supported him. However, the name of Abdülhamid II thereby went down in the annals of history among the immortal.

Realizing that a Jewish Palestine was an unattainable objective with Sultan Abdülhamid II in power, Hertzl convened the First Zionist Congress in Basle (Switzerland), which resulted in the formation of the Zionist World Organization and the determination to create a Jewish National State in Palestine, definitively discarding Argentina as an alternative option. In order to fulfil the planned objective, the Jews would work to bring down the Ottoman Empire, unless the Sultan changed his attitude.

The resolutions passed at the First Zionist Congress were featured in Rashid Rida's Cairo newspaper, Al-Manar, which also carried a warning about the dangers of Jewish immigration to Palestine.

In 1898 Hertzl convened the Second Zionist Congress in Basle, during which it was decided to established the Jewish National Fund, the aim of which was to promote the teaching of Hebrew and to entrust to Hertzl himself the task of searching for European backing for the creation of a Zionist State.

Hertzl greeting the Zionist intellectual, Dr Norad, at the First Zionist Congress, held in Basle (Switzerland) in 1897.

The Sultan stands up to Great Britain

Sultan Abdülhamid II was aware of the Zionist intentions and, in order to palliate them, he decreed the prohibition of issuing visas to visit Palestine for longer than 30 days to every non-Ottoman Jew, as well as the repatriation of anyone who stayed beyond that stipulated time.

The reaction of the Zionist movement was to convene the 4th Zionist Congress in London and, at its opening session, Hertzl praised the attitude of Great Britain—"the State that understands the Jewish movement and that provides aid and backing … "

Indeed, Great Britain once again exerted diplomatic pressure on the sultan's government, asking for the decree prohibiting the immigration of Jews to Jerusalem to be repealed. However, instead, the sultan ratified the decree but, in exchange, he agreed to allow Jews to settle in northern Palestine.

AH 1316
AD 1898

The death of Hertzl

Large waves of Jewish immigrants reaching Palestine in 1903 benefitted from the exception made by the sultan by which Jewish immigrants were allowed to settle in northern Palestine.

Hertzl never lost hope that one day he might manage to reach an arrangement with Sultan Abdülhamid II, but death robbed him of the opportunity to see his dreams come true and he left this world in 1904.

AH 1322
AD 1904

Hertzl's tomb in Palestine after his coffin was brought from Europe.

3. The end of Sultan Abdülhamid II

A dividing state

At a Congress organized by the colonial powers held in 1905, the conclusion was reached that the continuity of Islamic demography was the main reason for its strength and its historical victories. In order to put an end to this continuity it would be necessary to create a dividing state that would split the Muslim world in two, one part Asian and the other European. Everything possible should be done to widen the gulf between the two. Palestine was finally chosen as the state that would drive a wedge between all the Muslim countries.

One of the first Jewish settlements (kibbutz) in Palestine.

Kemal Atatürk

Ataturk and "Unity and Development"

AH 1325
AD 1907

Sultan Abdülhamid II, aware of foreign intrigue against his country, did his utmost to develop the infrastructure of the Ottoman Empire and improve its communications networks. In 1908, the railway line connecting Medina with Palestine, Syria and Turkey was inaugurated. But this policy did not please the Zionists in the region because they saw it as an attempt to reunify the Ottoman territories against colonial interests; they then resorted to reviving Turkish nationalism, represented by the Turkish Youth Movement and its political arm, the Committee of Union and Progress. One of its most brilliant leaders was the officer Kemal Atatürk, elected to put an end to the Sultan's aspirations.

Kemal Atatürk (the father of the Turks), nicknamed "the Conqueror", was the hero of the Dardanelles wars during the First World War and the commander in Turkey's victory over Greece.

The removal of Sultan Abdülhamid II

Representatives of the Unity and Development party in parliament, together with other members of parliament, voted to depose Sultan Abdülhamid II and to replace him with Abdülmecit, the son of the previous Sultan, Mehmet Reshat.

AH 1327
AD 1909

In July of that year, the Grand Mufti of the Ottoman empire ratified the measures taken in this respect by parliament. In fact, *de facto* power remained in the hands of the Committee of Union and Progress and, more specifically, in the hands of three Jewish ministers, appointed by this party, in a government with 13 ministers, which included only one Arab minister, representing 50% of the imperial Ottoman territory. The new sultan was simply a puppet in the hands of the governing party.

Statue of Kemal Atatürk, the Conqueror.

215

Atatürk conquers the capital of his homeland

Abdülhamid's dismissal and the challenging formation of the new government caused discontent among the people. Over the course of six months, this turned into a general uprising against the new sultan and against Unity and Progress which materialized in the assassination of several leaders of the governing party and the return of Sultan Abdülhamid to act as head of state. But Atatürk, who was the army chief of staff, moved his units, conquered the capital, Istanbul, removed Sultan Abdülhamid II from office again and deported him out of the vast Ottoman territory. Curiously, the commander-in-chief of the armed forces was an Iraqi Arab named Mehmet Shawkat Pasha.

The return of Unity and Progress to power began with a set of laws, measures and orders, the first of which was a decree promulgated in Tel Aviv itself (Israel's current capital), that left the way open for Jews to immigrate to Palestine, with no numerical or geographical restriction, and it also allowed unrestricted buying and selling of Palestinian real estate between Arabs and immigrant Jews.

Palestine remained an orphan after the dismissal of Sultan Abdülhamid II, who wrote in his book entitled *Memoirs,* "My firmness of purpose in prohibiting Jewish immigrants from settling in Palestine and the determination of Zionism in creating a national Jewish state in Palestine were the reason for my dismissal".

One of the first Jewish settlements (kibbutzim) in Palestine.

The edition of the newspaper "Palestine"

That was the year when "Palestine" was published, a newspaper dedicated to making Arab Palestinians aware of the dangers involved in installing Zionist settlements for the future of the Palestinian people and for all the Arab-Islamic nations and their relations with other countries in the world.

Meanwhile the Unity and Progress party that was in power in Istanbul continued to allow the infiltration of Zionist Turks into high spheres of the Ottoman state apparatus, as well as permitting the intensive construction of kibbutzim throughout Palestine.

AH 1329
AD 1911

An Arab rally in Jerusalem
in Ottoman times, 1908.

217

A Muslim caravan
from Jaffa, on its way
to Jerusalem, 1908

The First World War and the British mandate

1. Sharif Hussein's Movement

The Ottomans intervene in the war

In August 1914, the First World War broke out. The Ottoman state intervened as an ally of Germany, knowing in advance that Turkey had no interest in this war. Nevertheless, they took part without any political strategy. The Itihad party and the Turkish officers who were members of it put pressure on the Ottoman state to intervene in the war, under the recommendation of the Donmeh Jews who wanted to defeat them. The war exploded throughout Europe and spread to the Islamic east. The Muslim Arabs allied themselves with the Ottomans, in spite of the hatred that had existed between Turks and Arabs.

Jews praying before the Wailing Wall, 1908.

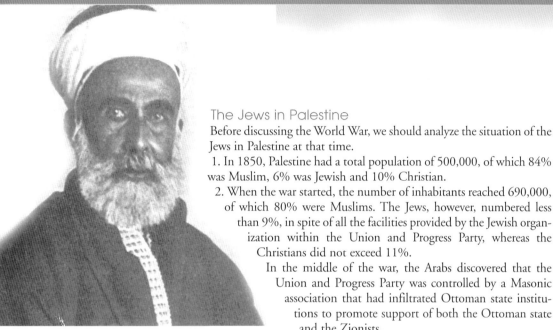

Sharif Hussein.

The Jews in Palestine

Before discussing the World War, we should analyze the situation of the Jews in Palestine at that time.

1. In 1850, Palestine had a total population of 500,000, of which 84% was Muslim, 6% was Jewish and 10% Christian.

2. When the war started, the number of inhabitants reached 690,000, of which 80% were Muslims. The Jews, however, numbered less than 9%, in spite of all the facilities provided by the Jewish organization within the Union and Progress Party, whereas the Christians did not exceed 11%.

In the middle of the war, the Arabs discovered that the Union and Progress Party was controlled by a Masonic association that had infiltrated Ottoman state institutions to promote support of both the Ottoman state and the Zionists.

AH 1333
MARCH 1915

1. Sharif Hussein's Movement

The Arabs, aware of the background to the Ottoman participation in this war, adopted a negative and even separatist attitude. Sharif Hussein, the governor of Mecca and Medina (Hijaz), took the initiative and sent his son Faisal to Damascus. He affiliated with a group named the Arab Youth Association, which agreed to revolt against Turkish rule and return the caliphate to the Arabs in the person of the Sheriffs, the descendants of the Prophet, as represented by Sharif Hussein.

Indeed, Faisal, Sharif's son, succeeded in his mission. (p. 222)

Jamal Pasha "the Butcher"
and some of his staff.

Professor Muhammad 'Abdu.

Jamal ad-Din al-Afghani.

The leaders of Syria offered him support, providing his father declared war on the Turks. However, the Ottoman governor, Jamal Pasha, found out about this and immediately arrested and hung many Syrian Arab leaders, which increased Arab hatred towards the Turks, especially when the majority of the Arabs knew nothing about the movements of Sharif Hussein, nor the preparations for the revolution. Because of this, the revolution spread everywhere; many well-known Arab and Muslim celebrities throughout the Arab world took the initiative to participate. These included, for example:

1. Muhammad Rashid Rida, of Lebanese origin.
2. Muhammad 'Abdu in Egypt.
3. Jamal ad-Din al-Afghani, the founder of the Al-Manar newspaper.
4. Muhib ad-Din al-Khatib, famous for his great literary works.
5. Al-Haj Amin al-Husayni, who encouraged thousands of people in Palestine and Syria to take part in the revolution.
6. Sa'id al-Karmi, the mufti of Tulkaram.
7. Sa'id ad-Din al-Khatib, the imam of the al-Aqsa mosque.
8. Numerous Muslims from all over the Islamic world also took part in the revolution.

Preparations for the great Arab revolution began under the direction of Sharif Hussein. He preferred to call it an Arab—and not an Islamic—revolution, as he said: "We are Arabs before we are Muslims". In spite of this, he never adopted laicism in the sense of separating religion from state, but, as he remarekd on another occasion: "We fight in the name of God and to protect our Islamic laws. We fight to liberate Arabs from Turks." Thus, Hussein managed to unite the Arabs under the flag of religion and nationalism.

2. The great Arab revolution

AH 1333
AD 1915

Lawrence of Arabia

Great Britain was immersed in war against the Germans and the Turks and began a series of negotiations with Sharif Hussein, whom they supplied with troops for the imminent declaration of the revolution. Repeated delegations of English officials promised him the establishment of an independent Arab state under his own rule, immediately after the end of the war.

They sent one of their clever political-military experts, the famous "Lawrence of Arabia". He held long negotiations with Sharif Hussein, trying to convince him to declare the revolution as soon as possible. But the Arab leader refused to make any military move without reaching an official agreement with Great Britain and being told of the details of the establishment of the Arab state, such as what its borders and territories would be under his sovereignty.

Nevertheless, Britain avoided providing the information requested by Sharif Hussein. He refused to budge, unless he received guaranteed answers to his questions. The stalemate remained, until the British presented the following plan:

Southern Yemen and the Gulf Emirates were to come under British sovereignty and would not be part of the future Arab state. Southern Iraq would have an unusual administrative status under English sovereignty. As for Syria, excluding the Lebanon, it would be placed under the sovereignty of Sharif Hussein. At that time, there were many Christians living in Lebanon. For this reason, Britain reserved it as an important, strategic ally.

Lawrence of Arabia, the British secret service envoy to the Arab territories, sent to prepare the way for the British military campaign against the Arab world.

223

Sharif Hussein accepted the British explanations, except what was said about Lebanon. By his reckoning, it would have to be an Arab territory, as it was located in the heart of the region. But Great Britain asked for the negotiations on this matter to be postponed until the Turks had been driven out of the region. In addition, through their specialist representative, Lawrence of Arabia, they once again asked for the revolution to be declared as soon as possible. And, while negotiations were underway, Great Britain was secretly preparing a conspiracy against the Arabs.

The Sykes-Picot agreement

AH 1334
AD 1916

The government of Great Britain was crafty and intelligent. While negotiating with Sharif Hussein, they signed another agreement with France that was hammered out between the British Foreign Minister Sykes and his French counterpart, Picot. It involved carving up the future Arab world between the two colonial powers. This was later called the Sykes-Picot Agreement, according to which Iraq, Transjordan and the region of Haifa and its surroundings would be controlled by Great Britain, while Syria and Lebanon would be ruled by France. As for what was left of Palestine, this would be a territory under international administration.

Declaration of the Great Arab Revolution

AH 30/07/1334
AD 01/06/1916

Whilst the British and French were finalizing their colonial agreement, Lawrence of Arabia and his collaborators from the English secret service were finalizing preparations for Sharif Hussein to declare the Revolution. Political associations in Syria and numerous political and religious leaders from the Arab world supported the revolution. The whole world aspired to putting an end to Turkish injustice directed against the Arabs and against the essence of Islam, and to stop immigration to Palestinian territories.

The great mistake that the Arabs made was to trust Great Britain when it promised to free them from the Turks, as the Sykes-Picot agreement was soon revealed by the Egyptian press. This caused great consternation in the Arab world. Britain tried to calm Sharif Hussein and denied the events reported in the

Some officers from the Great Arab Revolution.

224

The Great Arab
Revolution gets
under way.

Egyptian newspapers. However, nothing mattered any longer to the Arab leader because the war had started and there was no turning back.

Lawrence of Arabia and the Arab forces headed by Sharif Faisal, Sharif Hussein's son, with the support of the armed Arab tribes, managed to cross the Arab desert and attack the port of Aqaba, the main stronghold of the Turks and the greatest obstacle for the English forces in Egypt, who had just defeated the Germans at El Alamain, near the Libyan border. They attempted to occupy Palestine and Syria, but were repulsed by the Turks. Nevertheless, Lawrence of Arabia, backed by both the Arab tribes and Sharif Faisal, was able to attack and take Aqaba by land. The Turks never expected an Arab assault from the desert. This victory was a surprise for the British. Lawrence immediately went on to Cairo to inform General Allenby that everything was ready for the British to enter Palestine and Syria. The Arab and British armies were soon to make their way towards these territories. Meanwhile, Great Britain was finalizing in absolute secrecy the third agreement with the World Zionist Organization, according to which they guaranteed they would grant them their part of the booty of Palestine, in return for the American Jews agreeing to bring the United States of America into the First World War.

The Zionist Christians in the British government, the Prime Minister Lloyd George—or "Lord George"—and Foreign Minister Balfour, as well as the Home Secretary, the Jew Herbert Samuel, put pressure on the British government to make a commitment to the Organization and thus satisfy their plans for Palestine.

Sir Herbert Samuel (with the
white plume) steps onto
Palestinian soil for the first time.

AH 1335
AD 1917

Lenin and the Communist Revolution

Russia intervened in the First World War by attacking Turkish and German borders. In October 1917, Lenin, who had the support of the Jews, was able to overthrow the absolutist power of the Czars and found the Communist state. This led Russia to withdraw from the world war and concentrate on its internal matters.

AH 1335
AD 1917

The Balfour Declaration

In Eastern Arabia, the Arab armies led by Sharif Faisal and the British army led by Allenby occupied Palestine and, on the same day, they both entered Damascus. These conquests heralded the accomplishment of the hopes of the Arabs, who aspired to creating a great Arab state and recovering the Caliphate. However, on 2 November 1917 (AH 1335), Great Britain declared, via its Foreign Minister Balfour, who was a Christian Zionist, its commitment with the World Zionist Organization: Palestine was going to be the homeland of the Jewish people. Strangely enough, the above-mentioned declaration was made public before Great Britain occupied Jerusalem and all the Palestinian territories in December 1917. When General Allenby, who was commander-in-chief of the English forces, reached Jerusalem on 9 September 1917, he made another revealing statement that was even more surprising: "The Crusades have ended now" (in spite of the fact that they had ended some 800 years before).

The Arabs could not conceal their anger towards the politics of Great Britain in the area. The newly appointed King of Syria, Sharif Faisal, began arduous negotiations with the English to withdraw their earlier declarations and to respect the agreements they had signed.

Balfour, the British Foreign Minister.

Lenin.

British NCOs with General Allenby in Palestine.

3. Great Britain deceives the Arabs

The British conspiracy

AH 1336
AD 1918

Great Britain came back with a new trick. This time they told the Arab leaders, in June 1918, that the territories they were occupying (Palestine and southern Iraq) would be governed according to whatever the inhabitants wanted and that the Arab states under Ottoman rule would be independent. This referred to northern Palestine, Jordan, Syria, Lebanon and northern Iraq. This "new lie" echoed positively among the Arabs, who trusted Britain when the latter accepted that King Faisal, Sharif Hussein's son, was to declare the birth of the agreed Arab state in Damascus. This event was merely a formal declaration, as effective power still lay

The Versailles Treaty (1919) – The end of the First World War.

The Zionist delegation
at the Peace Congress
in Versailles (1919).

with the English. In September of that year, Britain convinced France that Palestine should stop being an international area, in keeping with the "Sykes-Picot" agreement, and, in return for withdrawing their support for King Faisal, the leader of the new Arab state, they would not object to France occupying Syria and the Lebanon.

Syria and Lebanon constituted the personal fief of King Faisal and, for this reason, Great Britain preferred to leave France in control of the conflict in that region. However, when King Faisal found out about this conspiracy, on November 1918, Great Britain and France quickly made a new promise, called the "Anglo-French Declaration", by which both powers would guarantee independence to the future Arab state.

The end of the First World War

The First World War ended in 1918, leaving the Arab world and the Ottoman state carved up. The Zionists had acquired greater strength worldwide and were supported most especially by the European nations. The Arabs continued to demand their independence, the revocation of the Balfour declaration, the cessation of Jewish immigration and the liberation of Arab territories from foreign colonialism.

But the colonial powers had planned a new map for the Syrian territories. France occupied Syria and Lebanon, whereas Great Britain occupied Iraq and Palestine and allowed the Jews to create the Hebrew University. It was there that General Lord Allenby gave his famous speech in which he announced that Palestine would be the Jewish homeland.

AH 1337
AD 1919

The First Arab Palestinian Congress

When the Arabs discovered the real colonial objectives of Britain and France, they convened the First Arab Palestinian Congress on 27 January 1919, to discuss ways of defending their land. They passed the following resolutions:

• To reject Syria being divided into small states as per the "Sykes-Picot" agreement.

From right to left: Tahasin Qadri, Lawrence of Arabia (a member of the British secret service), Colonel Bizani, King Faisal, Nuri as-Said and Rustum Haydar at the Peace Congress in Paris.

- Palestine was to be part of Greater Syria, as it always had been.
- Syria was to be an independent country and a member of the future state of the United Arab Countries.
- A national Palestinian government was to be formed.

The Palestinian Nationalist Movement decided to fight pacifically against the Zionist project and against Britain, to persuade the latter to revoke the Balfour agreement. However, the Arabs were unable to change anything and the status quo continued under French and British control. The victors of the First World War then decided to hold a peace congress.

The Arabs leave Palestine to its fate

On 6 February 1919, the Peace Congress was celebrated in Paris and was attended by King Faisal Ibn al-Sharif, leader of the Great Arab Revolution. He was persuaded to momentarily forget about Palestine, in exchange for a state in the Arab territories. So the king accepted that Palestine was to remain under international rule. That marked the first Arab capitulation with regard to the land of Palestine.

Politicians and historians attributed Faisal's position to the following reasons:

1. The military and political weakness of the Arabs and the need to find negotiated solutions.
2. The Arabs considered Britain to be a faithful ally, as they had fought together to drive the Turks out of their territories. Until then, nobody had yet found out about the Zionist project in Palestine.

229

Faisal I, the King of Iraq.

Coinciding with the Balfour
Declaration, on 2 November of
each year, the old city of
Jerusalem would hoist black
flags as a sign of mourning.

3. Great Britain emerged from the First World War as the most powerful state in the world and it was unthinkable that the Arabs could confront it, especially when hopes of peace spread throughout the world.

4. The Arabs had been subjected to Ottoman rule for a long time and therefore had no experience in state management. They were not used to politics nor its wiles.

5. Great Britain took advantage of the conflict and the rivalry that existed between the major families in Palestine, and especially between the Husseinins and An-Nashashibiyins, in order to weaken the Palestinians and to continue implementing their strategies in the region.

In these circumstances, King Faisal chose to look for peaceful solutions, as he believed that he would benefit from it. As a result, he sent a letter to the American Zionist leader, Frank Forter, stating: "We Arabs, especially the intellectual ones, contemplate the Zionist rebith optimistically. We will do all we can to help the Jews establish the homeland they deserve". Several commissions were formed to follow-up the Paris agreements. One of them was the King-Crane Commission which went to the region to study the case *in situ*. But this was merely a fact-finding mission. Up to what point were people prepared to accept the establishment of the Jewish state in Palestine? The majority outrigthly rejected the Balfour decla-

ration and any Jewish settlement on Palestinian soil. As the Palestinian people were on the verge of exploding, the commission warned the international community that the situation could get out of hand at any moment if the Jews were not stopped from emigrating to Palestine.

Revolts and resistance movements

1. Amin al-Husayni, a budding leader

The Uprising of the Moses Festivity

The Jewish settlers boasted publicly that Palestine would be theirs, which aroused patriotic feelings among the Palestinians. Coinciding with the celebration of the Moses festivity, held every year, the Arabs reacted against the settler provocation by organizing a popular revolt, known as "The Uprising of the Moses Festivity" and "the 1920 Revolution", which left five Jewish settlers dead and 211 injured.

The occupying British forces took revenge on the population and cruelly killed 4 Palestinians and caused 24 serious injuries. The leading figure in this uprising was Amin al-Husayni, who later became the undisputed political leader and mufti of Jerusalem. The government in London paid no attention to the report drawn up by the British military governor in Palestine, which blamed the Zionist settlers for the outbreak; instead, they destroyed the report and condemned the "visible heads" of the uprising to 15 years imprisonment.

The socio-political situation in Palestine became further embroiled when, at the San Remo Conference, a resolution was passed ratifying the Balfour Declaration and its implementation, changing the Palestinian statute of military government to that of a civil administration under the direction of the Jewish Zionist Herbert Samuel, former British Home Secretary, who had been appointed British High Commissioner in Palestine. He lost no time in putting the Zionist project into practice.

The first decision Herbert Samuel took, on 20 October 1920, was to legalize the sale of land to Jewish settlers and to authorize the immigration of 16,500 Jews per year. The Zionist project took shape and spirit when the British administration edited a postage stamp with the name of Palestine in Arabic, English and Hebrew.

Amin al-Husayni with the newly appointed King of Iraq, Faisal I, in Haifa.

The then mufti of Jerusalem, Amin al-Husayni, implemented a series of measures to confirm the Arab-Muslim nature of Jerusalem. The most important of all was the renovation of the west wall of the al-Aqsa mosque, which the Muslims call the Al-Buraq Wall and which the Jews call the Wailing Wall. Curiously, the Jewish community protested about this before the British administrator.

The Jaffa Uprising

AH 1339
AD 1921

Faced with the adverse attitude of the British administration, the Palestinian political leaders sent a delegation to London to meet the minister of foreign affairs, Sir Winston Churchill, with the intention of making him revoke and withdraw the Balfour Declaration and its derivations, but the response was a totally negative one.

In view of this and, faced with continuous Zionist provocations, on 1 May 1921, a popular, Islamic-orientated Jaffa uprising broke out and quickly spread to northern Palestine. The result of this uprising was that the insurgents killed 47 Jews and injured 146, whereas the Jewish settlers and British forces killed 48 Muslims and injured 73. The settlers were unable to confront the Palestinians on their own.

British Rule

AH 1340
AD 1922

The intense political activity under the leadership of al-Husayni, and the need to form a representative organ of all Palestinian Arabs, led to the creation of the Supreme Islamic Council, the forerunner of the Palestinian National Movement.

In order to thwart attempts at grouping together and organizing the Palestinian resistance, in June 1922 Britain published the *White Paper*, after approval from the World Zionist Organization. This document consisted of a constitution and certain political guidelines to be followed. It confirmed the continuation of British rule in Palestine as an irrevocable statute, and the Balfour Declaration that led to the establishment of

The city of Jaffa
from the sea.

Palestine a Jewish State as a non-negotiable objective and process.

This *White Paper* was sent to the League of Nations (the predecessor of the United Nations Organization) and, on 22 July 1922, the content and spirit of the document were ratified. Great Britain tried to calm the Arab dissatisfaction by creating the Palestinian Legislative Council, made up of 23 deputies and only 10 seats, for the Arabs that constituted 78% of the whole population, and with no legislative authority to review British rule, the Balfour Declaration, Jewish immigration or any matter of a financial nature. The Zionist settlers obviously received the British proposal with satisfaction, whereas the Arabs rejected it as a whole.

Population trends in Jerusalem up to 1922

In 1922, the Palestinian population amounted to 757,000 inhabitants, of which 78% were Arabs, 11% Jewish settlers, 10% Christians and 1% British. In other words, the absolute majority of the inhabitants were Arab.

Amin al-Husayni.

The Palestinian delegation sent to Churchill – the British Minister of Foreign Affairs: Musa Kazim al-Husayni appears in the photo.

235

2. Izz ad-Din al-Qassam, a new leader

AH 1340
AD 1922

Political action continues

At their 5th Congress, the Muslim Palestinians decided to continue fighting for the independence of Palestine and to achieve unity among the Arab countries. They rejected the creation of a national Jewish State and Zionist immigration to Palestine.

While political action took its course, Izz ad-Din al-Qassam, who was Syrian, encouraged the people to actively resist Zionist immigration and to engage in an armed struggle against the British occupants.

AH 1343
AD 1925

Islamic Jihad Movement

The visit by Mr. Balfour, the Foreign Secretary, to inaugurate the Hebrew University, sent the Palestinians into a rage—they reacted by arranging rallies and a general strike throughout the country. Al-Qassam took advantage of the situation to persuade the people that armed struggle was the only effective method of persuading the occupant, and to urge them to follow the Syrian example against the French occupant.

To turn his aspirations into reality, in 1925 al-Qassam founded the Islamic Jihad Movement, whose motto was: "Jihad, victory or martyrdom".

Members of the
4th Arab-Palestinian
Congress, held on 25.3.1921.

236

Al-Qassam attacks the French in Syria

Al-Qassam, who was born in Banias, Syria, in 1871, was a born fighter. He fought against the English in Syria for three years (1918–20), then against the French when they took over from the English there. He was condemned to death by a French military court, which issued an order for his arrest. He escaped to Palestine and went to live in the town of Yagur, near Haifa, where he devoted himself to education, organizing community prayers as imam and speaker at the Friday service, and issu-

Delegation from the Fourth Arab Palestinian Congress.

ing marriage certificates. His work earned him a reputation and popularity throughout Palestine.

Al-Qassam as symbol of the Jihad

That year, the Muslim Youth Organization of Palestine was founded as a branch of its Egyptian counterpart. Al-Qassam was elected chairman of that organization, as well as of the Islamic Jihad Movement.

Al-Qassam was indeed a symbol of jihad. He rejected peaceful solutions, even though other Arab parties opted for them, as did Amin al-Husayni for example, the mufti of Palestine, who had hopes of solving the conflict. For this reason the 7th Arab-Palestinian Congress was held that same year. It was the last one at which Britain was once again urged to revoke the Zionist project, but the Palestinians were completely ignored.

Members of the
3rd Arab-Palestinian Congress,
held in Haifa on 14.1.1920.

AH 10/03/1348
AD 15/08/1929

The Buraq Uprising

Under the British protectorate, the Zionists dared to attack the Mosque of Al-Aqsa and were able to occupy the west side of the Buraq wall (the Wailing Wall). They declared this was an exclusive part of their holy places. On 15 August 1929, a great revolution called the "Buraq Uprising" was triggered throughout Palestine. In it, one hundred and thirty-three Jews were killed and three hundred and sixty-nine were injured. And, yet again, the British intervened to quash the uprising, leaving a total of a hundred and sixteen Arabs dead, and two hundred and thirty-two injured.

In view of this tension, the Arabs' political leaders went into action to control the situation and calm the spirits of the Palestinians. This, together with the English repression, put an end to the revolt and everything went back to normal. Nevertheless, it should be pointed out that Amin al-Husayni and his followers were the real protagonists of that revolt.

British show of force in Jerusalem.

The vindictiveness of the British

Instead of establishing peace, as had been promised, Great Britain condemned the leaders of the Buraq Uprising to life imprisonment and gave permission for mass Zionist immigration. This had two consequences: Firstly, it increased Palestinian hatred of the British government and of Zionist Jews, and, secondly, it also sparked an increase in the number of young people wanting to sign up with jihad organizations. All hope was lost that Britain would stop supporting both the Zionist project and Jewish immigration.

In spite of all this, political action continued. An Arab delegation led by Musa Kazim al-Husayni (Abdel Kader's father) went to London to resume negotiations. Faced with the threat of revolution and jihad, the British officially agreed to revoke the Balfour Declaration. However, immigration, the establishment of Jewish settlements and the flow of incoming military supplies continued to grow.

Accordingly, the jihad movement attempted to counter the British machinations. Many Muslim leaders joined under the direction (p.240) of the great Lebanese fighter, emir Shakib Arslan, to deal once again with the situation of the Arab world. Shakib Arslan published a book entitled *The present situation of the Islamic world,* considered to be one of the most important works written in the early 20th century. The author analyzed in depth the situation of the Islamic world and future prospects for the region. He reached the conclusion that the Anglo-Zionist plan posed one of the most dangerous conspiracies ever orchestrated against Muslims.

The Lebanese leader sent secret letters inciting organizations to join in the armed struggle. They were aimed not only at saving Palestine but also all colonized Arab countries. Everyone agreed with these revolutionary ideas to initially liberate Syria and Palestine. The rebel leaders were going to be Shakib Arslan and Amin al-Husayni. Several Arab and Muslim leaders from the Arabian Peninsula, Syria, Egypt and Iraq joined the plan. Participants came from as far as India, where Mawlana Shawkat, the leader of the Islamic Movement of India, was a prominent figure.

However, this very important plan failed for several reasons. Firstly, due to the lack of sufficient resources; secondly, due to the presence of colonial forces; thirdly, due to the lack of organized planning.

AH 1349
AD 1930

Musa Kazim
al-Husayni

General Islamic
Congress,
Jerusalem (1931).

Solidarity between
Muslims and Christians in
Palestine because of
Zionist conspiracies.

From left to right:
1. Muhammad Rashid Reda
2. The Indian intellectual and poet, Muhammad Iqbal.
3. The famous Syrian leader, Shukri al-Quwatli.

General Islamic Congress in Jerusalem

AH 1350
AD 1931

On 17 December 1931, an important congress, presided over by the mufti of Jerusalem, Amin al-Husayni, was held in Jerusalem. Delegations from twenty-two Arab and Muslim countries were present and they warned, in a communiqué to the Islamic nations, of the dangers of Zionism and the need to endow the Palestinian cause with an Arab and Islamic dimension. Among the most outstanding delegates were Muhammad Rashid Reda, the Indian intellect and poet Muhammad Iqbal, the Indian leader Mawlana Shawkat Ali, the Tunisian leader Abdel Aziz ath-Thaʿalibi, the former prime minister of Iran, Seyyed Ziaʾeddin Tabatabaee and the Syrian leader, Shukri al-Quwatli.

Immediately after this congress, an international commission was formed to investigate the problems that existed between the Arabs and the Jews. Another commission, called the "Buraq Commission", analyzed the reasons for the Buraq revolt. This commission confirmed that the Wailing Wall is indeed the west wall of the Al-Aqsa Mosque, also known as the Buraq wall, and that it belongs to Muslims. But Great Britain rejected this conclusion and once again declared that they supported the Zionist cause. Tensions boiled over again, but Britain managed to control the situation by its well-known methods of repression. Many leaders were detained and deported to the Seychelles.

Members of the
Independence Party.

AH 1351
AUGUST 1932

Al-Qassam organizes armed resistance

The Palestinians lost all hope in the effectiveness of peaceful means to get their rights reinstated. They then founded the Independence Party, the first Palestinian political party that proclaimed its aversion towards Great Britain. But it did not last long, as its efforts at provoking an armed struggle failed. Nevertheless Amin al-Husayni issued a communiqué stating:

"There is still hope left, but the time has now come to fight for the supreme cause". He thereby declared jihad, although other leaders, such as Musa Kazim al-Husayni, opted for more peaceful measures. The jihad started with underground groups organized by al-Qassam, the Muslim Youth leader. The scout movements also joined him.

Repressing a Palestinian
demonstration in 1933.

Companions of Musa Kazim al-Husayni trying to protect him from the British police. This is what caused his death.

General strike

Britain continued to turn a deaf ear to Arab claims. It supported Jewish immigration and armed Zionist activism. However, rallies in Jerusalem and Jaffa continued unabated and the general strike was unanimously followed throughout Palestine. Britain ended the strike with repression, which left 35 Palestinians dead and 255 injured. In spite of this cruelty, rallies continued throughout Palestine and British repression became increasingly savage. Those taking part in peaceful rallies were battered, including the Palestinian leader, Musa Kazim al-Husayni, who had just turned 80. Kazim died from his wounds in March 1934.

AH 1353
AD 1933

Al-Qassam goes into action

The Zionist clan in the British government started the Judaization of Jerusalem. The Jews and the British reached a strategic agreement to increase the number of Jewish settlements in Jerusalem and to quash any group that tried to prevent the process.

Meanwhile, Amin al-Husayni publicly led the jihad in Palestine. At the same time, al-Qassam founded an underground movement. After his death, it was known as the "Izz ad-Din al-Qassam Movement" and it spread throughout rural Palestine.

AH 1354
AD 1934

The al-Qassam Uprising

Amin al-Husayni combined peaceful methods with those of jihad, although he tended more towards the latter. With collaboration from the Ulama Palestinian Congress of Jerusalem, he presented a report, signed by all the Palestinian parties, asking the British governor of Palestine to stop Jewish immigration, to refrain from allocating Palestinian territories to Zionist settlers, to once again form a parliament reflecting demographic reality and to establish an independent Palestinian government. Al-Qassam, for his part, finalized preparations to declare an uprising staged by 200 active members and 800 sympathizers. On 10 October 1935, and from the Jenin heights near Haifa, he proclaimed the revolution with the idea of first liberating Haifa, where he was planning to site the national Palestinian government.

Preparations for al-Qassam's plan lasted ten years. Several commissions were created, including one responsible for locating volunteers, and another in charge of their underground military training in the mountains.

Funeral of Kazim al-Husayni at the Damascus Gate, Jerusalem.

A third commission dealt with financial matters; a fourth one had the task of gathering information, and the fifth commission handled international affairs, with the aim of achieving recognition of the new state at Arab and international level.

Al-Qassam's project was elaborately thought out. He took the necessary steps to avoid any information leaking out until it was time to declare the revolution. But, in the end, the plan failed when one of his followers attacked a small patrol comprising a British and a Jewish officer and several soldiers, killing the Jewish officer. The British thus became aware of the Palestinian military threat. They moved motorized units towards the mountain regions where the patrol had been attacked, and some mujahideen were forced to engage British forces without receiving any orders. The British attacked the spot where the mujahideen had concentrated by land and air. Al-Qassam and his followers fought heavily, but they were no match for the British forces.

On 20 November 1935, the British asked al-Qassam to surrender but he refused, and uttered a famous expression for which he is renowned: "It is a matter of jihad—victory or martyrdom". He went on fighting for six hours with fifteen of his followers in an unequal battle. In the end, he and some of his companions were killed, while the others were injured and later arrested. Thus, due to the reckless behaviour of one of its members, the revolution was over.

Izz ad-Din al-Qassam.

Abdel Kader al-Husayni

Those events had a great impact throughout Palestine. Everyone did their utmost to take part in the jihad. Amin al-Husayni, for example, founded the Arab Palestinian Party, an underground military faction. Another organization, the Holy Jihad, headed by Abdel Kader Musa Kazim al-Husayni and backed by sheikh Amin al-Husayni, emerged in 1935.

The Zionists, for their part, created an organization called Irgun, led by Jabotinsky. This was a Jewish nationalist military organization that split off from the Hagganah (a Jewish military organization formed and backed by the British). Irgun was more radical and obtained lots of weapons from Belgium which the British themselves discovered at a shed in the port of Haifa.

Abdel Kader al-Husayni.

AH 1355
AD 1936

The Arab High Commission

That year, al-Husayni called a six-month-long general strike which began in Nablus and spread throughout Palestine, the upshot of which was the agglutination of all Palestinian parties under the umbrella of the Arab High Commission. Initially, the Commission called for the creation of a Palestinian government and parliament. Its first communiqué stated its three main objectives:

- First   To bring a halt to Jewish immigration to Palestine.
- Second   To bring a halt to the allotment of Arab land to the settlers.
- Third   To create a national Palestinian government appointed by an elected Palestinian parliament.

Farhan as-Saadi takes over the leadership from al-Qassam

Al-Qassam's followers were reunited under the direction of Farhan as-Sa'adi, a close friend of al-Qassam's. The new leader soon built up the capability to wage guerrilla warfare, which got under way when a band of young men from the Qassam brigades attacked a convoy of Israeli armoured vehicles on the Nablus-Tulkaram road, which was under surveillance by the British. The casualities inflicted were three dead and seven wounded.

Members of the Arab High Commission, founded in 1936.

Palestine
Distribution of the Jewish and Palestinian populations, with the percentage for each of the 16 Palestinian districts, 1946.

Number of inhabitants

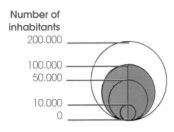

Jewish   Palestinians

This map was drawn up according to the British government's official report entitled "Supplement to a survey of Palestine" (Jerusalem Government printer, June 1947). It was published as an official document by the League of Nations, number 93 (b), in August 1950.
According to British statistics, in 1946 the number of inhabitants in the southern region of the Negev amounted to approximately 100,000.

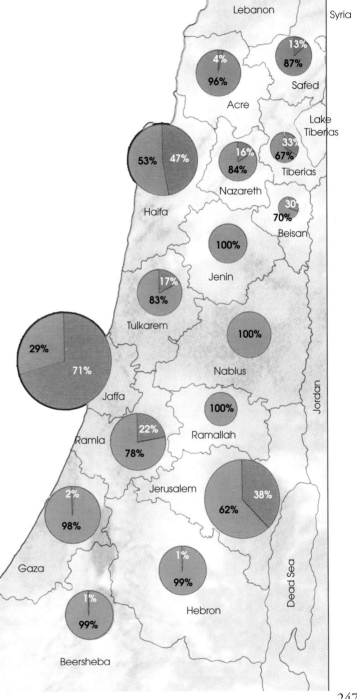

Lebanon
Syria

Acre
4%
96%

Safed
13%
87%

Lake Tiberias

Tiberias
33%
67%

Nazareth
16%
84%

Haifa
53% 47%

Beisan
30
70%

Jenin
100%

Tulkarem
17%
83%

Nablus
100%

Jordan

Jaffa
29%
71%

Ramallah
100%

Ramla
22%
78%

Jerusalem
38%
62%

Gaza
2%
98%

Hebron
1%
99%

Mediterranean Sea

Dead Sea

Beersheba
1%
99%

3. The Qassam brigades make their mark on the uprising

Farhan As-Sa'adi, who headed the Qassam brigades, declared armed resistance. Military operations continued until Britain was able to capture and execute him one day during Ramadan, even though he was aged 80. This sparked a number of marches and strikes throughout the Palestinian territories. On 19 May 1936, the Qassam brigades declared all-out war on the settlers and the British. They intercepted military convoys on bridges and along roads, and cut telephone and telegraph lines. There is said to have been up to 50 operations a day.

The Qassam brigades made their mark on the great 1936 Uprising.

Left:
Fawzi al-Kaukji
(in the centre).

Right:
Members of the
armed Zionist
Hagannah, learning
how to handle
weapons, before the
State of Israel was
established.

Abdel Kader al-Husayni heads military operations

Meanwhile, Abdel Kader al-Husayni was leading other military operations from his headquarters in Bir Zeit. Operations were directed against Jewish and British economic interests and their military barracks. In turn, British forces mounted major attacks on rebel areas. They had support from two Jewish military organizations, Irgun and Hagannah, which blew up Palestinian houses and centres, and killed anyone they came across. Faced with so much cruelty, Arab volunteers arrived from Iraq, Jordan and Syria. Fawzi al-Kaukji, a Lebanese, turned up with 150 armed men from various Arab countries.

In August 1936, some four thousand operations had been carried out by nationalist forces, leading to casualties among their ranks of 3,000 dead and 3,000 taken prisoner, with 400 dead among the British and the Zionist forces. Having been unable to achieve their objective, representatives of the British forces approached the leaders of Arab countries, asking them to intervene in order to defuse the situation. On 10 October 1936, the Arab leaders made a joint appeal to the leaders of the revolution, to Amin al-Husayni, and to the Arab High Commission, which read:

Abdel Kader
al-Husayni with
some commanders
of the revolt.

"We, together with our brothers the Arab kings and emir Abdullah of Jordan, ask you to keep calm and to stop shedding blood. We rely on the goodwill of our friend, Great Britain, and their manifest desire for justice to prevail in Palestine".

The Arab High Commission replied favourably and, two days later, military operations were suspended.
On 11 November 1936, a British royal commission, known as the Peel Commission, arrived in Palestine to investigate the reasons for the great Arab revolt. Its work, in the course of which all Arab and Jewish rulers and military leaders were contacted, lasted eight months and the objective was to establish peace.

The Peel Commission recommends the partition of Palestine

AH 1356
AD 1937

The Arabs expected the Peel Commission to recommend the constitution of a Palestinian parliament and state that would respect the rights of the Jewish community but, paradoxically, on 7 July 1937, the Commission recommended dividing the territory into two states, an independent Jewish state, and another Arab one annexed to Jordan and under its sovereignty.

The Arab High Commission tried in vain to convince Great Britain to revoke the Peel resolution. Faced with a negative response from the British government, on 23 July 1937, it declared its rejection of the division, while reaffirming its intention to continue its efforts to achieve a Palestinian state while fully guaranteeing Jewish religious rights.

In April, at the Arab General Congress held in Bludan (Syria), attended by 450 delegates, the proposal to partition Palestine between Arabs and Israeli settlers was rejected, and a resolution was passed calling for an end to Jewish immigration and the assignment of Arab land to Zionists, and for the British to leave. These resolutions were flatly ignored by Britain.

The Peel Commission

Al-Hajj Amín al-Husayní.

The Qassam brigades take up arms again

Given the futile promises made by Britain, the Qassam Brigades again went into action and declared a jihad. On 26 September 1937, they killed General Andrews, the British governor. On 1 October 1937, Abdel Kader al-Husayni led his brigades along coastal roads to the British army command in Jerusalem. He subsequently proclaimed jihad across the whole of Palestine.

Persecution of Amin al-Husayni

On October 1, 1937, Great Britain decided to dissolve the Arab High Commission and all the Arab political and paramilitary organizations. Palestinian celebrities were deported, while Amin al-Husayni was persecuted everywhere. He escaped to Lebanon and led the uprising against the British from there.

During the truce, Britain seized the opportunity to extend Jewish immigration to Palestine, especially from Europe. It also backed Jewish military organizations, especially the Hagannah and the Irgun. This is how preparations to confront the Palestinian resistance began. The Irgun arranged the murder of many Palestinians, whereas the Hagannah took the initiative in defending Jewish settlements in Palestine. Great Britain entrusted the Zionist British officer, Orde Wingate, with the task of training Jews in military combat, sowing the seeds of the future Israeli army.

On 11 November, British military courts were set up for the purpose of weeding out all opposition. Arab homes were searched and, if any type of weapon was found, the house was ordered to be demolished and the young people who lived there were executed. The Arabs, of course, were unlikely to take such persecution without a fight.

AH 1357
AD 1938

Britain sends more troops to Palestine

In order to counter operations mounted by the Arab resistance, military reinforcements were sent from Britain and Egypt.

The Zionist British officer Orde Wingate organized night squadrons of Hagannah members whose mission it was to murder Palestinians and to mine the markets and Arab neighbourhoods. The Palestinians responded by doing likewise to the Jewish settlements.

The British and Zionist forces in Palestine were surpassed by the efficiency of action of the resistance and, as a result, they called on international Zionist organizations to urge the mass immigration of Zionist soldiers and to ensure an abundant supply of capital and armaments for the Jewish settlers. But, colonial tyranny only further complicated the situation. There were 5,780 armed clashes in 1938, leading to the death of 10,000 British troops and a similar number of Zionist soldiers, with over 12,000 dead among the Palestinian nationals, whose forces were then engrossed by the arrival of 10,000 new volunteers.

The British forces (42,000 soldiers, 20,000 policemen and 18,000 colonial guards), together with 60,000 armed Zionists, decided to comb the Palestinian cities and villages in a punitive exercise. The world's leading power at that time, held up by 50,000 Palestinian citizens, went on to demolish 5,000 Palestinian homes. Britain did the utmost to introduce a Zionist State on foreign land, against the will of its legitimate owners, while the neighbouring Arab states could do nothing about it.

British reinforcements in Palestine.

AH 1358
AD 1939

The British courts put
Palestinians on trial.

The "Palestinian Peace Groups", an English stratagem

In a bid to spread discord and division among the Palestinians, the British authority created a Palestinian organization called the "Peace Groups", whose mission it was to intimidate the Palestinians and warn them of the futility of armed resistance. They were invited to seek a consensus for peace with the British and the Zionists, while, at the same time, doubt

was cast over the strategy and aspirations of Amin al-Husayni and the groups led by Abdel Kader, al-Husayni and the Qassam brigades. However, the Palestinian people were aware of the British ploy to attempt to wean them away from the armed struggle.

Britain adopts a new ploy

At the beginning of 1939, the uprising entered its fourth year and Britain realized it was losing control of the situation. It decided to change tactics—in February 1939, the decision was announced to implement measures in favour of the just Palestinian claims. The plan to partition the Palestinian territory between Arabs and Jewish settlers was withdrawn, and Arabs who had been exiled as prisoners to the Seychelles were released, on condition that they did not return to their homeland. They also convened round table discussions in London attended by delegations representing Arab countries, Palestinian Arabs and Jewish settlers.

Despite the failure of the talks in London, military action died down, especially when, in May 1939, Britain stated its decision to abandon the Balfour Declaration and withdraw the project to create a Jewish state in Palestine.

The British government noticed how Arabs had reacted favourably to the new policies and how this had calmed the insurgents. To gain the confidence of the Palestinians, they published their intention to eventually create an indivisible Palestinian State administered by Palestinians and to reduce the number of Jewish emigrants to 75,000 over the following five years, after which immigration would be forbidden without permission from the Arab authorities of Palestine.

The British pacification policies went very much beyond their verbal promises when they also announced the prohibition, for a period of 5 years, on selling property to Zionist settlers.

Zionist scepticism left no room for settlers to gauge the true extent of Britain's new strategy in Palestine. Discontent spread among their ranks, as did the desire to oppose the new British policies. The Arabs, for their part, sought to put Britain's political word to the test when the latter announced that they would immediately release all political prisoners and allow expatriates to return to their homeland, including Amin al-Husayni.

Mass grave in Nazi
concentration camp.

Hitler declares war.

Zionist settlers defy Britain

When, on 17 May 1939, the British colonial secretary, Malcolm MacDonald, presented his project for a Palestinian State, the armed Zionist organizations showed their violent disapproval in a number of assassinations designed to impress the British authorities. The spokesman for the armed Irgun group declared that "the Jewish State will become a reality, not through British efforts but through those of the Jews". In his declaration he urged the Jewish settlers to invade and occupy the whole of Palestine.

To appease Irgun, Britain sent a delegation to Palestine to inform the Jewish settlers that none of their promises to the Arabs would be fulfilled and that the true objective was to put an end to the resistance. Irgun accepted the explanations of the British representative with certain scepticism. Abraham Stern, a Zionist leader known for his rebelliousness and extremism, left Irgun together with his followers and formed an armed gang known as the "Stern Gang". Its leader was soon to declare war on the British in Palestine on the pretext that Jews were fully entitled to choose the time and place when they would proclaim the foundation of the Jewish State, with or without British approval.

4. The Second World War

With the outbreak of World War II, European countries were one by one invaded by Nazi Germany. However, Britain was able to hold out by involving the USA in the war.

The Jewish dilemma, with an incalculable number of people murdered and persecuted by the Nazis, had put the British government in a very awkward position—on the one hand, they needed the support of the Arab countries in the war but, on the hand, they were under pressure from the international Zionist movement to provide safe haven for their Jewish allies who were fleeing from the Germans. To solve this problem, Britain channelled the exiles to other British colonies far from Palestine, but the Zionist movement regarded the British plan as reneging on their promise to create a Jewish state in Palestine. Jewish extremist organizations then conspired to commit the diabolical act of blowing up a ship carrying Jews to a British colony in order to dissuade their coreligionists from heading anywhere other than Palestine.

Amin al-Husayni, under persecution from the British in Lebanon, moved to Iraq, then to Iran and from there to Turkey on his way to Germany, where he met Hitler at the Führer's request. Both Germany and their ally Italy declared their support for the Palestine resistance and the entitlement of the Palestinians to a sovereign state. This was intended to have an annoyance value for the British authority in the Middle East.

The Germans train the Arab Army

AH 1360
AD 1941

Amin al-Husayni encouraged the Arabs living in Europe to enlist in the Arab Army that German officers were going to train. Indeed, hundreds of volunteers were recruited and trained as an assault force against armed Zionist groups and their British allies all over the Islamic East, and especially in Palestine.

USA backs the covetous Zionists in Palestine

AH 1361
AD 1942

The Zionists took advantage of Nazi anti-Semitism to win support from the American people for the Jewish cause in Palestine. To achieve their objective, the Zionists arranged a world congress in Baltimore where it was agreed that, to settle the Jewish problem, there was no other alternative than to create a Jewish State in Palestine.

Left: Nazi persecution of the Jews.

Right: Anti-Semitism in schools.

Adolf Hitler

AH 1363
AD 1944

Anti-semitism

Both the Democrat and Republican Parties gave their full support to the resolution passed in Baltimore. Both parties put pressure on Britain to withdraw the promise made to the Arabs, to continue with the plan to divide Palestine among Jews and Arabs and to refrain from obstructing Jewish immigration to Arab countries.

In view of the imperious need for American support in the war against Germany, Britain had no alternative but to accept what the USA dictated. The British revoked all agreements with the Arabs concerning Palestine and allowed the free passage of 90,000 Jewish immigrants into the country over a 2–3 year period.

Hitler arms the Arab army

Faced with this massive number of immigrants, Amin al-Husayni asked Hitler to send weapons. He gave orders to his army stationed in Libya to provide 30,000 weapons to al-Husayn's envoys.

The Zionists plan to drive the British out of Palestine

The Jewish settlers, with an army 60,000 strong, decided to drive the British out because they had become a hindrance. The first step was to assassinate British officials and blow up several British military centres.

On 19 May 1942, the leader of the Jewish terrorist organization Hagannah, David Ben-Gurion, in a gesture that clearly challenged the British authority, dared to declare that the territory of the Jewish state ran from the Nile to the Euphrates, exactly as it was described in the Old Testament. Ben-Gurion called on all young Jews around the world to flock to the newborn state.

The USA and Britain back the Jewish state

Britain realized its role in Palestine had come to an end, particularly on seeing the Jewish capable of creating their own independent state. In May 1944, the British Labour party voted to encourage the Palestinians to abandon their lands, in exchange for large sums of money. This is how the path for Jewish immigration was opened yet again. The two American parties, in their election campaigns, proclaimed that Zionists were entitled to emigrate and establish the state of Israel throughout Palestine. In October 1944, Israel's flag was raised for the first time on Palestinian

Left: David Ben-Gurion, the first Israeli prime minister, 1948.

Right: Harry Truman, the US President in 1945.

soil. In September, the Zionists assassinated Lord Moyne, the British representative, who was on an official visit to Cairo. Britain took this to be a serious warning for them to leave Palestine as soon as possible.

AH 1364
AD 1945

End of the Second World War

Once the Second World War was over and the Germans defeated, the Arab Army that had been trained by Germany was dismantled.

Ben-Gurion, at a meeting with Zionist leaders in the USA, was guaranteed aid to buy modern armaments for the newly formed Israeli army. Harry Truman, the recently elected President of the United States, asked the British prime minister, Lord Attlee, to authorize the immigration of 100,000 more Jews to Palestine. The new weapons and the increasing num-

The end of the Second World War.

259

ber of Jewish immigrants helped Hagannah pressure Britain to abandon the country. Irgun, for its part, perpetrated acts of sabotage against the British, with the same objective as the rest of the Zionists.

Faced with a change in the political-military situation of Palestine, the Arab League protested to the USA and Britain, but the British government replied by withdrawing their White Paper and revoking their decisions regarding the creation of a united Palestinian state, the Balfour Declaration and Jewish immigration to Palestine. However, both governments attempted to whitewash the situation by forming an Anglo-American commission to study the Palestinian case on the ground and propose suitable solutions.

5. Revolution and Conspiracy

AH 1365
AD 1946

The return to the uprising

A general strike was convened throughout the country in February 1946. The Arab League founded the Arab High Commission for Palestine and recognized it as the official representative of the Palestinian people. The Arab countries could not take any more serious measures, as the majority of them did not have national sovereignty.

Al-Husayni reappears in Egypt

With the help of friends, Amin al-Husayni escaped from France, where he was under house arrest, and took refuge in Egypt. Every Palestinian joyously celebrated the return of their leader. Under the auspices of the Arab League, he was appointed president of the Arab High Commission, but the mutual antipathy between him and the Iraqi government, the British chief of staff in Jordan and influential British figures in Egypt, prevented him from exercising his duties.

Palestinian resistance intensifies.

40,000 Yemenite Jews immigrated to Palestine in one year.

Jewish immigration intensifies

The number of Jewish immigrants rose by 61,000 as a result of the new American and British policy in the Anglo-American Commission on Palestine. The Arab League responded timidly to this biased policy with a communiqué exhorting Palestinians to arm in order to defend their national interests, but, on 18 February 1946, Britain denounced the attitude of the Arab League in a letter addressed to the UN, submitting the case to the latter for an appropriate resolution to be taken. The Arab League, in turn, sent a letter to the UN making Britain responsible for the deteriorating situation in Palestine. Britain rejected this claim and asked the UN to include the Palestinian problem in the Security Council's agenda, after an advisory commission had been created to inform the UN of the real Palestinian situation and prospects for a political solution.

Hasan al-Banna, the founder of the Muslim Brotherhood movement.

The Commission recommends the Partition of Palestine

AH 1366
AD 1947

On 3 July 1947, the Advisory Commission recommended ending British Rule in Palestine, the partition of the country into two states—one Jewish and the other Palestinian Arab—and submitting Jerusalem to an international administration. The Arabs rejected the partition of their country, as did the Jews, because of the status intended for Jerusalem. And, in a demonstration of strength, Hagannah committed a series of assassinations and acts of sabotage against the Arabs.

On 6 September 1947, the Council of Arab States decided unanimously to reject the recommendations, to continue supporting the Palestinians with arms and logistics and to authorize the incorporation of Arab volunteers into the Palestinian resistance. Britain and other European countries, led by Czechoslovakia, armed the Jewish settlers. In view of the deteriorating situation, the UN reconsidered its resolution on partition.

On 26 September 1947, Britain announced its decision to pull its troops out of Palestine on 15 May 1948. The Arab High Commission denounced the hasty British measure, but the Jewish Agency, for its part, accepted the partition of Palestine into two states in a communiqué issued on 2 October 1947. The USA and the Soviet Union followed the "example" of the Jewish Agency. Of course, violence would soon break out.

Jewish immigrants arriving at the port of Haifa on the eve of the proclamation of the State of Israel in 1948.

Hasan al-Banna calls for an armed struggle

The leader and founder of the Muslim Brotherhood movement in Egypt, Hasan al-Banna, mobilized Egyptian volunteers to join the ranks of the Palestinian Resistance. A few days later, more than 10,000 volunteers had enlisted, but the Egyptian army blocked their passage to Palestine. To prevent a clash between Egyptians, al-Banna gave orders for some of the volunteers to secretly infiltrate Palestinian territory and for others to head towards the Suez Canal region and attack the British there. The heroic action of the volunteers went down in the annals of Middle East history.

The Partition

On 29 November 1947, under pressure from the USA and the Soviet Union, the United Nations General Assembly passed resolution number 181, with two thirds in favour of the partition of Palestinian territory into two states—one Jewish, with 54% of the surface area, and the other Arab, accounting for 46%. However, the number of Jewish settlers was not taken into account. Indeed, they did not exceed 32% of all inhabitants, as opposed to the 68% of Palestinians. Neither was it taken into account that Arabs owned 93.5% of the surface area of Palestine at that time.

Hagannah appealed to young Zionists throughout the whole world to head for Palestine to occupy military and administrative positions in the future Jewish State.

However, the USA decreed an embargo on the sale of arms to all Arab countries in order to prevent possible supplies reaching the resistance, while the Jewish community in the USA donated 250 million dollars to their coreligionists in Palestine.

In turn, Britain finalized the withdrawal of its troops on the date that had been agreed on with the Jews—15 May 1948.

Rallies by the Arab masses against their respective governments, because of their ineffectiveness in light of the new situation, forced the Arab League to agree to provide the military department of the Arab High Commission with 10,000 guns and 4,000 volunteers.

B-117 fighter-bombers, made in America, with the Israeli emblem, in the 1948 war.

Lord Wingate, head of the Jewish terrorist organization, Hagannah.

Arab defence forces in 1949.

The year of defeat

AH 1367
AD 1948

The vicissitudes of the defeat

The colonial occupation of the Arab world, the Balfour Declaration in 1917, Zionist immigration and the creation of Jewish armed groups (Hagannah, Irgun and Stern), which later joined to form the Israeli army, well-trained and armed by Britain, constituted a decisive factor in crushing the Palestinian revolution of 1939 and the elimination of most of its leaders, particularly Izz ad-Din al-Qasam.

In January 1948, Britain delivered 20 fighter-bombers to the newly created Jewish army at strategic places, before withdrawing their forces. America, in turn, sent armoured vehicles to equip the Jewish army. These events and actions cleared the way for the proclamation of the Israeli State.

1. Abdel Kader Al-Husayni leads the Battle of El-Qastal

On 2 April 1948, the Hagannah attacked the town of al-Qastal (from the English word 'castle') to the west of Jerusalem, one of the most strategic places in Palestine, and all its inhabitants were driven out. This military ac-

tion was the beginning of a plan, whose aim was to occupy as much of the territory as possible before the British army withdrew on 15 May 1948.

Abdel Kader al-Husayni and his 56 volunteers could do nothing to liberate the people. Owing to the unequal balance of forces, he asked the Arab High Commission for help but, as al-Husayni himself relates, he was warned against taking any heroic military action without approval from the Commission's military department. He was advised not to return to al-Qastal, alleging that this might compromise Arab governments with Britain. But he answered the Commission, saying: "I shall go to al-Qastal, attack it and restore the town, even if it costs me my own blood. Your attitude has made me hate life. I would be honoured to find death instead of seeing the Zionists occupy my land and the leaders of the Arab League betraying the Palestinian cause. We are more entitled to the arma-

An explosion at a Jewish market in Jerusalem in February 1948 that left 57 dead and 100 injured.

ments that you keep in your dustbins. History will condemn you for not having attended to Palestine. I would prefer to die in al-Qastal than to see your lack of concern and your complicity".

The Cairo newspaper, al-Masri, stated that Taha al-Hashimi, from the Commission military department, joked about al-Husayni's impetuosity, saying:

"Well, we have weapons and ammunition, but we are not going to hand them over to Mr. Kader for the time being. However, we will study the case after 15 May 1948 (the date of the British withdrawal)". Abdel Kader al-Husayni's reply was categorical: "But Pasha Taha, if you do not act straight away, after 15 May 1948 you are going to need a force ten times the size of what we are now requesting to defeat the Zionists. And, even if you have it, you are not going to win. May God be my witness to the fact that I am telling you the truth.

"Pasha Taha, I make you responsible for the loss of Jerusalem, Jaffa, Haifa, Tiberias and other parts of Palestine". Then he addressed other members of the Commission:

"You are betraying the Palestinian cause. You will be pleased to see us dead or decapitated". Qasim ar-Ramadi, who accompanied him, also addressed the Commission:

"May my blood wash the heads of the General Secretary of the Arab League, Abd ar-Rahman Azzam, Taha al-Hashimi and Ismael Safwat (commanders of the military department of the Arab High Commission), who would be pleased to deliver us to our enemies to be slaughtered like sheep; but we will fight with all our strength and the Commission's weapons will remain in the arsenals and in your dustbins. We shall return to Palestine to fight for victory or the honour of martyrdom".

Meanwhile, al-Husayni was able to assemble 500 Arab volunteers and, on their way to al-Qastal, they passed an Arab military garrison at Ramla and asked for help. The military commanders told him they could do nothing for him before 15 May 1948, according to their orders. However, on 8 April 1948 he and his forces attacked the town of al-Qastal and took it back from the Zionist army, which sustained 150 dead and 80 wounded. Al-Husayni also fell in combat. The following day, Hagannah occupied the town again with huge reinforcements and gave the Arab volunteers there no options whatsoever.

2. The massacre at Deir Yassin

AH 1367
AD 1948

The Jewish terrorist group, Hagannah, under the leadership of Menahem Begin (the Israeli prime minister in the late nineteen seventies), together with female members of the Stern Gang, committed one of the most shameful massacres in history at the village of Deir Yassin, near al-Qastal. Eye-witnesses declared: "The people from Hagannah took the village when its inhabitants were celebrating a wedding. The first thing they did was to put the bridal couple and 33 guests with their faces to the wall and machine-gun them down in cold blood".

Zidan, aged 12, the sole survivor in a family, reported: "The Jews forced us to stand up, with our faces to the wall and they machine-gunned us all. Everyone dropped down dead, except us children, because we hid under the adult corpses. But, I got shot in my side. They kept on firing. Minutes later, a bullet made the head of my four-year-old sister explode. The rest of my relatives—my parents, grandparents, uncles, aunts and cousins—have all lost their lives".

Halima 'Id, 30 at the time, said: "I saw a Jew shooting my brother's wife, who was giving birth, in the neck. He then slit open her abdomen with a dagger and, when Aisha Ridwan tried to take the baby out, he killed it too. Hanan Khalil, who was 16 at the time, commented: "I saw a Zionist slitting the body of my neighbour, Jamila Habash, from head to foot, with a knife he was carrying. Then he killed our neighbour Fathi the same way". The head of the Red Cross delegation, Jacques de Reynier, saw the terrorists at Deir Yassin after the massacre, and said: "I saw young people and teenagers of both sexes armed with sub-machine guns and grenades. Their hands were still stained with blood. I saw a young Jewish woman who had the look of a true criminal. She showed me her hands, which were dripping with blood, and shook them as if they were two medals".

"I went into a house in the town and found it to be completed ruined. The bodies were cold; furniture was piled up and there were pieces of hand grenades and cartridge cases everywhere. I could see the massacre was committed using sub-machine guns, grenades and knives or bayonets. When I was about to leave, I heard someone groaning, it was a 10-year-old girl whose body had been shattered by the effected of a grenade. When I was about to lift her, an Israeli officer stopped me but I paid him

no attention and carried on with my task. Out of the whole village, which had a population of 400, I could only find two women alive; one of them was elderly and had taken refuge under a heap of firewood".

The "hero" of the massacre was Menahem Begin, who became prime minister of Israel. He said: "The operation at Deir Yassin gave spectacular results. The Arabs were struck by panic; they fled before us, as soon as they heard we were coming. Out of the 800,000 Arabs living in Israel, only 165,000 were left, and all that was thanks to the operation at Deir Yassin. Truly that operation was one of the most decisive factors in our victory".

The murder of 250 innocent civilians did not move the conscience of even one government in the whole world to condemn the massacre.

Jewish settlers
in Safed.

3. Preparations for the Proclamation of the State of Israel

AH 1367
AD 1948

Menahem Begin, the Israeli prime minister.

The Zionists proclaim the state of Israel

On 16 May, one day after the proposed withdrawal of Great Britain, the Jewish National Council announced its decision to create an independent Jewish state in Palestine. However, the fighting and uprisings continued. The Israelis continued to receive arms from Europe and especially from the United States of America.

British backing

On 18 April, Britain started to pull out of several Palestinian villages, thus opening the doors to the Israelis. On 22 April, Zionist forces occupied Haifa and drove the Palestinian inhabitants out. On 30 April, members of the Jewish terrorist organization, Hagannah, took over west Jerusalem and drove the Muslim Arabs out of their homes.

Jewish mercenaries training with mortars.

Arabs decide to reject the Jewish state

The events in Palestine gave rise to huge rallies in the Arab and Islamic world. Under popular pressure, on 1 May, Syria, Lebanon, Iraq and the political committee of the Arab League decided to send troops to take over from the British occupation forces, but not before 15 May, the last official day of British rule in Palestine, out of respect for the international resolution.

France gives support to the Zionists

Meanwhile, French planes loaded with weapons reached the Hagannah. The Jewish forces continued occupying other regions of Palestine and drove the Arabs out. Up to 200,000 were exiled. Resistance against the occupation still lingered, but its strength waned with the massive immigration of well-armed Zionists.

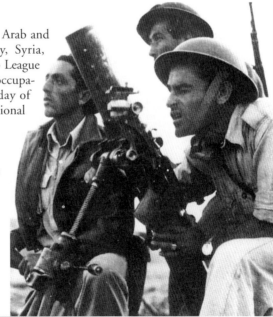

Egyptians take part in the battle

On 10 May, Jewish forces occupied Jaffa, which prompted the Islamic resistance forces from Egypt to attack and defeat Zionist forces for the second time in the Negev. The Arabs saw the Jews fleeing before them, in a region that was of no strategic interest to them and far from Egypt.

Arab countries declare a state of emergency

On 11 May, Hagannah occupied Safed and its surroundings. Consequently, a state of emergency was declared in the Arab countries and there was a general mobilization to liberate Palestine. On 12 May, Egypt announced it would send forces after 15 May. Just before that date, the Jordanian army took the initiative and attacked some Zionist garrisons, but that incursion had scant repercussions in view of the scope of military operations and the steady rate at which Hagannah seized one town after another. Baisan was the most important of them. Preparations were made to occupy the rest of the towns in Palestine, and Jerusalem in particular.

The fall of Jaffa

There was a general revolt in this city and everyone who could hold even a knife took part. However, as there was no real Arab support, Jaffa fell for the second time, with casualty figures of 770 Palestinians dead and several wounded.

Palestinians
forced to leave
their homes.

PART FOUR
Palestine under the Zionist occupation

CHAPTER ONE
The loss of Palestine

The loss of Palestine

1. The Arabs join the war

AH 1367
AD 1948

On 14 May 1948, Jordanian forces attacked several Israeli settlements, which ended up surrendering. Analysts think the Arab army would have been capable of quickly recovering the whole of Palestine if their assault had been swifter and more energetic.

Proclamation of the State of Israel

On 14 May 1948, the British High Commissioner left Jerusalem to return to Britain, leaving the road open for the proclamation of the State of Israel the following day. The Israelis did not wait until 15 May 1948. Just as the High Commissioner was leaving, at four o'clock in the afternoon, Ben Gurion proclaimed the State of Israel in Tel Aviv. Eleven minutes later, President Truman declared recognition of the State of Israel on behalf of the United States. This proved the matter had been prepared long before the announcement.

The state of the Arab armies

On 15 May, after the pullout of the British army, the Arab forces decided to intervene. The Arab League had reached an agreement by which the Syrian, Lebanese and Iraqi forces would head for central Palestine, while the Egyptian army would move on Ascalon, and the Jordanians on Ramallah and Jerusalem.

Prior to dealing with details of these military movements, we should clarify some points:

Ben Gurion proclaiming the birth of the State of Israel in Tel Aviv, 1948.

1. Most of these countries were subject to British colonialism and a British officer commanded one of their armies.
2. A certain number of officers in these armies had directly coordinated the future configuration of Palestine with the British.
3. One of the Arab armies was led by fifty high-ranking officers, forty-five of whom were British.

However, before the war started, the Arab forces entering Palestine issued an official announcement, declaring:

1. The dismantlement of the guerrilla organization headed by Amin al-Husayni.
2. The dissolution of the Salvation Army and the Arab High Commission, which had represented Palestinians in Palestine.
3. The disarmament of all Palestinians, so that combats would be limited exclusively to official forces.

Disarmament of the Palestinians by Arab armies

Instead of directly engaging the Israeli forces, the Arab armies began to disarm the Palestinians. In addition, the combined Arab forces, comprising the Syrian, Jordanian, Lebanese and Iraqi armies, did not exceed 24,000 soldiers, all of which were disorganized and equipped with old weapons that sometimes went off in their own faces.

On the contrary, the Jewish army numbered 70,000 soldiers, who were trained and well armed by some European countries and the United States. Therefore, it was a question of an unequal war in every respect.

We should remember that, up to that time and in spite of the Israeli military operations led by the Hagannah and supported by the British, 82% of the territory still remained in Palestinian hands.

War breaks out

War broke out on 15 May 1948. The State of Israel was proclaimed and British rule came to an end. Wherever the British army moved out of a region, it was delivered directly into Israeli hands. This continued until the withdrawal from Palestinian soil was complete.

Egypt enters Palestinian territory

The Arab armed forces, headed by the Egyptians and Jordanians, entered Palestine with the intention of liberating the country. Meanwhile, Lebanese troops managed to liberate some Palestinian villages on the border with Lebanon.

Emigration of the population from Faluya to Gaza under the auspices of the United Nations, 1948.

The Muslim Brotherhood fights in Palestine

The Arab forces, including the Syrian branch of the Muslim Brotherhood, under the direction of Mustafa As-Saba'i, invaded Palestine. In Iraq, Muhammad Mahmud Aswaf, leader of the local Muslim Brotherhood, encouraged the Iraqis to enlist in the war and founded the Association for the Salvation of Palestine. He managed to assemble 15,000 volunteers to fight in Palestine, while the Arab armies numbered only 24,000 soldiers.

The Iraqi government prohibited Aswaf's volunteers from entering Palestine unless they joined the Army of Salvation, led by Amin al-Husayni. But, while Aswaf was negotiating how to integrate his forces with those of al-Husayni, an order came from the Arab armies dissolving the Army of Salvation, putting paid to the aspirations of the Iraqi volunteers.

The Muslim Brotherhood forces, led by Abd al-Latif abu Qurah, managed to enter Palestine by crossing over the river from Jordan. They set up their camps near Jerusalem. The Egyptian Muslim Brotherhood, headed by Ahmad Abd al-'Aziz, with the consent of the Egyptian government, which had to yield to massive pressure from the people, also entered Palestinian territory. These forces had been trained by an officer, Mahmud Labib.

Palestinians watching the Hagannah military positions, January 1948.

Jewish emigrants from Yemen,
in a Palestinian town square
(1949-1950).

The young volunteers displayed heroism, in contrast with the half-hearted attitude of the Arab armies in all the battles they took part in. Their contribution was really decisive. There were also 250 volunteers from Bosnia. Inside Palestine, the people rebelled and followers of the leader, al-Qassam, organized themselves and enlisted in the "Army of the Supreme Fight".

2. The Arabs stop the war

AH 1367
AD 1948

On 17 May, two days after the proclamation of the State of Israel and the outbreak of war, the city of Acre fell. On 19 May, the Israelis seized Old Jerusalem and moved into the city but, owing to the intervention of Jordanian forces and the Jordanian Muslim Brotherhood, the Israeli forces found themselves besieged.

On 22 May, the Security Council called for a ceasefire. The superpowers exerted pressure on the Arab countries to accept it, which they finally did. The ceasefire was called with 100,000 Israelis besieged inside Jerusalem. Thus, the Army for the Salvation of Palestine, under the auspices of the Arab League, pulled back, but the battle continued to be waged by Islamic soldiers and volunteers.

However, they had won a series of great victories. The Egyptian forces, for example, had occupied Beersheba, Gaza and part of the Negev, while forces from the Egyptian Muslim Brotherhood had taken part in the siege of Jerusalem. Before the cessation of hostilities was declared, the Iraqi army had recovered Jenin, while Jordanian troops controlled Old Jerusalem after surrounding the Israelis in the western sector. They also liberated Jericho, attacked Jerusalem and encamped near Lydda and Ramallah.

After the ceasefire, the British General Glubb Pasha, commander of the Jordanian forces and general commander of the Arab forces in Palestine, said: "If the Arabs had allowed their forces to finish the job and continue fighting on 15 May, they would probably have annihilated the emerging state of Israel".

The first truce, under the ceasefire which the Arab countries had imposed on their troops and the other soldiers, lasted four weeks, while they waited for the results of the negotiations. It was 11 June 1948.

Jewish immigrants
from Europe, 1948.

Israelis take advantage of the negotiation period

On 16 June, the Israelis opened 75 military training camps in Europe. In the space of four weeks, the newly trained soldiers were ready to go to Palestine. On 27 June, all Israeli forces joined together with those that had enlisted in Europe to form the Israeli defence army. They numbered over 70,000 soldiers.

While the Arabs were waiting for the results of the negotiations, the Israelis continued to arm themselves and carry out top-level training. Planes loaded with provisions and new weapons arrived from America and Europe. The negotiations ended with a declaration by Count Bernadot, the United Nations mediator, who proposed a political solution—the division of Palestine. It was rejected by both the Israelis and the Arabs. Negotiations resumed as the Israelis rearmed. The Arab forces were not reinforced, and received no new armaments.

An Israeli combat tank destroyed in the 1948 war.

Fighting resumes

The truce ended on 9 July 1948 and fighting resumed, but the Arabs were surprised by the modern armament of the Israelis, including aeroplanes and heavy artillery. In an overwhelming assault, the Israelis were able to reverse the siege of Jerusalem and save the 100,000 soldiers besieged there. They were so efficient that they even dared launch attacks on Cairo, Damascus and Amman. The Iraqi forces were ordered to retreat from the areas under their authority. Glubb Pasha ordered the Jordanian forces to lift their siege at Ramallah and Lydda. This all took place with only a few skirmishes and the Arab forces ended up retreating.

The second truce

On 15 July, the Security Council decided on a second truce. Rallies were held in the Arab world. Britain mediated between the conflicting parties and agreement was reached. However, on 17 May, Count Bernadot, the United Nations mediator in Jerusalem, was assassinated by the Stern gang, which admitted their responsibility in an official communique.

General Government of all Palestine

The Palestinians refuesd to recognize the State of Israel and, in an attempt to preserve Palestinian government, declared a General Government for all Palestine, led by Amin al-Husayni. But Arab governments not only refused to recognize it; they also forced its president to leave Gaza, under military threat from King Faruq of Egypt, still under the authority of Great Britain.

The fall of the Palestinian cities

The Palestinians carried out several operations against the Israelis, who responded by intensifying their attacks on the Negev with support from European non-Jewish mercenaries. There were many of them and Israel paid each pilot 5,000 pounds a month, which was quite a high salary at that time. The Israelis owned planes but they lacked pilots, so they paid an extra 50 pounds to the pilots for each sortie.

The overwhelming drive by the Israelis led to the successive fall of the Palestinian towns that had previously been recovered. On 22 October, Beersheba fell and, on 5 November, al-Majdal and Ascalon. Besides, out of a total of 585 Palestinian villages, the Jews destroyed 478. They committed 34 massacres of women and children and seized 78% of Palestinian territory, when they were only entitled to 54%, according to the United Nations resolution that had been agreed and ratified by the group of Arab States.

One of the dangerous consequences of that disaster was the exile of 500,000 Palestinians, just when the Security Council had declared a permanent truce, which was accepted by the Arab countries. This is how the greatest calamity occurred and Palestine was sold.

In this unfortunate situation, the fighters (mujahideen) had to return to their respective countries, where they were received and led straight to prison. On 11 February 1949, the main inspiration behind and founder of the Muslim Brotherhood, Hassan al-Banna, was assassinated, and the majority of his Egyptian followers were apprehended.

Palestinians
leaving their
homes.

3. Direct consequences of the 1948 war

AH 1367
AD 1948

The ceasefire and recognition of Israel

On 24 February 1949, Israel and Egypt officially agreed to a ceasefire. Lebanon also adhered to the agreement. However, Syria refused to negotiate an agreement until 23 March, when General Husni az-Za'im, who had taken over state leadership after leading a military coup, officially signed it. Jordan followed suit on 4 April and indeed most countries in the world officially recognized the State of Israel, which became a member of United Nations. Thus, the State of Israel was established in Palestine on the back of Arab weakness, and it was rebuilt over the rubble of Palestinian villages.

Israeli soldiers
in the 1948
war.

Moshe Dayan,
the former
Israeli defence
minister.

280

Destruction of Arab cities

Moshe Dayan, who was to become Israeli defence minister, actually said: "There is not one single Israeli village in this land that has not been built on top of the siting of an Arab village, nor before having evicted the people so that a new Israeli settlement could be erected ".

AH 1368
AD 1949

The deportation of Palestinians

The Palestinian people were dispersed inside and out of Palestine. Those who remained there clashed with sophisticated armament and the violence of the Israeli army. Organizations, parties, formations and armed brigades sprang up abroad, in the diaspora, to such an extent that every Palestinian was said to have joined at least two organizations.

Under Israeli pressure, a huge wave of Palestinians emigrated to Jordan and the Gulf states. Al-Husayni's followers progressively moved away from him because of a series of defeats they had suffered. However, al-Husayni, in spite of his patriotic loyalty and perseverance, could do nothing when faced with Arab faint-heartedness.

The Palestinian people change their strategy

As a result of the national disaster, the Palestinian people realized that they had to rely on their own resources, so they concentrated on teaching and education, learning trades and professions. From a statistical point of view, Palestinians are the most educated Arab people today—they are better educated and trained than Arabs elsewhere. The evicted Palestinians realized the value of good education for their children since no state was prepared to take care of or defend them, or become responsible for their cause.

Abdullah Ibn al-Hussein,
the first King of Jordan.

King Abdullah of Jordan

On 12 October 1949, on the initiative of Jordan, a congress was held in Jericho. The congress was attended by pro-Jordanian Palestinian personalities who recognized Abdullah ibn al-Hussein as King of Jordan.

A Syrian tank destroyed
in the 1948 war.

281

The immigration of Yemeni Jews to Israel was financed by international Jewish capital.

AH 1369
AD 1950

The decision to compensate the Palestinians

On 11 December 1949, the United Nations issued resolution number 194 which guaranteed the refugees the right of return to Palestine, but, under the umbrella of Jewish sovereignty. The resolution included economic compensation for those who did not wish to return, in exchange for expressly stating so. Evidently, Palestinians responded to such an offer by rejecting it, as it meant they would be selling their land, their homeland and their identity.

Integration of the West Bank (Transjordan) into the Kingdom of Jordan

On 4 April 1950, the West Bank (the west bank of the river Jordan, accounting for 22% of Palestine) was officially incorporated into the Kingdom of Jordan. At the same time, Egypt announced that it would retain administrative authority over Gaza, where the local population was concentrated in just 1.5% of the whole Palestinian territory.

Western commitment to the Israelis, to the detriment of the rights of the Palestinian people

On 25 May 1950, The United States, Britain and France jointly announced their commitment to protect Israel. They also declared that anyone who violated the truce would be sanctioned, and voiced their opposition to any attempt to supply arms to the Israelis, Palestinians or Arabs, thereby suspending arms supplies to the Arab world, while they continued to reach Israel. On 5 July 1950, Israel announced it would welcome Jews from anywhere in the world who wished to emigrate to Palestine, and allow them to obtain Israeli nationality.

Male and female Jewish settlers in the Negev desert, southern Palestine, 1948.

4. The Islamists remobilize

AH 1369
AD 1950

Chaim Weizmann, first
President of Israel.

The Suez war

The activity of the Islamists defending Egypt's national interests increased at the end of the forties, with intensified operations against the British presence in the Suez Canal. As for Palestine, the Islamic officer Abd al-Mun'im Abd ar-Ru'uf went to Gaza, then under Egyptian administration, to train a large number of Palestinians and prepare them for a new battle against the Israelis. That war lasted four years, up until the fall of the monarchy in Egypt in 1952 and the takeover by Gamal Abdel Nasser.

The July Revolution

That year, the Egyptian officer Gamal Abdel Nasser headed a coup staged by the "Free Officers" which ended in the abolition of the monarchy. The Free Officers took over power under the command of General Muhammad Naguib, who was close to the Muslim Brotherhood. The latter had pledged their support for the revolution and had backed it with all their resources. Like the majority of the leaders of the revolution, Nasser was very close to them. Later on, Nasser managed to depose Mohammad Naguib and take over the seat of power, without tarnishing the solid relationship he had with the Islamist Egyptians.

AH 1371
AD 1952

Ben Gurion and Abba
Eban leaving the
United Nations
headquarters, 1951.

A refugee school set up by the
United Nations, 1953.

Peace proposals

As of the beginning of the second half of the 20th century, the international community did its utmost to bring about lasting peace in the region. Peace proposals multiplied and many countries made contributions to the process. The first peace initiative came from Norway, but the Arab people rejected it as the terms of the agreement did not respect the integrity of Palestinian territory.

AH 1372
AD 1953

The supreme fight (Jihad) against Zionist occupation

That year, the resistance reappeared and fighting resumed. The first act of war came when a bus transporting Israeli military personnel was blown up near Beersheba, resulting in the death of 13 soldiers. Israel realized what was happening and the danger it posed. They reacted with the massacre of Qibya on 14 October 1953 when they blew up 34 houses and killed 67 Palestinians, while many others were exiled.

The proposal by US president Johnson

After that massacre, Johnson presented his proposal for a lasting peace plan in the region, but the Arab people paid no attention to it and continued with their military operations in Palestine.

Yitzhak Ben Zvi, the
second President of Israel.

284

5. Gamal Abdel Nasser

AH 1373
AD 1954

Nasser attacks the Muslim Brotherhood

During the last month of that year, Nasser struck a heavy blow against the Islamist forces in Suez and Egypt—eighteen thousand of them were arrested in just one day. As a result, the operations directed against the British and Israelis in Gaza came to an end, and non-clerical, left-wing tendencies came to the fore.

The Gaza massacre and peace proposals

The various peace projects put forward were rejected by the Muslims and Arab countries, including one presented by Jama. While Israel continued with Palestinian repression and displacement, a new massacre was reported in Gaza on 28 February 1955 which produced 49 Muslim martyrs.
The Dallas peace plan then emerged, followed by the so-called Eden proposal, while the Jama plan was again presented. They were all rejected by the Arab countries and the Palestinian people for not meeting their requirements.

Left:
Gamal Abdel Nasser, former president of Egypt.

Right:
Hasan al-Hudaibi, leader of the Muslim Brotherhood at the time of Nasser.

The 1956 war

Nasser's star shone on 27 July 1956 when he declared the nationalization of the Suez Canal which, up until then, had been run by a British company that was raking in all the revenues. Nasser turned it into a national company that belonged to Egypt. This sparked a crisis between the Egyptian leader and Britain. Subsequently, Israel, France and Britain reached a secret agreement to jointly attack Egypt for various reasons.

1. Israel wanted to put an end to Islamic and Egyptian guerrilla forces in Gaza as they were the nub of active resistance. They also planned to occupy the Sinai and impose their influence on the Suez Canal.
2. Britain wanted to recover the Canal because it was a huge money-spinner and the profits fed British banks.
3. France sought an end to Egyptian backing of the Algerian revolution as it wished to secure its total authority throughout Algerian territory.

The Israelis annex more Arab territories.

These were the interests that led to the design of trilateral hostility against Egypt and which induced France to provide Israel with vast amounts of arms. On 29 October, at Kafr Qasim, Israel committed yet another mas-

sacre, in which 39 Palestinians lost their lives. That same day, in another surprise attack, the Egyptian airports, Gaza and part of the Sinai were taken with overwhelming ease. The weakness of the Egyptian army became evident and its prestige was rock-bottom. The 1956 war allowed Israel to reach the Suez Canal.

The occupation of Gaza, Sinai and the Suez Canal

Three countries completed their strategy when France and Britain requested Israel and Egypt move back to a distance of 10 kms. from the banks of the canal. Egypt refused to do so, whereas Israel withdrew its army at once to the required distance. By using Egypt's denial as a pretext, France and Britain started to shell Port Said and were therefore able to occupy the whole canal and complete the operation by occupying Gaza and Sinai. Arab weakness remained quite clear.

Meanwhile, the United States, after emerging as one of the great powers after the Second World War, took advantage of the impasse and intervened in to favour their interests. Their voice was heard and they gave a severe warning to those in charge of the trilateral British-French-Israeli assault that they should move back to the positions prior to the assault. Far from taking any notice, Israel replied with a savage massacre at Khan Yunes, where 275 Palestinians were slaughtered like sheep.

Battered ships in the Suez Canal.

AH 1376
AD 1957

The withdrawal from Sinai and Gaza

The Israeli occupation triggered Islamic resistance in Gaza, where young people were trained and prepared by Islamic mujahideen. Pressure from the resistance and from international quarters prompted an American call for Israeli, French and British forces to withdraw. They did this on 6 March 1957, after guaranteeing free maritime passage through the Suez Canal and the Gulf of Aqaba. The Sinai and Gaza were returned to Egyptian sovereignty.

Nasser and the Egyptian army took that withdrawal as a victory of Egypt over Israel and the victory was widely celebrated. The firm authority of the Egyptian command was emphasized and Nasser's star began to shine once again. After these events, the Egyptian forces returned to Gaza and again put pressure on the Islamic movement. It finally split into two groups—the first focused on their ideology of patience and education in the faith, whereas the second one could find no alternative other than to take up arms, since it could not rely on support from the Arab states. This group chose to adopt an armed Islamic stance to avoid being imprisoned and oppressed as people who openly professed Islamic resistance.

Egyptians returning
to Al-Arish after the Israeli
withdrawal in 1957

Egyptian prisoners-of-war at Sharm al-Sheikh, 1956.

French forces advance towards Port Fuad (Egypt), 5/11/1956.

Left to right:
Georges Habash,
Hani al-Hassan,
Mahmud Abbas (Abu Mazen),
Khalil al-Wazir (Abu Jihad).

6. Palestinian organizations

Al Fatah

AH 1377
AD 1958

It was then that the Fatah Palestine National Liberation Movement was born in Kuwait. It consisted of Islamist Palestinians close to their newly elected president, Yasser Arafat. Several Islamic leaders joined that movement and its founders included Sulayman Hamad and Khalil al-Wazir ("Abu Jihad"). Four of the five leaders were members of the Muslim Brotherhood.

The Arab Nationalist Movement

AH 1378
AD 1959

That year, the Arab Nationalist Movement headed by Georges Habash was founded at the American University in Beirut. One of the five founders of that movement was the outstanding Kuwaiti doctor Ahmed al-Khatib. The Palestinian Commission appeared in the organization chart of this ideological formation. When the plan for uniting Egypt and Syria failed, the movement adopted a Marxist-Leninist leaning, including the idea of popular action and revolution. Simultaneously, the General Union of Palestinian Students was founded, and several ideological organizations and movements started to spring up here and there.

The increase of underground activities and movements prompted the Arab League to declare the need for a single official entity for Palestinians to cover all organizations, aimed at guaranteeing their control.

Left to right:
Yasser Arafat,
Salah Khalaf (Abu Iyyad),
Levi Eshkol,
Ahmad ash-Shuqayri.

AH 1381
AD 1962

The unification of al-Fatah

Al-Fatah was divided into groups and cells throughout the world, but it was brought under a single command structure presided over by Yasser Arafat. Prominent figures in its directorate were Hani al-Hassan, Salah Khalaf (Abu Iyyad), Khaled Hassan, Khalil al-Wazir (Abu Jihad), Mahmud Abbas (Abu Mazen), Salim az-Za'nun, the founder of the Fatah headquarters in Kuwait, Kamal Adwan and Abu Yusuf an-Nayyar.

Al-Fatah moves further left

AH 1382
AD 1963

On 16 June 1963, owing to grass-roots opposition to his policies, the founder of Israel, Ben Gurion, resigned and was replaced by Levi Eshkol. Meanwhile, al-Fatah became increasingly less religious, especially after its members were asked to choose between joining the Islamic Movement (a group of Islamic associations) or continuing in the Fatah movement. The majority decided to join the Islamic Movement, thus isolating al-Fatah, which became gradually more anti-clerical. In my opinion, al-Fatah's withdrawal was the result of a mistaken strategy adopted by the Islamic Movement because it laid the foundations for trends contrary to Islamic action.

That year, Ahmed Hilmi 'Abd al-Baqi died. He was the representative of the General Government of Palestine before the Arab League. He was replaced by Ahmed ash-Shuqayri as the president of that titular government.

AH 1383
AD 1964

The National Front for the Liberation of Palestine

That year saw the creation of a new Palestinian organization with a Marxist-Leninist ideology under the name of the National Front for the Liberation of Palestine. Its military wing was called "Youth Revenge".

The Palestine Liberation Organization

During the same year, the Arab Summit resolved to set up a single structure that would agglutinate all the different organizations, because so many were being founded that they were becoming unwieldy and difficult to control for the Arab governments. Ahmad ash-Shuqayri was entrusted with the task of uniting them.

On 28 May 1964, with the direct support of President Nasser of Egypt and the assistance of 422 representatives of the Palestinian people, ash-Shuqayri founded the Palestine Liberation Organization (PLO) and announced the following decisions:

1. Approval of the national Palestinian agreement and the election of Ahmad ash-Shuqayri as president of the PLO.
2. Confirmation of the armed option to liberate Palestinian territories.
3. Confirmation of the territorial integrity of Palestine.
4. Creation of an army for the liberation of Palestine.
5. To publicize and promote the Palestinian cause worldwide.

The Palestinian people received the PLO very favourably because of their solid, clear decision to confront the Israelis.

Al-Asifa Organization

On 17 June 1964, from its headquarters—which were still in Kuwait—al-Fatah decided to initiate military action against Israel, although this was done on the understanding that responsibility for the operations was attributed to a ghost organization nicknamed Al-Asifa, thus averting direct retaliation against al-Fatah. On 31 December 1964, al-Fatah began its first military action and simultaneously sent a report in the name of Al-Asifa to the United Nations in which it claimed the start of a military campaign and declared itself to be the military force behind the Palestinian people.

Ahmad ash-Shuqayri

Habib Bourguiba.

Left,
Bourguiba Mosque
and Mausoleum.

Bourguiba's peace proposal

That year, for the first time ever, a project for peace with Israel was put forward by an Arab nation. Until then, the Arabs had never dared present anything like it. It was put forward by the Tunisian President Bourguiba, who pledged his recognition of Israel as an independent state.

King Hussein
receiving Abdel
Hakim Amer,
commander-in-chief
of the joint Arab
forces, 1964.

293

Arab governments imprison Palestinian guerrillas (fedayeen)

At about the same time, there was a violent backlash against al-Fatah and its members among Arab governments, some of which issued search and arrest warrants against members of al-Fatah. The organization reacted by sending a forceful protest report to the Arab Summit. It called for the cessation of the persecution of Palestinian guerrillas, the liberation of prisoners and the lifting of the information blackout to which al-Fatah had been subjected. However, Israel replied with violent, repressive operations and the demolition of Palestinians' houses and residences in the occupied territory.

The spread of al-Fatah operations

AH 1386
AD 1966

On 13 November 1966, Israel attacked several Palestinian towns, leaving 18 Palestinians dead, 54 injured and 125 houses destroyed. Al-Fatah reacted with huge military operations that lasted for two years, in which there were 200 interventions against Israeli forces in Palestine.

Egyptian tanks abandoned at Abu Ayilah, in the Sinai, 1956.

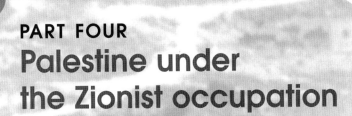

Palestine under the Zionist occupation

CHAPTER TWO

The 1967 disaster and the escalation of Palestinian guerrilla warfare

The Israeli invasion
of Jerusalem.

The 1967 disaster and the escalation of Palestinian guerrilla warfare

AH 1387
AD 1967

1. Prelude to the 1967 war

The Marxist National Front for the Liberation of Palestine formed an alliance with other Palestinian forces that then became the Popular Front for the Liberation of Palestine. Meanwhile, the radio station Sawt Al-Arab (The Voice of the Arabs) lavished such praise on Nasser that it was thought he was to lead Palestine to freedom and drive the Israelis into the sea, making a personal appearance in Tel Aviv and thus returning the sovereignty of Palestine to the Arabs.

Israel threatens the fedayeen

Israel was angered by the continuous infiltration of fedayeen from Syria and Egypt. Thus, on 10 May 1967, the Israeli army chief-of-staff, General Rabin, threatened Syria with occupying Damascus and taking measures against the Syrian regime if such infiltration continued. The Israeli prime minister, Levi Eshkol, made similar statements.

Nasser responds to the Israeli threat

Nasser was by then the top leader in the Arab world. On 22 May 1967, he urged the United Nations to withdraw their forces from Sinai and he announced his intention to blockade the Strait of Tiran, the only access Israel had to the Red Sea. The announcement posed a serious strategic threat to Israel, which then reacted by issuing a series of statements claiming that Nasser's measure was considered a declaration of war.

Nasser's response to the Israeli reaction was firm and full of unequivocal calls for war. On May 22, on leaving his meeting with the president of the United States, Israel's Minister of Foreign Affairs, Abba Eban, declared: "The choking of the Strait of Tiran is a declaration of war, since the condition of our withdrawal from Sinai in 1956 was that the sea straits should remained open. We believe this is a violation of the agreement and therefore it is a declaration of war."

King Hussein of Jordan, President Nasser of Egypt and Yasser Arafat, the PLO leader.

The Arab "Ring States" form a coalition

On May 30, King Hussein of Jordan visited Egypt to sign a mutual defence agreement, and an alliance was proclaimed between the "ring states" (Syria, Egypt and Jordan) against Israel. Nasser asked the United Nations observers and their forces to leave at once, which they did. The Arab countries declared their intention to wage a decisive battle and liberate Palestine once and for all. Their armies assembled on Israel's borders, while countries like Iraq, Kuwait and others sent backup troops to Egypt.

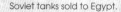

Nasser at a meeting with Soviet President Brezhnev. Soviet socialism was appealing to the Egyptian leader.

The Arab armed forces

All indicators for victory were clearly in favour of the Arab countries—together they had assembled a huge force, both in number and equipment, but especially because they were led by Nasser, who had won the confidence of the masses to liberate Palestine and drive the Israelis out. Egypt alone had a much larger army than Israel. It had 450 planes and 1,200 tanks, as opposed to Israel's 300 planes and 800 tanks. Besides, the Egyptian army had 346,000 soldiers, not to mention the Jordanian, Syrian and Lebanese forces and the support coming from other Arab countries.

Soviet tanks sold to Egypt.

2. The course of the war

AH 1387
AD 1967

On 6 June 1967, a war broke out which Arabs referred to as the "major setback". While the Egyptian radio station, Sawt Al-'Arab, issued bulletins heralding a great victory for the Arab armies and announcing that several hundred Israeli planes had been shot down, a very different situation was emerging from the battle-field. From the first night of war, while Arab soldiers were relaxing, the Israeli air force carried out a surprise attack that destroyed military airports and every Egyptian, Jordanian and Syrian plane that was on the runway. Huge losses were sustained, attended by a seri-ous military collapse. Six days later, the catastrophe be-came obvious and the battle ended in total defeat, al-lowing the Israelis to occupy the West Bank, Gaza, the Golan Heights and the rest of Palestine.

The occupation of Sinai and the Golan

In the space of six days, Israel occupied the 61,000 square kilometres of Sinai, an area larger than the whole of Palestine, and the geostrategic, 1,150 metre-high Golan Heights. In this respect, Israel said: "The Golan is a far greater threat than the Egyptian front. Tel Aviv can be shelled from there, and most of Palestine can be seen as if it were a valley in the open".

The 1967 Six-Day War began with an intense air raid on Egyptian airfields, on 5 June 1967. The picture shows three Egyptian MiG-21s destroyed on the ground.

Israelis occupying the Golan Heights.

Palestinians
humiliated by
Israeli soldiers.

Israelis on the esplanade of the Al-Aqsa Mosque

The Israelis entered the al-Aqsa Mosque and shouted proudly and freely: "It was as easy as cake—Muhammad's religion has gone". And they hummed the words:

"Muhammad died and left behind the girls", mocking the weakness and defeat of the Arabs. And they continued, shouting, "Khaybar, Khaybar", in reference to having taken revenge for the battle of Khaybar.

Sharon with
Ben Gurion.

Israeli soldiers
in occupied
Jerusalem.

The balance of the war

The consequences of that disaster were enormously distressing for the Arab world. Some of them can be summarized as follows:

1. Destruction of the Egyptian, Syrian and Jordanian air forces—393 planes, of a total of 416, were reduced to scrap on the airfields within the first eighty minutes of Israeli air strikes.
2. Destruction of 80% of Egyptian military hardware.
3. A death toll of 10,000 Egyptians, 6,100 Jordanians and 1,000 Syrians, plus thousands of wounded.
4. 330,000 Palestinians in exile and the confiscation by Israel of their lands, which were then divided between the Jewish population.
5. Israel had the opportunity to extend the building of settlements.
6. Nasser's fall from stardom and a radical change in Arab claims—their demands for the liberation of Palestine, occupied in 1948, now became a demand for the liberation of the territories occupied in 1967. The initial call for the liberation of all Palestine had now been forgotten.

These events sparked tension in the streets, and criticism directed at Arab regimes and their armies. To win back credibility among the people, Arab leaders pledged their support for the fedayeen, whose popularity soared after 1967, the date when Al-Aqsa was humiliated and Jerusalem occupied by Israel.

That scandalous defeat was a catastrophe for the Arab-Islamic nation. But, if you look back at Islamic history five centuries earlier, it might become apparent that, despite all, the 1967 disaster marked the dawn of an Islamic and Arab resurgence. After such a catastrophe, perhaps minds and hearts would be awakened to greater awareness, heralding a return to the true spirit of Islam.

The commander-in-chief of the Egyptian forces surrendering to the Israeli army.

The Israeli army advances in the Golan.

Egyptian prisoners-of-war
being transported by
Israeli forces.

The arrogance of Israel

Victory led the Israelis to act arrogantly. Thus, on 26 June 1967, they proclaimed the unification of east and west Jerusalem, which they held to be their eternal, non-negotiable capital. In Damascus, the Palestinian command held an urgent meeting and decided to change over to guerrilla warfare to confront the Israeli challenge. The first measure taken by the Popular Front for the Liberation of Palestine was the hijacking of a plane. Fedayeen operations were stepped up in Palestine. Despite a moderate start, with an average of 12 military operations a month, their efficiency was greater than it had been in the pre-1967-war era.

Israeli soldiers cleaning
their weapons in Sinai,
after the occupation.

Israeli soldiers advancing towards Palestinian cities, 1967.

The Arab Summit of the Noes

In July 1967, the heads of the Arab States held a summit in Khartoum at which the resolutions taken became known as the "Arab noes":

– No reconciliation, no negotiation, no resignation.

These resolutions were later withdrawn. The Security Council met on 2 November 1967 and issued a series of resolutions, one of which was Israel's obligation to move back from some territories that they had occupied. However, it was not specified that they should pull out of all the occupied land. The ambiguity of the resolutions stemmed from the fact that the term "occupied territory" was used without the definite article (the), so that just which territories were referred to was not clear.

The Arabs started a diplomatic struggle with the United Nations, the aim of which was to have the definite article included, so that "territories" would not be left undefined. They also sought express mention of all the territories. That diplomatic war ended up by being called the "Definite Article". Finally, the Security Council called for an end to hostilities and respect for the sovereignty of every state in the region.

3. Dangerous developments

AH 1388
AD 1968

President Tito of Yugoslavia.

Israeli anti-aircraft
missiles, 1967.

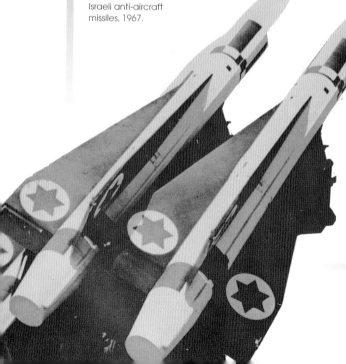

Peace proposals

New peace proposals included one put forward by the Yugoslav leader, Tito. It was flatly rejected by the Israelis—as victors in the war, they declined to negotiate with the Arabs, and were not prepared to forfeit any of their gains.

Israel attacks

On 15 February 1968, Israel attacked 25 villages and Palestinian refugee camps in Jordan using napalm, which is prohibited by international law. That assault cost the lives of 56 Palestinians and wounded 82. Al-Fatah responded by stepping up their operations against the Israelis.

The battle of Karama

Some progress was made when the Jordanian secret service leaked information to al-Fatah about Israel's intention to attack guerrilla cells at the Karama camp, located in Jordanian territory. The Jordanian secret service recommended withdrawing the forces stationed at the camp, but al-Fatah decided to confront the situation. On the day of the Israeli assault, al-Fatah and Jordanian forces pushed back the Israelis, killing an undetermined number of attackers, inflicting heavy material losses and forcing them to raise the siege on the camp.

The garrisons of the sheikhs

News of this action spread quickly and helped to dispel fear of the Israeli army, which was now perceived to be defeatable. Fedayeen activity increased and huge bases were built in Jordan and Lebanon. They were also used by the Islamic Movement, although the latter never joined the ranks of al-Fatah. Their own bases were known as the "garrisons of the sheikhs".

Bold action

While such clashes increased, the Israelis started excavating under the Al-Aqsa Mosque, in search of Solomon's Temple. The Arab governments, which had once arrested and imprisoned members of al-Fatah, officially recognized the movement after 1967. It grew in strength and eventually headed the Palestine Liberation Organization, founded by the Arab League and directed by Yasser Arafat. This was the heyday of fedayeen action against Israel, to the extent that around 199 operations were carried out a month—an average of 8 a day.

Al-Fatah leads the Palestinians

Al-Fatah then led the struggle against Israel, as Nasser's influence had declined markedly after the 1967 disaster. The Organization, which was growing steadily, decided that the only way to create a Palestinian state was through armed struggle. However, after starting out as an Islamic organization, al-Fatah gradually adopted other ideologies.

AH 1389
AD 1969

Members of al-Fatah training in the use of weaponry.

Arson at the Al-Aqsa Mosque

Israel readied the army and police force to confront al-Fatah. Meanwhile, Jewish extremist groups appeared, supported by Zionist Christians. One of them, the Australian Wyns Michael, set fire to the al-Aqsa mosque on 21 August 1969. The fire destroyed important parts of the building, including Nureddin's mimbar, which Saladin had placed in the mosque, a symbol of the Muslim struggle against the crusaders, and the dome and part of the walls and furniture. The Islamic world reacted by expressing its indignation in the form of mass rallies. The Arab heads of state condemned this deed before the United Nations. An Arab-Islamic summit was then held at which the Islamic Congress Organization, taking in all the Islamic countries, was founded. Its task was to endow the Palestine cause with a strategic and Islamic orientation, but lacked the necessary means to enforce its decisions.

The Green Belt Operation

With the intention of restoring some of the Arabs' wounded dignity and in response to the fire at the al-Aqsa mosque, the Islamists, in collaboration with al-Fatah, simultaneously attacked three Israeli garrisons, resulting in an undetermined number of dead and wounded. The Israeli responded with the Deir Yassin operation, and the Islamists, together with Fatah, attacked the Israeli officers club at Deir Yassin, with a death toll of 60 Israeli military personnel and the destruction of several military vehicles and fuel stations.

Hijacking planes

The Popular Front (PFLP) hijacked an Israeli plane en route to Algeria. Israel responded by destroying 13 planes parked at Beirut airport. Operations against Israel were now mounted from Lebanon and Jordan. In contrast, Egypt imposed heavy restrictions on any fedayeen action. Jordan harboured so many Palestinians and their military camps that the latter became a state within a state—Palestinians held their own military parades in Amman, without authorization from the Jordanian government. The situation was similar in the Lebanon, where the Lebanese eventually came out in opposition to the Palestinian presence in their country. Their attempts to control the situation sparked serious clashes with Palestinian forces. Aware of the volatile situation, the Arab countries convened a summit, which resulted in the Cairo Agreement of 1969, signed by

Arafat and the Lebanese president in the presence of Nasser, by which the Lebanese government would allow the Palestinian resistance to continue its activities, but only in southern Lebanon and Beirut.

Southern Lebanon

The Palestine Liberation Organization centred its activity in southern Lebanon, an area dubbed the "land of reconquest". In fact, this region, with many, densely populated Palestinian refugee camps that fed the Palestinian resistance, had been controlled by the PLO ever since the 1967 war.

AH 1390
AD 1970

Nine Palestinian operations per day

1970 was a year of intense guerrilla activity, with a rate of 279 Palestine resistance operations conducted every month—approximately 9 per day. Many bases were set up in Lebanon and Jordan. One of the largest was the "Jerusalem base" in Jordan, run by Abdullah 'Azzam. Objectives in central Israel could be reached from there, as evinced in the operation carried out on 5 June 1970, which resulted in the destruction of two tanks and a minesweeper.

Israel shells Jordan

In September 1970, the Palestinians were accused of an unsuccessful attempt to assassinate King Hussein, Nasser died and the Popular Front hijacked four commercial western aeroplanes, which they diverted to Jordan and blew up. The Israeli rage and desire for revenge ended in intense shelling of Jordan. The objectives were not only Palestinians camps but also airports, bridges and the country's infrastructure.

An opressed people.

Wasfi at-Tal,
the Jordanian
prime minister.

Black September

King Hussein's dissatisfaction with the fedayeen action and the disasters they had brought about on his country prompted him to take drastic action in order to put an end to the Palestinian armed presence on Jordanian soil. A war broke out between the Jordanian army and the fedayeen forces which led to the death of 3,000 Palestinian guerrillas, and all the Palestinian resistance bases were shut down. The upshot of this confrontation was that the Palestinian Liberation Organization was deprived of its most strategic military bases, precluding any further possibility of infiltrating the long Israeli border at its most vulnerable point. Yasser Arafat and his commanders were forced to leave Jordan incognito, with the help of Arab leaders.

The end of Arab nationalism

The Arab world then went through a period of change which saw the demise of the Arab nationalist movement after the death of Gamal Abdel Nasser. The Black September Organization was then founded. Its activities began with the assassination of the Jordanian prime minister, Wasfi at-Tal, during a stay in Cairo, and the kidnapping of the Israeli Olympic team, which was about to take part in the 1972 Munich Games. The kidnapping ended tragically with the death of the kidnapped athletes and their abductors by the Israeli and German secret services that were trying to liberate them.

Israeli soldiers pose with a photo of
the Egyptian leader, Nasser.

Israeli soldiers celebrating their victories near the Wailing Wall.

Sealing the borders

These events produced a shift in the theatre of operations against Israel to the southern Lebanon after the Jordanian, Syrian and Egyptian borders were closed to the Palestinian guerrillas. Lebanon then became the main centre of fedayeen action. There, the PLO also fought against the Lebanese army, which was not strong enough to contain them. Ultimately, the Arab countries bordering Israel did their best to clamp down on fedayeen activity.

Israel's revenge

Israel decided to take punitive action against all Arab countries that harboured the fedayeen and their guerrilla bases. To this end, it shelled factories, bridges and power stations in Lebanese territory. King Hussein attempted to defuse the crisis by a proposed annexation of the West Bank by Jordan.

AH 1391
AD 1971

Levi Eshkol, the Israeli prime minister, during the 1967 war.

309

Jordanian
anti-aircraft battery
in the 1967 war.

The 1973 war and the age of misfortune

AH 1393
AD 1973

1. Prelude to war

The Popular Front continued their hijackings of commercial aeroplanes and their radius of action spread beyond Palestine. They attacked Lydda airport, killing 31 Israelis and wounding 80. Israel responded with a surprise landing on the coast of Beirut in April 1973, carried out by a special operations unit. It infiltrated Beirut and reached al-Fatah's headquarters, where it killed three of the main leaders—Muhammad Yusuf an-Najjar, head of foreign affairs of the PLO, Kamal Nasser and their official spokesman, Kamal 'Udwan.

Meanwhile, Egypt's President Sadat, who had succeeded Nasser, was preparing to recover the Sinai, taking advantage of Israel's concern about major fedayeen operations inside Palestine, which came mainly from Lebanon. The Egyptian president managed to secretly reach an agreement with Syria on a precise strategy to be adopted. Their aim was to carry out a joint and simultaneous assault, with Egypt liberating Sinai and Gaza, in the south, and the Syrian army recovering the Golan in the north. Apparently, neither Lebanon nor Jordan, nor any other country, was informed of this plan.

Syria was concerned about the geostrategic importance of the Golan Heights, the invasion of which involved serious risks, as it was well defended by the Israelis. In effect, the Israelis thought the Golan would not be invaded.

On the Egyptian side, Israel had a very solid defence line called the "Bar-Lev Line" which it considered impossible to traverse. They boasted that such a remote possibility would require cooperation from Russian and American engineers, as well as Egyptian sapper equipment.

Golda Meir, the
Prime Minister of Israel
(1969-1974).

Anwar el-Sadat

Syrian forces
operating in the Golan.

The Bar-Lev Line

The Bar-Lev line was an artificial water obstacle with multiple pipes through which flowed incendiary fuel. When activated, it reduced any material near the shore to ashes. Behind the line was a sand barrier some 20 metres high on the east bank and, behind that, 35 buried fortresses equipped with anti-aircraft and anti-tank defences. The line was surrounded with minefields, tanks and anti-aircraft missile batteries. Israel could thus rest assured that the Egyptians would not be capable of clearing that obstacle.

Oil as a weapon

The anger of the Arab people towards the Israelis continued to mount. King Faisal of Arabia pointed out that oil could be used as a weapon. He sent Egypt financial support amounting to 600 million dollars. An exchange of fire between the Syrian and Israeli aviation ended in 13 Syrian planes falling into the sea. As agreed with Egypt, the arrangement was that Syria should wait until the end of October before entering the war.

Arab soldiers.

AH 1393
AD 1973

2. The War of the 10th day of Ramadan

6 October 1973

Egypt and Syria carried out a combined, surprise attack on the Jewish holy day of Yom Kippur. Most of the Israeli forces were on leave and their chiefs-of-staff confided in the impregnability of the obstacles installed, which they thought neither the Egyptian nor the Syrian armies were capable of crossing.

The fall of the Bar-Lev line

The assault was quick. In less than eighteen hours, the Egyptian army crossed the Line and took control of the Suez Canal. Forty hours later, the Bar-Lev line fell to chants of "God is great". The Egyptians hardly sustained any casualties.

The Egyptian strategy was to seize the Canal and destroy the Bar-Lev line, followed by a second phase in which the objective was to recover the Sinai. The Egyptian army was disconcerted at the ease with which the Bar-Lev line had fallen. It pressed on towards Sinai, egged on by Sadat, to complete its liberation. However, the Egyptian chief-of-staff, General Ash-Shadhli, thought it wiser to scale back the speed of their advance, as originally intended, to avoid becoming vulnerable to the Israeli air superiority. His cautiousness was ignored by the politicians, who insisted they should continue to advance. Israel counterattacked and destroyed 250 tanks from the air.

Sharon with his head
bandaged, 1973.

The Syrian front

The Syrian army, in the course of a surprise attack, was able to penetrate the Golan Heights and recover Mount Hermon.

The USA intervenes in the war

The USA rushed to set up an air shuttle to supply Israel with the most modern war material. The supply line was so intense that there were only a few minutes between the arrival of each aircraft carrying material. It also provided Israel with satellite information on Arab troop movements.

The Defr Suwar breach

With that material and intelligence support, Israel was able to secure a bridgehead over the Canal and cross over to the other shore. I had occasion to watch that scene on television when in the United States. While the Arab radio stations were announcing a complete victory, I could see with my own eyes how the Israeli army was opening a breach on the Sinai front near the Canal. They then destroyed the Egyptian anti-aircraft defences, after which their aircraft were free to ply Egyptian air space unchallenged, thus consolidating the siege of the third Egyptian army in the Sinai.

Israeli forces attack
the Syrian army
during the 1973 war.

Israeli soldiers wounded during the 1973 war.

The siege of Ismailia

The Israeli forces besieged the city of Ismailia, where the Islamic movement led the armed resistance and organized the city's defences, in view of the collapse of the Egyptian army. The first line of resistance was around the mosques and the Israelis refrained from invading the city.

Syria retreats

Faced with the disaster of the Egyptian front, the Syrian forces that had taken over the Golan Heights lost heart and soon abandoned them. Israel took advantage of the situation and recovered the Golan. It also seized eighteen new Syrian villages. Damascus was at the mercy of the Israeli army. However, all sides involved sustained heavy losses.

Demystification of Israeli supremacy

In certain respects, the 1972 war somehow represented a "moral victory" for the Arabs because it dispelled the myth that the Israeli army was invincible, which compensated for everything that had been lost in the 1967 Six-Day War. Actually, if it had not been for the Americans, who provided Israel with precise information about Arab troop movements, the outcome of this war might have been very different.

Oil as a weapon

The Arab oil ministers met in Kuwait on 17 October 1973 and announced their decision to reduce Arab oil production by 20%, followed by a further reduction of 5% every month, until Israel pulled back from the occupied Arab territories. The true merit of that decision was essentially due to King Faisal of Saudi Arabia.

The ministers decided to completely suspend the oil supply to those countries that supported Israel, including the United States, the country that suffered most from the consequences. I was living there at the time and I remember that the price of oil went up by 70%. Americans were forced to tighten their belts. An example of this was the decision taken by car manufactures to produce smaller-sized vehicles to save fuel. In any case, the impact was too heavy for the American economy to bear.

Israeli field gun in the Golan during the 1973 war.

The aftermath of the 1973 War

The war had severe military and political consequences, noteworthy among which were:

1. The Arabs lost more territories and could not recover those occupied in 1967.
2. It was a morale-booster for Arab soldiers after having defeated the Israeli army in the early stages of the war.
3. The myth that Israel was invincible had been dispelled, making the possibility of a new war against Israel viable.
4. Arab oil proved to be an effective and practical weapon against Israel and the countries that supported it.
5. Direct negotiations between Arabs and Israelis opened the doors to a negotiated peace between them, based on "land in exchange for peace", which was conceded in exchange for "the noes of Khartoum".

The prime minister of Israel at that time, Golda Meir, was said to have wept at the news of the defeats inflicted on Israel at the outset of the war. The Israelis were convinced that, without American aid, the outcome would have been very different.

Negotiations between the two sides ended in an agreement by which Israel was to withdraw 30 km east of the Canal, and Egypt to the west, leaving a token force of 7,000 soldiers 7 km. east of the Canal. The UN

The Israeli delegation.

The Egyptian delegation signing the 1973 armistice document.

Battle scene
from the 1973 war.

forces were to separate the two armies in the area stretching some 22 km east of the Canal. Israeli forces would control the rest of Sinai.

The Arabs recognize Arafat

In October 1974, at a meeting of the Arab states held in Rabat, the Palestine Liberation Organization headed by Yasser Arafat was recognized as the sole legitimate representative of the Palestinian people. Activity by all other Palestinian bodies other than the PLO was banned. This decision was a blow to Arab sentiment towards the Palestinian cause, as it meant that the liberation of Palestine was the sole responsibility of the PLO, a fact now endorsed by all the Arab nations.

Yasser Arafat stood out as the official mouthpiece for the Palestinians. His protagonism increased the following month when he was invited to deliver a speech on behalf of the people of Palestine before the UNO, which had admitted the PLO as an observer member. However, the "Magna Carta" of the PLO and al-Fatah continued to clearly state that the only way of liberating Palestine was through military action.

Gestures of Arab flexibility

With those political gains, the Arabs started showing their willingness to accept a peaceful solution. They were even prepared to accept a stage-by-stage plan that included the establishment of a Palestinian state in one part of Palestine. Fedayeen action was notably reduced.

Wrecked Arab tanks.

Civil War in Lebanon

In April 1975, civil war broke out in Lebanon. It lasted well into 1990, that is, 15 years of conflict between the various parties and factions—Druzes, Maronites, Sunnis and Shiites. The Palestinians were also involved in that conflict, which considerably sapped activities geared to the Palestinian cause. A Christian Phalangist–Maronite alliance was formed whose declared aim was to put an end to the Palestinian presence in Lebanon, to which end they would mount assaults on refugee camps and fedayeen bases.

UN Resolutions

Meanwhile, the Palestinian cause was achieving political success at the United Nations in terms of independence, sovereignty, repatriation and the recovery of rights by whatever means, including the use of military force. That same year, the UN General Assembly voted in favour of considering Zionism as a form of racism.

Fedayeen action continues

Al-Fatah continued with its military action. On 5 March 1975, an operation called Safoi was launched in Tel Aviv which ended in the deaths of 50 military personnel and 50 Zionist settlers.

AH 1396
AD 1976

The Palestinian–Lebanese conflict

In Lebanon, fighting became an everyday thing. On 14 January 1976, Lebanese Phalangists invaded a camp and killed a great many Palestinians. They also surrounded other camps, such as Jisr al-Basha and Tel az-Za'tar. The military clash between Maronites and Palestinians ended up spreading to all the political forces in Lebanon.

The Jews in Al-Aqsa

In Jerusalem, an Israeli court granted Jews the right to pray on the esplanade of the al-Aqsa Mosque. This decision sparked street protests and extremely violent clashes between Jews and Muslims in Jerusalem.

The Syrian–Palestinian conflict

With the Syrian intervention in Lebanon, Palestinians were targeted and Syrian forces limited their movements, which caused a tense situation and even skirmishes between them. This, together with the closure of the Arab borders with Israel, destroyed the operating capacity of the Palestinian Resistance.

Israeli repression

The Palestinian situation worsened when 'Land Day' was announced on 30 March 1976. Violent rallies took place in Palestine which were quelled by Israeli forces, leaving a toll of 6 martyrs and 1,500 people injured.

The Syrian president, Hafiz al-Asad.

The fall of Palestinian camps

At the same time, the Lebanese Phalangists, who continued trying to occupy the large Tel az-Za'tar camp, finally achieved their objective with the help of some Arab forces. Hundreds of Palestinians died in the clash. The same thing happened at the Jisr al-Basha camp, and its seizure weakened Palestinian action even further.

Tel Aviv, 1959.

3. Peace and resignation

Sadat in Israel

Sadat, who after the war was known as "the October hero", paid an unexpected visit to Israel on 19 November 1977 in search of a negotiated peace. He was received by the greatest and best-known mass murderer in Palestine, Menahem Begin, and his collaborators. Sadat was invited to deliver a speech in the Israeli Knesset.

Saad Haddad, dissident officer and self-proclaimed head of the South Lebanon army.

The dismemberment of the Arabs

Sadat returned to Egypt without a peace agreement. Nevertheless, the Arab world came under intense pressure because of condemnation of his visit. Israel, on the other hand, was encouraged and satisfied that the Arabs had sought their friendship, but the Arabs only grew more divided.

Israel occupies southern Lebanon

In 1978, al-Fatah carried out a naval landing on the Israeli coast, led by a fedayeen Palestinian named Dalal Maghribi, in conjunction with a group of Palestinian guerrillas. The operation ended with the killing of 37 Israelis, while another 82 were injured. Israel retaliated with an attack in southern Lebanon. They sent in an army of 25,000 soldiers, who destroyed dozens of villages and killed 700 Lebanese and Palestinians. Israel went on to occupy the southern region of Lebanon, handing over 41 Lebanese military posts to international forces and occupying a border strip which they eventually placed under the command of the dissident officer, Saad Haddad, an ardent sympathizer of Israel and head of the South Lebanon Army. Shortly after those events, the Security Council issued resolution number 425 urging Israel to pull back at once from southern Lebanon and to hand the area over to the international peacekeeping forces.

AH 1398
AD 1978

Carter, Sadat and Begin
at the time the peace
accords were signed at
the White House,
1/9/1978.

The Camp David accords

Sadat continued negotiating with Israel under the patronage of the United States. On 1/9/1978 he signed the famous Camp David accord with Menahem Begin, by which peace was restored between Israel and Egypt and the Sinai was returned to Egyptian sovereignty. However, Gaza was not included in the accords, which sparked direct confrontation between the Palestine Liberation Organization and Egypt. The Arab countries expressed their opposition to the Egyptian initiative, which caused a rift in their diplomatic relations. Egypt was even expelled from the Arab League and its headquarters were moved from Cairo to Tunis.

4. The weakening of Al-Fatah

Ahmed Yassin in the political scene

Meanwhile, fedayeen action continued in Palestine, where the elderly Ahmed Yassin, founder of the Islamic Association, became a household name. He also founded the Islamic University in Gaza which ended up by becoming the greatest Islamic stronghold in Palestine.

AH 1400
AD 1980

The birth of the Islamic Jihad Movement

The Islamic Jihad Movement (journalistically known as the Islamic Jihad) was founded by Dr. Fathi Shikaki and Abd al-Aziz Awda, on their return from Egypt. Both were influenced by the ideas of Sayyid Qutb, the ideology of the Khomeini revolution and the ideas of the Egyptian Jihad movement.

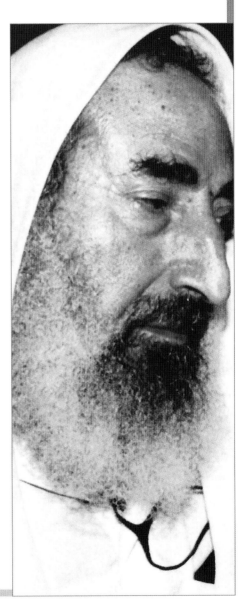

Ahmed Yassin, the founder of the Hamas Islamic Resistance Movement.

The Muslim intellectual, Sayyid Qutb.

The Iran-Iraq war

The Iran-Iraq war had entered its eighth year. It was undermining the strength of both countries, as well as the Gulf states. The latter could no longer continue with their financial support of the PLO, particularly because of oil prices.

AH 1401
AD 1981

Israel attacks southern Lebanon

Israel took advantage of these events to intensify its attacks on Palestinians in both Palestine and Lebanon. The offensive on 8 July 1981 involved an air and sea assault against fedayeen strongholds using aircraft and heavy artillery. King Fahd then presented a peace project which met with scant approval and had to be withdrawn, given the tense atmosphere that prevailed.

Sadam
Hussein.

Khomeini.

AH 1402
AD 1982

Al-Fatah scales back its activity

That year, a group of Jewish fanatics tried to invade the al-Aqsa mosque. Tensions flared when an Israeli soldier named Allan Goodman burst into the mosque enclosure carrying a sub-machine gun and opened fire on the caretaker. He then rushed inside and fired at the congregation that was praying there. This unfortunate event prompted Khalid al-Hassan, the PLO representative, to put forward a peace plan which included an international conference about the Palestinian cause. That was when al-Fatah started to back down from military operations to seek peaceful solutions.

Fedayeen operations

In response to Israeli provocations, the fedayeen in southern Lebanon and the Palestinian and Lebanese

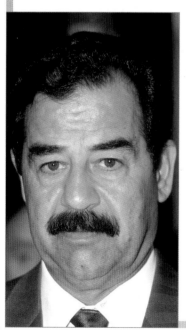

resistance launched missile attacks on Israeli settlements in Galilee, while the Abu Nidal group assassinated the Israeli ambassador to London on 3 June 1982 in the course of a risky operation.

The fedayeen in southern Lebanon eased their pressure on the Lebanese government and instead focused its actions against Israel, in view of which Israel considered the possibility of occupying southern Lebanon.

AH 1401
AD 1981

5. Israel invades the Lebanon

AH 1402
AD 1982

On 2 June 1982, Israel attacked the Lebanon by land, sea and air. Its ground forces advanced on two fronts—one along the coast, and the other across the mountains. The main objective of the invasion was to end the guerrilla warfare and drive the Palestine Liberation Organization and its leader, Yasser Arafat, out of the Lebanon.

The Israeli army in Lebanon.

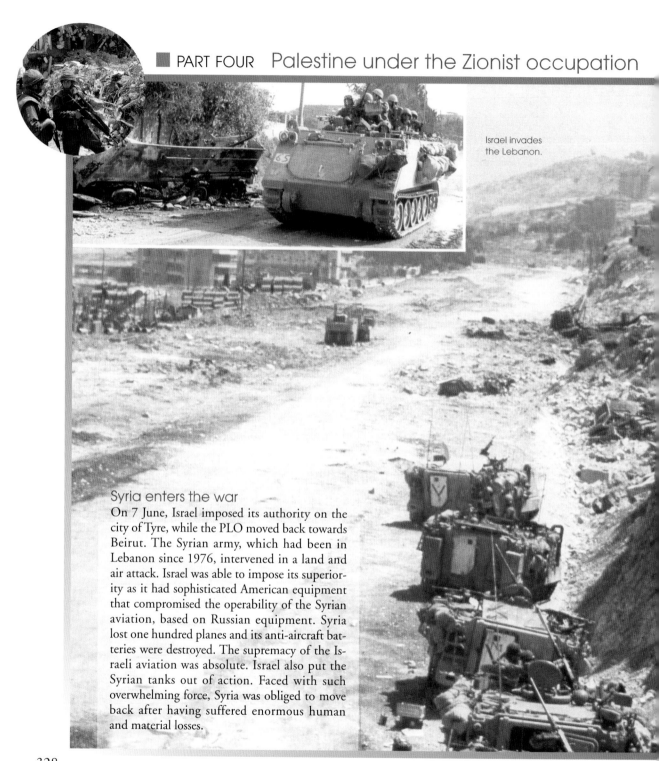

Israel invades
the Lebanon.

Syria enters the war

On 7 June, Israel imposed its authority on the city of Tyre, while the PLO moved back towards Beirut. The Syrian army, which had been in Lebanon since 1976, intervened in a land and air attack. Israel was able to impose its superiority as it had sophisticated American equipment that compromised the operability of the Syrian aviation, based on Russian equipment. Syria lost one hundred planes and its anti-aircraft batteries were destroyed. The supremacy of the Israeli aviation was absolute. Israel also put the Syrian tanks out of action. Faced with such overwhelming force, Syria was obliged to move back after having suffered enormous human and material losses.

328

The siege of Beirut

Southern Lebanon easily fell to the Israelis and, although the resistance continued its guerrilla warfare, Israel's military superiority ended up overwhelming all resistance. Beirut was placed under siege, but the Israeli forces refrained from entering the city because of the risk of repeated surprise attacks from the resistance once they were inside. (Their troops were limited in number and combat training of each soldier cost a hundred thousand dollars). The siege lasted two months, during which the outskirts and residential neighbourhoods were shelled.

Israel bombards Beirut.

Consequences of the siege

The consequences for Beirut of Israeli bombardment:

1. Its infrastructure was destroyed and the PLO withdrew from the Lebanon.
2. The PLO chose a political solution, accepting US conditions for a pullout from the Israeli siege.
3. Israel became embroiled in a military gridlock in southern Lebanon.
4. The PLO, Fatah and the Palestinian people suffered internal rifts and divisions, and factions emerged in support of either the Egyptian or American solution.

Israeli soldiers striking Lebanon with missiles.

The Arabs propose recognizing Israel

At a meeting held in Fez, the Arab countries put forward a plan for a peaceful solution which, for the first time ever, included tacit recognition of Israel's entitlement to the lands it had occupied in 1948, and which asserted that all countries in the region had the right to live in peace. Once the Arab countries had confirmed their intention to make concessions, the PLO endorsed the plan and negotiated the organization's withdrawal from Beirut. With support from the Lebanese Phalangists, Israel continued besieging the Palestinians and Yasser Arafat at his home in Beirut.

The attempt to desecrate Al-Aqsa

While world attention was focused on events in Beirut, a fundamentalist movement called "Kach", and another, the "Temple Mount Faithful" tried to desecrate and destroy al-Aqsa, but the Palestinians and the mosque guards managed to intercept and prevent them from entering the precinct.

Arafat renounces the armed struggle

Under pressure from the critical situation caused by the continuous bombardment, on 25 July, from his home in Beirut, Yasser Arafat declared his acceptance of all UN resolutions on Palestine, and the PLO's willingness to stop fighting and dedicate themselves to political action. Nevertheless, Israel did not agree to everything and demanded that all armed Palestinians should leave Lebanon, which was still being shelled.

The PLO withdraws from Lebanon

On 21 August 1982, the PLO agreed to withdraw from Lebanon, providing the USA guaranteed a peaceful withdrawal under the supervision of international forces. Israel and the US accepted and the first group left Beirut en route to Cyprus. The rest left by boat, bound for different destinations. Finally, Yasser Arafat abandoned Beirut on 30 August and settled in Tunis. Thus, the Palestinian armed presence in the Lebanon more or less came to an end.

A group of Palestinian prisoners in the Lebanon.

6. The massacre at Sabra and Shatila

The plight of the Palestinian camps in Lebanon
The Palestinian refugee camps remained on Lebanese soil, but without military protection. Their situation was untenable in economic and sanitary terms. Each camp provided shelter for between 20 and 30 thousand refugees who were left unprotected once the military organizations moved out.

Siege of the camps of Sabra and Shatila
Israel took advantage of the situation. On 15 September, the Israeli forces, led by Ariel Sharon, surrounded the camps of Sabra and Shatila. An agreement between Sharon and his friend, the leader of the Phalangist party, concluded that Israel would surround the camps but not enter them. The Phalangists then invaded and massacred their inhabitants.

Israeli troops at the camps of Sabra and Shatila.

AH 18/11/1402
AD 16/09/1982

The massacre at Sabra and Shatila

Israel did not dare invade these camps, to avoid its soldiers falling to guerrilla forces. The mission was thus delegated to the Lebanese Phalangists akin to them, and they limited themselves to merely surrounding the camps. On 16 September 1982, the well-known massacre at Sabra and Shatila took place. Eight hundred people, including men, women and children, were murdered in cold blood. Some sources calculated the number of victims to be around 3,500 dead but, what is generally accepted, is that the number was huge. The entire world condemned the massacre, but without lifting a finger.

Israel's support

September 16, 1982 was a Thursday. In the late afternoon, both camps were invaded and the massacre was carried out by the Phalangist Lebanese militia. With Israeli soldiers surrounding the camps, it was impossible for anyone to attempt entry or exit. For 36 hours, women and girls were raped and mutilated and old people and children were subjected to humiliating ordeals. By night, the Israeli soldiers launched flares to help the militia in their mission, in addition to offering them logistics, ranging from food to weapons.

The massacre at the camps of Sabra and Shatila

No compassion

On the morning of Friday 17 September, the first signs of the massacre appeared when a group of women and children fled towards the Gaza hospital at the Shatila camp, where they informed doctors of what had happened. The massacre continued until midday, Saturday 9 September. Ariel Sharon referred to the "cleaning-up operation" with his famous motto: "No compassion!"

How the killing started

Um Ghazi Yunis Madi, one of the survivors of the massacre, comments: "They invaded the camp on 16 September at half past five. Initially, no shots could be heard as they used axes and knives for the slaughter. They buried people alive with excavators. We fled barefoot as they were shooting at us. They killed my husband in the bedroom and my three children. They decapitated one son and they burned another after having amputated his leg, and I found my third son with his belly split open, just as they had done to my brother-in-law." Another woman, Sumayya Qassim Bashir, related:

"They murdered my husband in that massacre. The most horrible sight I've ever seen was when my neighbour, Mrs. Munira 'Amr, was

The massacre at the camps of Sabra and Shatila.

The Israeli army's "cleaning-up exercise" at the camps of Sabra and Shatila.

murdered after seeing them behead her baby in front of her. It was only four months old".

Death and rape squads

The thugs lined the people up on the sports field and execution squads were assigned to them. A great number of women were raped. Many people, especially women and children, waved white flags as a sign of surrender, but 50 women became the first victims of the massacre.

The attack on the hospitals

The criminals were not satisfied with killing refugees in their homes, but attacked the hospitals of Acre and Gaza, where they murdered doctors and patients and forced 40 patients to board lorries—none of them were ever heard of after that.

The destruction of houses

Later on, with Israeli help, excavators were called in to demolish a large number of houses. Then they drove south of Shatila to dig mass graves in broad daylight. The massacre was carried out on the Hebrew New Year.

The Israelis demolishing houses with their inhabitants still inside.

The testimony of an American journalist

Roberto Suro, a special correspondent in Beirut for the American magazine, "Time", related what he had seen personally on entering the camps:

"There was just a heap of ruins and the corpses of men, women and children piled one on top of the other. Some had bullet holes in their heads, others were beheaded; some had their hands tied behind their backs, or to their feet. There were detached heads. We saw the corpse of a woman with her son in her arms. Just one bullet had killed her. The corpses were separated and Israelis bulldozers were removing them. I stopped to watch how a woman shouted in front of a corpse torn into pieces: 'My husband... God... who is going to help me now... they have killed my husband and all my children... What can I do, my God...' "

The correspondent added:

"We saw a three-year-old girl lying like a rag doll on the road. Her white dress was stained with mud and blood. A bullet had hit her in the back of her head and it went through her brain. We saw naked women whose feet and hands were tied behind their backs and we saw a baby hurt in the head that was wallowing in a pool of blood and beside it there was a baby's bottle of milk on a table. Near a bedroom, the limbs of a child had been cut off and carefully placed in a circle with its head in the middle".

Jewish–Christian fanaticism

Commenting on this massacre before the Israeli Knesset, Menahem Begin said: "They were two-legged animals."

One of the leaders of the Maronite brigades told the American correspondent: "We certainly had waited many years to enter the camps in western Beirut. The Israelis chose us because we were better than them when it came to house-to-house operations."

And, when the journalist asked him if there were any prisoners, he answered: "In this type of operation there is no need to take any prisoners."

A full description of this massacre would fill tomes, and this is not the place for it. We have no alternative but to weep freely over the atrocity, which the whole world was well aware of. Today, we focus on those mas-

Menahem Begin.

sacres as a historical lesson in Judeo-Christian extremist hatred, their criminal acts against humanity, and against Arabs in particular.

Lebanon on the road to peace

AH 1403
AD 1983

On 17 May 1983, the Lebanese administration signed a peace agreement with Israel which could not be implemented because it was rejected by the Lebanese resistance and Syria. The territory in southern Lebanon that was not under Israeli and Lebanese control became a safe haven for some young Palestinians and members of the Lebanese resistance.

Resistance in the south

Some young Palestinians and the Lebanese resistance attacked Israeli forces in southern Lebanon. On the other hand, Syria's hatred of the PLO led Syrian forces to northern Lebanon in an attempt to put an end to Arafat's supporters who had taken refuge there.

Israeli unease about the resistance

In the south, Israel tried unsuccessfully to put down the Lebanese resistance because of the guerrilla tactics they used. The latter's assaults on Israeli forces were deadly—Israel sustained heavy losses and was forced to move out of the region.

Israeli tanks in the suburbs of Beirut.

Detention of the elderly Ahmed Yasin

In Palestine, militants of the Islamic Movement were reorganized under the direction of the elderly Ahmed Yassin. Israel finally discovered the new armed organization and arrested this senior citizen, who was sentenced to 12 years' imprisonment, despite the fact he was handicapped and could only move his head and tongue. However, he managed to fill youngsters with enthusiasm and organize their ranks.

The elderly Ahmed Yassin, founder of the Hamas Islamic Resistance Movement.

Birth of the Islamic tendency

While the PLO was being dismantled and divided, and armed struggle was abandoned in favour of peace moves, Islamic action became increasingly popular and attracted many adepts, turning into the main competitor of the PLO and Fatah.

An Israeli spy plane shot down in Lebanon, 1982.

The Amal Movement besieges the Palestinians

In southern Lebanon, events took a different turn when the Amal movement encircled the Palestinian camps. The siege lasted from 1985 to 1988. It resulted in the weakening of the PLO and the strengthening of Amal-related movements, as well as the fulfillment of an effective role by Islamic movements on the Palestinian scene. The Palestinian presence in southern Lebanon was thus limited to the camps, which were already devoid of military organizations.

1145 exchanged for 3!

Meanwhile, a faction of the Popular Front for the Liberation of Palestine (General Command) managed to capture three Israeli soldiers, for whose release they demanded that Israel set Palestinian prisoners free. On 20 May 1985, Israel agreeed to release 1,145 prisoners, including the elderly Ahmed Yassin, in exchange for the three prisoners held by the General Command.

AH 1405
AD 1985

Nabih Berri, the leader of the Lebanese Amal Movement.

The Lebanese resistance.

All these events contributed to the weakening of Palestinian military effectiveness. Although certain operations did continue, in most cases these were dispersed and ineffectual due to the practical disappearance of support from armed organizations working outside of Palestine.

Despair.

The first Intifada

CHAPTER ONE
The first Intifada

The first Intifada

AH 1407
AD 1987

1. Reasons for and objectives of the Intifada

The glider operation

On 25 November 1987, Khalid Akar of the PFLP-GC embarked on a dangerous operation. He flew a glider that was undetectable to Israeli radar and landed near the Israeli Gibyor barracks, where he killed 6 soldiers and wounded 8 before being shot himself. That incident contributed to a boost in Palestinian morale. The fighting spirit against Israel was revived, together with enthusiasm to rekindle the resistance.

Palestinian children resisting the occupation forces.

344

A helpless Palestinian family after the Israelis have destroyed their home.

Reasons for the Intifada

The following reasons stand out, among many others, to explain the outbreak of the first Intifada after several years of inactivity due to Palestinian weakness:

1. A policy of oppression and humiliation on the part of the Israeli authorities after invading southern Lebanon, in addition to that of destroying houses, eviction, detention and expulsion.
2. Israel's decision to merge the economies of the West Bank and Gaza with that of Israel, turning both territories into a market for Israeli products.
3. Economic subjugation of the Palestinian people, making them job-dependent on Israel, so that many Palestinian workers were employed on Jewish settlements, driven by lack of job opportunities, poverty and unemployment.
4. The rise in Zionist extremism, frequent attempts to invade al-Aqsa, continuous efforts to Judaize Jerusalem and the upsurge of attacks on mosques and Islamic monuments.
5. The growth of the Islamic conscience in the Arab world and the arousal of fighting sentiments among Palestinians.
6. The desperation of the Palestinian people over the peace solutions and the growing feeling among Palestinians of the need to take the initiative, without waiting for the Arab states to act on their behalf. The conviction that, for forty years, negotiations, congresses and decisions had proved to be fruitless.

8 December: A spark ignites the Intifada

All the above-mentioned reasons paved the way for the Intifada, but they were not direct causes. What sparked it off was an incident, on 8 December 1987, in which an Israeli truck driver purposely rammed two cars belonging to Palestinian workers. The truck driver crushed their vehicles, killing four occupants.

That seemingly unimportant incident—in comparison to the massacres perpetrated by the Israeli authorities—was unlikely to go down in the history books. Nevertheless, it was the straw that broke the camel's back and stoked the flames of the Intifada, igniting the fervour of ordinary Palestinian people and arousing their will to fight the Israelis.

The objectives of the Intifada

In the early morning of 9 December 1987, after the first prayer of the day (al-Fajr), the Intifada began when major rallies, organized by the Islamic Movement, set out from the Jabaliya camp. Israel forestalled them. Martyrs fell one after the other, but the Intifada was soon to spread. The Islamic Movement had set clear objectives for the Intifada:

1. To raise the people's morale and to strengthen their confidence in God's justice and the power of Islam.
2. To rid people of feelings of resignation, impotence and submission to reality and to insist on the need to fight against a tyrannical, occupying enemy.

Palestinian children training to fight.

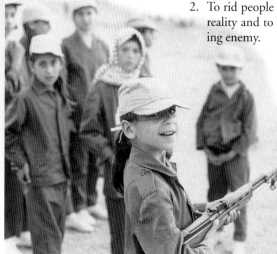

3. To reaffirm the Islamic identity of Palestine and its people, besides boosting their fighting spirit for the supreme cause.
4. To blunt the arrogance of the Israelis and shake them up psychologically.
5. To severely damage the Israeli economy.
6. To reduce the immigration levels and the construction of settlements.
7. To revive the Palestinian cause which was dead on Arab, Islamic and international levels.

Stones, the weapon of the Intifada.

AH 1408
AD 1987

2. Start of the Intifada

Stones as weapons

The Intifada broke out on 9 December 1987 and was based on the use of one weapon against the might of the Israeli forces—stones. The protagonists were children, imbued with strength, enthusiasm and upright conduct. Any one of them was capable of standing firmly in front of a tank and throwing stones at it. The Intifada cancelled out their sense of resignation, fear and humiliation which had become ingrained for over forty years. Resistance and confrontation took on a new meaning. The new generation was growing up in opposition to the previous generation, which had become used to the occupation and had sunk into inertia and resignation.

Hamas mobilizes the Intifada

On 14 December 1987, the Hamas Islamic Resistance Movement that was behind the Intifada revealed their instigation. The hallmark of Hamas consisted of action perpetrated from inside Palestine, without counting on external support from the Arab states or anyone else.

For the first time since Fatah had strayed from its Islamic orientation, Islamism was re-emerging. The composition of the In-

Poster calling
for the
liberation of
the Palestinian
people.

tifada was characterized by its mosaic of all sectors of the Palestinian people—and not only young men—capable of fighting like the fedayeen before them. It included children, women and senior citizens, all acting according to their capabilities, making it an uncontrollable popular movement.

The first communiqué from Hamas

On 15 December 1987, Hamas issued its first communiqué confirming to the Palestinian people that destiny was calling them to liberate the motherland and that it was now time for the Israelis to stop humiliating them and deporting them from their homes.

Israeli repression

The Intifada, which had international echo, dealt a severe blow to Israel, which embarked on violent suppression, shooting unarmed Palestinians, while pictures broadcast by international television networks reached the international public. Condemnation of Israeli violence was widespread. The United States urged Yitzhak Rabin, the then Israeli defence minister, to seek methods other than shooting unarmed Palestinian demonstrators. The new style consisted of breaking bones. Yitzhak Rabin declared that the new style was much more effective than firing shots and detaining people because breaking bones prevented young people from taking part in the rallies. Besides, this way they could not go back to throwing stones. What's more, this was not going to incite public opinion against Israel.

Israeli soldiers
arresting a
young
Palestinian
in Khan Yunis.

Israel continued to confiscate territories, destroy houses and engage in indiscriminate detentions, searches and terrorism. Nonetheless, the resistance continued with what could be termed low-profile methods—that is, stones, petrol bombs and knives. To this arsenal Hamas added the economic weapon which entailed launching an appeal for Palestinians to boycott and abstain from paying taxes, which caused heavy losses to the Israeli economy.

3. The PLO's position

The PLO responds

The PLO had kept silent about the Intifada until 18 January 1988 when it issued a communiqué assuming responsibility for the resistance action and the rallies, although historical evidence proves that these claims were unfounded since the true instigator of the Intifada was the Islamic Movement.

AH 1409
AD 1988

Exchange of prisoners

Members of the Islamic Movement reached an agreement with Israel to exchange prisoners.

The PLO negotiates

On 7 June 1988, the PLO asked Israel to resume negotiations in exchange for stopping the Intifada. Up until then, the figures for Palestinian casualties were as follows:

–   400 dead
–   1,200 injured
–   3,400 people permanently handicapped
–   1,700 cases of abortion
–   23,000 arrested

Dissociating the West Bank from Jordan

Israel, hard hit by the Intifada, demanded as a prerequisite for negotiations that Jordan should renounce the West Bank and return it to the PLO, which had also been pressuring Jordan to that effect, claiming it was the sole legal representative of Palestine and had started negotiating directly with Israel. On 31 July 1988, King Hussein consented to separating the West Bank from Jordan, so that the former was then administratively and legally controlled by the PLO.

A Palestinian child weeps after his family has been killed before his very eyes.

Hamas clarifies its position

Hamas had declared its commitment to liberating Gaza and the West Bank. Its phased objectives can be summarized as not rejecting a temporary truce with Israel but without permanently renouncing any of the Palestinian people's rights.

Proclamation of a fictitious Palestinian state

On 14 November 1988, the Palestinian National Committee directed by Yasser Arafat accepted two United Nations resolutions (242 and 181) that referred to the partition of Palestine. From Tunisia, Yasser Arafat declared the establishment of an independent Palestinian state and recognized Israel's right to set up their own state in one part of Palestine. Recognition of the new Palestinian state spread throughout the world. However, the state in question was fictitious as it was proclaimed from Tunisia at a time when the Palestinian people were oppressed and lacked any real sovereignty in their own land.

The Palestinian and Egyptian presidents.

Arafat recognizes Israel

The Palestinians paid no attention to this proclamation and the Intifada continued to run its course until 9 December 1988, when its first anniversary coincided with a general strike throughout Palestine. On 15 December 1988, Arafat went to the United Nations where he declared his recognition of the state of Israel and acceptance of the United Nations resolutions. He also declared his renunciation of any further acts classified as "terrorist" action.

4. The position of Israel and the PLO

Russian Jewish immigration

Arafat then agreed to direct talks with the USA for the first time. Israel took advantage of Arafat's position by opening its doors to Jewish immigration from the Soviet Union, which had already started to become dismembered. In all, a total of 630,000 immigrants were taken in.

Detention of the elderly Ahmed Yassin

The Intifada was growing in strength and popularity, while Israel resorted to savage repression to contain it. The elderly Ahmed Yassin was again arrested. Zionist movements became exacerbated to the point that a radical group tried to place the first stone for the reconstruction of the Jewish temple near the entrance to al-Aqsa on 17 October 1989.

Arafat refuses Hamas' conditions

In view of the new developments, the Palestine Liberation Organization invited Hamas to take part in the preparatory committee of the Palestinian National Council, which was to become the legislative body of the announced Palestinian state. But, on 7 April 1990, Hamas rejected the offer for several reasons, including:

1. The Legislative Chamber was not made up of elected members but of those directly appointed in advance by Yasser Arafat.
2. The Palestinian agreement did not contemplate an Islamic state but a lay one.
3. Hamas demanded that the PLO withdraw their recognition of Israel and upheld the principle of one Palestine, stretching from the sea in the west to the river in the east, and from the Negev in the south to Cape Nagor in the north, and they considered that only the Palestinian people were entitled to it.

However Arafat refused these conditions, which is how the National Council was held without Hamas.

Huge wave of Russian Jewish immigration to Palestine.

The remains of their
home – a photo
for posterity.

PART FIVE
Intifada and peace

CHAPTER TWO
The peace process

The peace process

1. The occupation of Kuwait prepares the way for peace

Iraq's occupation of Kuwait

On AH 11/01/1411 (AD 02/08/1990), the Arab community was struck with disaster when Iraqi troops occupied Kuwait. Division was latent in grass-roots Islamic movements, between supporters of the position taken by Iraq, with Sadam Hussein at its head, and detractors of the Kuwaiti invasion, not to mention the disgraceful image of the Arab world that such an event conveyed.

PLO support and Hamas rejection

The Palestine Liberation Organization viewed Sadam Hussein's occupation of Kuwait in a favourable light, which caused a rift between it and the Gulf states. They cancelled all aid they had been sending to the PLO, while Palestinians resident in Kuwait and other countries in the region were forcibly displaced by the aftermath of the occupation. Nevertheless, Hamas declared its complete opposition to the occupation of Kuwait and called for the hostilities to be halted as they would irrevocably entail the intervention of foreign forces in the region.

Iraqis watching the announcement of the occupation of Kuwait on television.

The massacre at al-Aqsa

Radical Israeli groups took advantage of Arab involvement in the new conflict, when attention was focused on the issue of liberating Kuwait, to place the cornerstone of the alleged Jewish Temple, only this time it was inside al-Aqsa. The mosque guards tried to avert the action, only to find themselves in the middle of crossfire in which Israeli soldiers used live ammunition to quell the riots, causing another massacre in which 20 Palestinians were killed and 115 injured. It happened in the tenth month of that year.

The liberation of Kuwait and the Palestinian position

AH 1411
AD 1991

On 17 January 1991, the battle to liberate Kuwait began. Sadam Hussein launched Scud missiles against Israel, which made the Palestinians happy, but those missiles were aimed at Saudi Arabia too. This caused anger in the Gulf countries, particularly at Palestinian jubilation just when people in Kuwait were suffering the effects of the invasion, and, above all, when certain Palestinian leaders declared that the occupation of Kuwait was a step in the direction of the liberation of Palestine and that Saudi Arabia would be the following objective. Such declarations were rash and only helped widen the gulf and spread discord among the Arab nations.

Israel's position

Israel was seized with terror when Sadam Hussein threatened to attack the country with chemical weapons. The United States asked Israel not to intervene and thus avoided stirring up popular Arab feeling against the coalition summoned to liberate Kuwait. Israel respected its commitment not to intervene in the war.

American initiative for peace

Three days after the liberation of Kuwait, the American president George Bush took advantage of the allied victory over Iraq to present Congress with a Middle East peace initiative.

Allied soldiers advance towards Kuwait.

Decline of the Intifada

The Intifada continued, though with less intensity, because of Israeli repression, while the PLO used it as a bargaining chip in talks. It was also weakened by a campaign of arrests among its leadership, particularly certain figures in Hamas. The arrests left Hamas without its leadership, but their positions were gradually filled by others, who were in turn arrested and then replaced by another generation of leaders, until the arrests reached the sixth and even seventh level of command of the Intifada. However, the newer leadership lacked the solidity and experience of the earlier command structures, which had the effect of gradually diluting the activities and strength of the movement.

Double life imprisonment for the elderly Ahmed Yassin

On 16 October 1991, an Israeli military court sentenced sheikh Ahmed Yassin to double life imprisonment. Going by the book, life imprisonment normally means thirty years. Israel added 15 more years to the sentence of a man who was already over sixty years old.

Jewish fanatics
burn mosques
and the Koran.

2. The Madrid Peace Summit

The Madrid Congress

On 30 October 1991, a peace congress was held in Madrid at which intense talks were aimed at negotiating an agreement between Palestinians and Israelis. All Arab states sent presidential envoys and their foreign ministers, as did the Gulf states, the European Union, the Maghreb and, of course, Israel. It was the first congress at which Arabs and Israelis sat down together in the presence of the American and Russian presidents and the British prime minister.

Photographs of assassinated schoolchildren.

Hamas's position with regard to the Madrid Summit

Hamas had, in advance, declared its firm position with regard to the peace summit, which can be summarised as:

1. Rejection of any peace agreement that did not address the aspirations of the Palestinian people, and which made the PLO a puppet in the hands of the occupying forces.
2. A military solution with a sound and durable strategy to contend with the occupation and liberate the land.
3. To direct military action against Israel alone.
4. To avoid clashing with the PLO, even when provoked by the latter.
5. To reject any conflict between Palestinians and not allow fighting to overspill Palestine's borders.
6. Non-intervention in the affairs of other countries, whether Arab or foreign, whatever their stance on the Islamic Movement or Israel, and an express ban on hijacking aircraft or similar outside Palestine.

Peaceful negotiations

At the Madrid Summit the PLO and Israel reached an agreement to resume negotiations, but those negotiations proved fruitless, except for an attenuation of Intifada action, because the Palestinian people were exhausted after so much resistance. A ray of hope filtered among the Palestinians at the prospect of a peaceful solution, of assuaging their grief and of lifting the pressure continuously exerted on them by Israel.

AH 1412
AD 1992

3. Al Qassam and Hezbollah

The Oslo negotiations

Running parallel to the negotiations between the PLO and the USA, others were being carried out in the strictest secrecy in Oslo between Arafat and Israel. They lasted for one and a half years and involved 14 official visits to 10 capitals.

Yitzhak Rabin elected prime minister

Yitzhak Rabin became prime minister of Israel after the general elections. During his election campaign he promised to give autonomy to the Palestinians in Gaza and the West Bank. Israel accepted the idea with satisfaction as it entailed weakening the Intifada by isolating it into two separate areas, after which it would be easier to contain.

Deportation of the Hamas leaders

On 17 December, Israel deported over 400 Hamas leaders, together with some leaders of the Islamic Jihad Movement, and confined them in southern Lebanon. They were abandoned there in the desert, on uninhabited land. Dr. Abdel 'Aziz ar-Rantissi was among them. He had been one of the most distinguished leaders of Hamas in Palestine. The news spread and was echoed internationally. World rejection of that incident was expressed. Those exiled set up their camp outdoors and refused to move in any direction other than towards Palestine. From there they started divulging statements on Palestine to the world through the press agencies.

Hezbollah

A new party, the Hezbollah, of Shiite ideology, appeared on the Lebanese scene. It started to conduct major military operations against the Israeli army and the pro-Israeli Lebanese army in southern Lebanon. Both armies suffered heavy losses inflicted on them by Hezbollah.

Al-Qassam and Hezbollah attack Israel

The 'Izz ad-Din al-Qassam Brigades were also carrying out several important operations inside Palestine. For its part, Hezbollah intensified its assaults from southern Lebanon with Katyushka rockets, capable of reaching Israeli villages. Whenever Israel hit Lebanese and Palestinian civilians, Hezbollah responded by striking civilians in Israel.

Accountability

In a massive operation code-named "Accountability", Israel again invaded southern Lebanon and attacked Hezbollah by land, sea and air. Hezbollah responded with extensive suicide operations. In the end Israel pulled back in accordance with a verbal arrangement reached with Hezbollah, by which Israel agreed to refrain from striking Lebanese and Palestinian civilians, in exchange for Hezbollah not firing Katyushka rockets at Israeli towns and villages.

The war between Hezbollah and Israel continues

The verbal agreement did not include Hezbollah scaling back their military activity. On the contrary, in one year alone, they carried out 900 operations, an average of nearly 3 a day. Israel always responded by shelling southern Lebanon and hostilities started all over again. As Hezbollah was well organized militarily, their responses to Israeli incursions were forceful.

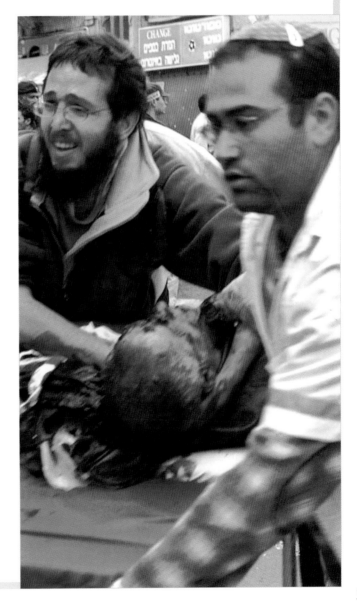

The results of a Palestinian fedayeen operation inside Israel.

1413 AH
1993 AD

4. The Oslo Agreements

The Oslo Process

Israel endured continuous attacks by Hezbollah from southern Lebanon and the Izz ad-Din al-Qassam Brigades in Palestine until, on 13 September, it was announced that the Oslo peace agreement had been signed, thanks to which Israel conceded to the PLO the right to self-determination in Gaza and the West Bank, in exchange for their official acceptance that, in the first stage of the accord, only Gaza and one town in the West Bank—Jericho—would be handed over to them.

The Palestinian organizations that were against the agreement met in Damascus and announced a new Palestinian trend opposed to the PLO. It comprised Hamas, the Islamic Jihad, the Popular Front and the Democratic Front, among others, amounting to nine in all. Every Islamic movement throughout the world declared its rejection of the agreement, while Fatah, the largest Palestinian organization, supported it.

Clinton, Rabin and Arafat at the time the peace agreement was signed at the White House, 13/9/1993.

Reasons for the Oslo Process

But, what were the reasons for the Oslo agreement? They can be summarized as follows:

1. A rift in the Arab bloc due to the support, by only some Arab countries, of the Camp David agreements between Egypt and Israel.
2. The exit of the Palestinian resistance from Lebanon, in 1982, and an end to the threats against Israel from southern Lebanon.
3. The collapse of Arab solidarity and the enormous economic and military losses caused by the first Gulf war in 1990.
4. The reversal in international support for the Intifada after the Gulf war and Palestinian support of the Iraqi side.
5. The collapse of the Soviet Union and its effect on the international balance of power, which was then tipped in favour of the United States, Israel's ally.

Israeli tanks block access
to a school.

361

Why the Islamic Movement was opposed to the Oslo agreements

1. The Movement saw it as a way of suppressing their resistance, as their struggle rejects any form of negotiation or renunciation.
2. The appearance of a fatwa, dictated by many learned religious experts (ulama), forbidding anyone from giving up a single span of Palestinian land. Those who issued the fatwa included Yusuf al-Ghardawi, Muhammad al-Ghazali and Omar al-Ashqar, among many others.
3. The Movement saw that the agreement included the recognition of Israel's right to 78% of Palestinian land.
4. The agreement did not clarify the status of Jerusalem, which remained unresolved, pending negotiations. The situation of the refugees and the Israeli settlements was not clarified either.
5. The agreement did not include the creation of a Palestinian state and consequently it did not guarantee Palestinians safety, and the exercise of their freedom.
6. The agreement deprived the Palestinian Authority of sovereignty in foreign affairs, border security and the right to legislate without approval from Israel, while the latter was entitled to enter the territories of Gaza and the West Bank whenever it pleased.
7. Another prohibition stated in the agreement was the formation of a Palestinian army, and its procurement of armaments, without prior authorization from Israel.
8. The agreement stipulated that Israel had the right to veto any legislation that the Palestinian parliament might pass if it opposed their interests. This was the most unusual clause.
9. The agreement also stipulated that the Palestinian Authority was obliged to refrain from any armed struggle against Israel, which would effectively turn it into an instrument in Israel's hands and lead to sectarian conflict between Palestinians.
10. The agreement did not consider the West Bank and Gaza to be Palestinian territories but Israeli ones where Palestinians would exercise autonomous government.

As the agreement provided for peace solutions between Arab governments and Israel, the Arab people opposed and rejected it, although the majority of Arab regimes approved it overall. This led to the establishment of a token Palestinian authority in Gaza and Jericho. In accordance with the agreement, and by way of prevention, the Palestine Liberation Organization agreed to outlaw any further military operations against Israel.

Israeli rally against the Oslo peace accord.

Young Palestinians hurling stones and petrol bombs at the occupation forces.

5. The end of the first Intifada

AH 1414
AD 1993

Israel assassinates Imad Aqal

Imad Aqal, one of the leading symbols of the Hamas command, was killed in a military operation. The American secret service had located his position, which allowed an Israeli force of 60 armoured tanks to surround it. Far from giving himself up, he fought back from the rooftops of several buildings. In the end, he was shattered by the impact of an anti-tank missile.

A witness who attended the martyr's burial said that his body revealed the impact of 70 bullets and numerous knife wounds.

Israeli relief over his death was short-lived, as Hamas responded two weeks later with a revenge operation, "Imad Aqal", in which colonel Meir Muntis was killed. The Israeli newspaper *Maarev* classified him as "The heart and soul of the fight against terrorism and a symbol of the Israeli army's struggle against the Intifada".

AH 1415
AD 1994

Peace with Syria

On the initiative of the USA, a meeting was held in Geneva on 16 January 1994 between Hafez al-Assad and president Clinton. The Syrian leader agreed to establish limited peace relations with Israel, providing it withdrew from the Golan. Rabin then presented a peace plan proposing a phased withdrawal, to be completed after negotiating a series of agreements, also in stages. However, this condition stalled the peace process with Syria.

363

The massacre at the Ibrahimi Mosque

A Jewish settler named Baruch Goldstein entered the Cave of the Patriarchs, Hebron, during dawn prayers and killed a guard and twenty-nine people kneeling in prayer, while wounding dozens in the congregation. The Kach and Kahane movements claimed responsibility for the massacre. Rabbi Burg issued an edict in which he praised the operation: "What Baruch Goldstein did is worship of God and part of Jewish religious duties."

Immediately afterwards, Hamas responded with 5 huge successive attacks headed by the engineer, Yahya Iyyash. The death of several Palestinian civilians ignited the scenario and Hamas replied by killing Israeli civilians and military personnel. The Islamic Movement later proposed putting an end to the massacres between both sides, but Israel refused and continued its policies of repression and persecution.

Remains of a Palestinian suicide mission against an Israeli bus.

Cessation of the Intifada

Under such pressure, towards the end of that year Hamas had to scale back its armed activity and reorganize, especially after the arrest of six of its commands. The PLO appealed to the Palestinians to stop the Intifada and pledged to restore their rights and safety. By 1997, 79 months after the Intifada had started, 1,392 Palestinians had been martyred, including 362 children, an average of one every day. The great Intifada had come to an end.

Consequences of the first Intifada

In spite of the huge personal and material damage sustained, the Intifada achieved great progress in arousing international awareness, which can be summarized as follows:

1. The international community became convinced of the need for addressing the Palestinian cause and discontinuing the occupation.
2. International sympathy for the Palestinian people and their just cause increased.
3. The Intifada uncovered Israel's false democracy, as it did their repressive methods.
4. The Intifada crystallized Palestinian identity and sowed the seeds for independence.
5. The Palestinian economy was rid of its dependence on Israeli institutions and an alternative Palestinian economy established. The process dealt a serious blow to the Israeli economy.
6. The Intifada revealed the identities of spies and disloyal Palestinians who were collaborating with the Israeli secret service.
7. It created a brave new generation, full of self-esteem, intent on bringing about freedom and independence and ridding the Palestinians of Israeli occupation.

Netanyahu and Arafat at the White House, 1 October 1997.

A Palestinian father burying his martyred daughter, killed by Israeli forces.

PART FIVE
Intifada and peace

CHAPTER THREE
The Palestinian Authority

1. Peace in Palestine and Jordan

2. Assassinations everywhere

3. Everyone against the Palestinian resistance

4. Hamas restructured

The Palestinian Authority

AH 1415
AD 1994

1. Peace in Palestine and Jordan

Arafat arrives in Gaza

On 5 July 1994, Yasser Arafat arrived in Gaza where he was received by crowds of Palestinians. He then took up his post as president of the Palestinian Authority, in accordance with the agreement between Israel and the Palestinians, under the patronage of the United States and since then has become a sponsor of the peace process.

Hussein and Rabin in Jordan.

Jordan agrees to the peace process

King Hussein signed the agreement with Yitzhak Rabin on 25 July 1994 in Washington that formally ended the state of war between Jordan and Israel, pending the final agreement being endorsed later on in Jordan. Meanwhile, Yasser Arafat assumed the leadership of the Palestinian Authority on 16 August 1994, beginning with a widespread campaign of arrests of members of Hamas, the Islamic Jihad and other forces opposing the peace process. Thus, for the first time, the peace accords turned the Palestinian-Israeli conflict into a Palestinian-Palestinian conflict.

Hussein, Rabin and Clinton during the Wadi Arabah peace agreement, 26/10/1994.

Hussein, Clinton and Rabin at the White House after signing the peace agreement, 25/7/1994.

The Wadi Arabah Agreement

On 26 October 1994, in Wadi Araba, Israel and Jordan signed a lasting peace agreement by which Jordan would obtain water rights, receive American support for its economy and have its geopolitical status enhanced in the region.

First of all, Gaza and Jericho

The final agreement, presumably to be signed after the peace agreement between Israel and Arafat in the USA, involved ceding Gaza and Jericho to the Palestinian Authority. However, these territories only accounted for 2% of the whole area of Palestine. A second round and, in particular, a third round of agreements were to be definitive in providing solutions for all the problems pending, especially that of Jerusalem, which Israel had refused to discuss previously and had asked to be postponed.

Jerusalem in mourning after the peace agreements

Desperate operation in Jerusalem

As Jerusalem was a fundamental, crucial issue for the Palestinian people, the Islamist response came three days later in a desperate operation in Tel Aviv, in which 22 people were murdered and 47 wounded. It was a severe blow to the Israelis, who believed that the peace agreements would put an end to the struggle for Palestine, but the operations continued.

Clinton, Hussein, Mubarak, Rabin and Arafat, moments before signing the peace agreement at the White House, 28/9/1995.

Dr. Fathi Shikaki, the Islamic Jihad leader.

Arafat assassinates Palestinians

The Palestinian Authority, in a show of strength, suppressed a huge rally organized by Hamas and the Jihad in Gaza. For the first time, Palestinians were dying at the hands of other Palestinians. The Authority killed 13 demonstrators and arrested 300. The Islamic resistance forces faced a great dilemma with the Palestinian Authority which had resolved to enforce the peace, even at the cost of suppressing the Intifada.

The Israeli embassy opens its doors in Jordan

In Jordan the peace agreements were crowned with the opening of embassies in both countries on 7 December 1994. The Israelis started to set up businesses inside Jordan and conduct surveys of the country's market in order to supply the goods they needed.

370

2. Assassinations everywhere

AH 1416
AD 1995

Assassination of Fathi Shikaki

Israel continued its Palestinian repression, even abroad. In Malta, on 26 September 1995, the Israeli secret service, the Mossad, assassinated Dr. Fathi Shikaki, the leader of the Islamic Jihad. It was in vain, as there was no interruption in resistance operations.

Yitzhak Rabin's funeral, 6/11/1995.

Members of the Palestinian police force.

Assassination of Yitzhak Rabin

The situation was further embroiled when a Jewish extremist murdered the Israeli prime minister, Yitzhak Rabin, at a huge festive gathering.

The motive was Israeli fundamentalist opposition to the peace agreement. The world was shocked to find that some Jews were so opposed to the agreement that they were prepared to murder their prime minister.

371

Yasser Arafat kissing the hand of Yitzhak Rabin's widow, during the funeral for the prime minister.

Condolences from the Arabs and Arafat

Rabin's magnificent funeral was attended by huge crowds, presidents and celebrities from different parts of the world. The Arab countries were represented by their respective delegations. Among those attending the burial was Yasser Arafat, who read the first sura of the Koran, "al-Fatiha", in memory of Rabin.

Negotiations between Hamas and the Palestinian Authority

On 18 December 1995, talks were convened between Khalid Mish'al, vice-president of the political wing of Hamas, and Salim Za'nun, in representation of the Palestinian Authority. The pursued objective was to convince Hamas of the need to abandon its military struggle and to take part in the imminent Palestinian elections, but the Islamic Movement refused to halt its armed activity. Negotiations between the two parties were left pending—Hamas increased its attacks on Israel and Yasser Arafat was unable to control the situation.

Jalid Mish`al, vice-president of Hamas' political bureau, 1995.

Israel assassinates Yahya Ayash

At the beginning of that year, Israel assassinated the engineer, Yahya Ayash, who was a leader of the Intifada and of the Resistance movement against the army occupation. The Israeli intelligence service (Mossad) placed a transmitter and an explosive device in a mobile telephone and delivered it to Kamal Hammad, one of their collaborators, with the intention of the latter giving it as a present to his maternal uncle, Yahya. This happened according to plan and Yahya was killed. The Mossad tapped and recorded all Yahya's conversations over this mobile phone, until one day Yahya started suspecting something. During his last call, Yahya Ayash said to his father: "Don't call me again on this mobile telephone" and, at that very moment, the explosive device hidden in the phone was triggered by remote control from an Israeli spy plane, destroying Ayash's head outright.

The traitor, Kamal Hammad, received compensation for his "good service" to the tune of one million dollars and a passport under a false name. Two hundred and fifty thousand Palestinians bid their farewells to Ayash at the cemetery in his city. Arafat was one of those who paid his condolences to the relatives of this great fighter.

AH 1416
AD 1996

Yahya Ayash, the brain behind the resistance operations.

373

The funeral
parade of the
assassinated
Ayash, in Gaza,
15/1/1996.

Operation Ayash

On 25 May, one month after the murder of Yahya Ayash, Hamas responded to the Israeli assassination in the territory controlled by the Palestinian Authority with two punishing operations. In the first, a bus transporting Israeli soldiers was blown up, killing twenty-four and injuring fifty. In the second attack, thirty-five soldiers were killed in Ashkelon. However, Israel retaliated with vindictive operations of the kind that had never been experienced in twenty-nine years of occupation. Hamas continued with the vendetta, mounting another operation that ended in the killing of sixty-four Israeli paramilitary troops.

Israeli repression against the Palestinian civilian population.

3. Everyone against the Palestinian Resistance

Israel and the Palestinian Authority suppress Hamas

Israel responded to Hamas' efficiency with cruel repression against Palestinian civilians, as did the Palestinian Authority, which imprisoned many Hamas members and sympathizers. However, the Resistance continued its strategy of punitive operations whenever Israel killed civilians. This strategy destabilized the Israeli government, which had no alternative but to seek help from those governments interested in finding a solution that would protect them from attacks originating in Lebanon and the occupied territories.

The Sharm el-Sheikh conference

At the request of Israel, an international conference was held at Sharm el-Sheikh (Egypt), in April 1996. It was attended by the Arab heads of government, the Palestinian Authority, Israel and the world powers, in an attempt to find a peaceful solution and put an end to the reigning violence. However, the resolutions adopted were geared to a search for ways of reining in Palestinian and Lebanese resistance operations in southern Lebanon, which had been stepped up to ten assaults a day against Israeli convoys.

Grapes of Wrath and The Massacre of Qana

The military successes of the well equipped and organized Lebanese resistance (Hezbollah) led the Israelis to invade by sea and air the strip of southern Lebanon adjoining their border which had been occupied several years before. They baptized this military operation "Grapes of Wrath" and, since the Resistance was not an easy objective, Israel took revenge against the civilian population and against the electrical and municipal facilities. It resulted in the death of 100 civilians, while hundreds were injured.

In April 1996, the Israeli army committed one of the bloodiest massacres ever committed by a State. That day, the Israeli aviation bombed the Qana refugee camp in Lebanon which was protected by UN forces. Hundreds of children and elderly people were killed. Israel could not silence the news as usual because the satellite television channels were there. However, defying international law, they insisted that they would continue their incursions until the Lebanese resistance halted its activities. The latter imposed the condition that they would stop shelling the Israeli bordering settlements if Israel halted its assaults against Lebanese civilians. Israel agreed, but did not respect the commitment.

A Hamas sympathizer.

The Palestinian Authority harasses the Resistance

In compliance with the Sharm el-Sheikh resolutions, the Palestinian Authority arrested over 1,000 Hamas and Islamic Jihad activists, suspended the academic year and sealed the charitable foundations belonging to these two organizations. However, Israel praised the measures taken by Arafat, the president of the PA.

Adapting the Palestinian Magna Carta

The Palestinian Authority, in compliance with the Sharm el-Sheikh accords, deleted all the articles in their Magna Carta that referred to

Dr. Musa Abu Marzuq, head of Hamas' Political Department, 1995.

non-recognition of the State of Israel. In other words, they deleted the ideological basis on which al-Fatah and the PLO had been founded.

Israel accedes to Hezbollah's demands

On 27 April 1996, Israel accepted the conditions imposed by Hezbollah and the shelling of the Israeli settlements stopped. This agreement boosted Hezbollah's credibility among local Lebanese inhabitants, who intensified their support of the Lebanese combatants.

Arrest of Musa Abu Marzuq

In May 1996, Israel, USA and the Palestinian Authority coordinated their action against Hamas, Islamic Jihad and all the related organizations. One result of this joint action was the arrest at New York airport of the head of Hamas' political bureau, Dr. Musa Abu Marzuq. Despite holding American nationality, on 8 May 1996 the examining federal judge ordered the extradition of the detainee—with no charges—to Israel, but Abu Marzuq appealed before the competent courts.

It is worth recalling that the structure of Hamas is similar to that of the IRA in that it has a military and a political wing. Moreover, both the USA and Britain maintain official contacts with the political wing of the IRA and do not consider it to be linked to the terrorist activities of its military wing. Nevertheless, this opinion was not upheld by any of the superpowers and the political wing of Hamas was declared to be "terrorist".

Military confrontation

On 19 May 1996, Israeli forces surrounded a Hamas guerrilla group in the Hebron Valley. The confrontation left 5 dead (3 Israelis and 2 Hamas members) and 11 wounded Israelis.

Netanyahu wins the elections

In view of the success of the Palestinian Resistance on the ground, the Israeli Labour party became over-stretched and unable to guarantee civilian safety within its borders. The Likud party took advantage of the political instability and included in their election programme extreme repressive measures against the Palestinians. This way, the elections were won by the Likud, headed by Benjamin Netanyahu.

Netanyahu
threatening to
strangle the
Intifada.

More tunnels underneath al-Aqsa Mosque

On the pretext of looking for archaeological vestiges pointing to the siting of Solomon's Temple, the Israeli authorities excavated beneath al-Aqsa in all directions, weakening its foundations to the extent that it was in danger of collapsing. On Friday, 25 September 1996, the authorities officiated the official opening of another tunnel underneath the west wall of the Mosque. The Palestinians who had turned up for Friday prayers protested against what they considered to be an act of sabotage against the holy place of all Muslims, but Israeli riot forces intervened, premeditatedly killing 62 members of the congregation and seriously injuring 1,600 others.

AH 1417
AD 1997

The Palestinian Authority imprisons more young Palestinians

According to the Human Rights Organization, at the beginning of 1997 the PA detained 1,600 Palestinians, out of which 700 were released without charges. Twenty of those arrested died from torture.

Friday prayers in Jerusalem.

378

Netanyahu whispers something in Arafat's ear.

4. Hamas restructured

Release of Abu Marzuq

While Abu Marzuq was under arrest in the USA, Hamas appointed Khaled Mashal, a graduate from the University of Kuwait, to succeed him as president of the political bureau, a position he still holds today. However, Abu Marzuq was released, with no further charges, in May 1997.

The PA show signs of corruption

While donations sent directly to inhabitants in PA territory reached their destination, financial support deposited in PA bank accounts was allegedly not received in its entirety by the Palestinian treasury.

In May 1997, the Treasury Control Commission, an organ of the Legislative Council, reported the disappearance of 326 million US dollars out of the 1,500 million for the annual budget. In view of this, the Legislative Council passed a vote of no confidence against Arafat's government.

Muhammad Jihad, one of the top Fatah leaders, declared that Arafat was surrounded by a gang of thieves. It was later revealed that financial and administrative corruption had invaded the state apparatus of the PA.

Khaled Mashal survives an assassination attempt

An Israeli Mossad operative took advantage of the climate of distrust in the PA to infiltrate into Amman. On 25 September 1997, he sprayed neurotoxic gas in the face of the new president of Hamas' political bureau, Khaled Mishal, in a street in the heart of the Jordanian capital. Khaled was struck down and lay unconscious until he was admitted to the ICU at a nearby hospital.

His bodyguard, with the help of passers-by, overpowered the assassin and handed him over to the Jordanian police.

King Hussein was notified and telephoned the Israeli prime minister, warning him that, if Mashal were to die, Jordan would break its diplo-

David and Goliath.

matic ties with Israel. He urged them to immediately send the antidote to the neurotoxic gas. As Israel could not afford to sacrifice its relations with Jordan, it rushed a delegation of top army officials with the antidote and so the life of Khaled Mishal was saved.

The elderly Ahmad Yassin is set free

The Jordanian government was enraged by the criminal act committed by Israel on its territory and demanded that the Israeli government release the elderly and paraplegic Ahmed Yassin, who had been condemned to life imprisonment, as a token of their goodwill. They were also to make an official pledge never to commit an act of terrorism on Jordanian soil again.

Israel accepted the Jordanian demands and indeed Yassin was set free and taken out of Israel, and his reunion with Khaled Mishal was filmed by international television camera crews.

As a result of this terrorist act, perpetrated by the state of Israel, support for the Palestinian cause has increased worldwide.

Netanyahu, Arafat, Clinton and King Hussein at the signing of the "Peace-for-Land" agreement on 23 October 1998.

Israeli extremists profane al-Aqsa and the Palestinian Resistance responds

AH 1419
AD 1998

The most striking trend of the first six months of that year was the increase in Israeli extremist and fanatical rage against Muslim holy places. At one such intentional incident, an Israeli hurled a pig's head wrapped in pages from the Koran inside the al-Aqsa Mosque. The Intifada responded with various military operations in different parts of the occupied territory, using remote controlled robots for the first time.

Because of the qualitative leap in the Resistance operations, Israel requested the USA to present a peace proposal for the Middle East that would calm the fury of the Intifada.

Arafat and Clinton in December 1998.

The Wye Plantation Agreement

In October 1998 a peace agreement was signed at the Wye River Plantation (USA). Although Israel had previously accepted and then postponed it, it heralded a new start to the dynamics of peace.

Intifada and peace

Al-Aqsa—the objective of Israeli terrorists

While the new peace initiative ran its course, not without some serious setbacks, Hezbollah stepped up its operations in occupied southern Lebanon, and Hamas grew in stature in the conscience of the Palestinians. Jewish extremists and fundamentalists plotted against al-Aqsa, but their ploys were aborted by Israeli police.

The Israeli government did not approve of attacks against al-Aqsa, for fear of exacerbating the ire of the Arab-Muslim crowds at a time when Israel was deeply involved in the peace process. It was also a period when they sought to make the country more credible and respectful of its commitments, providing the negotiations led to peace, in accordance with their wishes.

Jewish congregation at the Wailing Wall.

Barak, the new prime minister of Israel

On 19 May 1999, the Labour party candidate, Ehud Barak, took over from Netanyahu as head of the Israeli government. Barak, a hawk of the Labour party, promised voters he would put an end to the resistance and, to keep his promise, he signed an agreement with Jordan by which the Jordanian government would order the closing of Hamas offices in Amman. In September that same year they would sign the Sharm El-Sheikh Act with the PA by which the PA would control Hamas and Islamic Jihad, in exchange for putting the peace agreements signed earlier into practice; that is, the return of the West Bank and Gaza to the Palestinians.

Deportation of Hamas leaders

Khaled Mishal, Musa Abu Marzuq, Ibrahim Ghawsha and Muhammad Nazzal, all of whom held Jordanian nationality, were deported from Amman to Qatar. Because of this, twenty Palestinian intellectuals close to the PA signed a joint statement accusing the PA of allowing political repression, limiting freedom and turning a blind eye to corruption within the Palestinian administration.

The unusual thing is that, in spite of all the measures taken against the Resistance, military operations inside Israel have not stopped.

AH 1421
AD 2000
The Resistance improves Operational Activities

On 4 January 2000, the Israeli army was given a serious warning when, for the first time ever, two of its tanks were destroyed using modern remote-control technology. The Popular Front for the Liberation of Palestinian (PFLP) and the Islamic Jihad both claimed responsibility for various operations on the same day, which ended with 70 Israeli dead and 750 injured. Meanwhile, Hezbollah intensified its operations against Israelis until May, when the Israelis pulled back from southern Lebanon.

Ehud Barak, the Israeli prime minister.

Left: Ibrahim Ghawsha
Right: Muhammad Nazzal

From left to right: The late King Hussein of
Jordan, his son and successor, King Abdullah,
Hosni Mubarak, president of Egypt, Powell,
the US Secretary of State, and Shimon Peres.

PART FIVE
The Intifada and peace

CHAPTER FOUR
The second Intifada

The second Intifada

1. The spark that set the Intifada alight

One million Russian emigrants in Israel

In the year 2000, the Israeli authorities celebrated the arrival of Russian Jewish immigrants, numbering 1,000,000, among whom 92,000 were university graduates in nuclear, military and other sciences.

Sharon profanes Al-Aqsa

On 28 September 2000, the president of the Israeli Likud, surrounded by 3,000 soldiers, burst into al-Aqsa mosque. Muslim crowds considered this provocative act to be an outrage that could not be left without a suitable response.

The immediate reaction was a bloody clash between the people at the mosque and the Israeli security services, which left 5 Muslims dead and 100 injured.

The fact is that Sharon's irresponsibility was the culture medium from which the second Intifada emerged.

Muslims barring Sharon's entrance to al-Aqsa.

386

The outbreak
of the second Intifada

Both Arabs and Palestinians were disappointed with the development of the peace negotiations between their representatives and
those of the Israeli government, and they saw
Sharon's intrusion into al-Aqsa as a sign that
Israel did not want to negotiate real peace
but to gain time until the Arab will and
fighting spirit had been broken.

The logical reaction from the whole Muslim
world was to leave the PA to continue with
the sterile negotiations and support the Islamic Resistance with all the means available,
to the extent that the Kuwaiti parliament decided to suspend economic aid to the PA,
and send it directly to the Palestinians.

Mohammad Al-Durra –
Infanticide via satellite

His father was holding the child by his hand,
taking Muhammad al-Durra to school. He
was the target of Israeli snipers who saw this
boy as easy prey. His father, who had never
taken part in any resistance operations, tried
to protect his son with his own body behind
a wall, but the child killers shot and killed
the child and seriously injured his father.
French television broadcast live pictures of
the Israeli barbarity against the people of
Palestine.

Millions of viewers throughout the world
watched this macabre scene. The Israeli government said they regretted this chilling
episode, without further ado.

The mark of pain.

The 15-year-old Muhammad al-Durra,
assassinated by the Israeli army.

2. Israel and the PA confront the Intifada

Arafat against the Intifada

The first year of the second Intifada was catastrophic for Israel, not only because of the number of military operations conducted inside Israel but because of their scale.

The USA reconsidered its best efforts for peace, while the Israeli government put pressure on the Palestinian National Authority to stem the tide of the Intifada, accusing Arafat of being behind the resistance incursions. Arafat replied that his government was doing its best and that it had in fact averted 110 incursions before they reached their targets. The Intifada was by now unstoppable.

Israel assassinates Mahmoud Abu Hunud

On 14 November 2001, on their fourth attempt and with help from Mossad agents, the Israeli army murdered Mahmoud Abu Hunud, one of the leaders of the al-Qassam Brigades, using a guided missile that was fired at the car he was travelling in.

The assassinated Mahmoud Abu Hunud, a senior leader of Hamas.

A Palestinian boy leaps over a tear gas canister fired by Israeli soldiers, 31/8/2001.

The Abu Hunud Operation

Hamas and Israel carried out a tit-for-tat series of operations. On 2 December 2001, Hamas avenged Abu Hunud's assassination with four simultaneous incursions that left 25 Israelis dead and 250 injured. Israel was perplexed at the speed and precision of the Hamas operations. Sharon suspended an official visit to the USA and immediately returned to Tel Aviv, accusing the PA of being behind the attacks. To demonstrate their innocence and willingness to combat Palestinian guerrilla organizations, the PA detained more than a hundred Hamas leaders, including Ismael Abu Shanab. However, Israel violated their earlier commitments, shelling Gaza and the West Bank with air-to-ground missiles and besieging with ground troops the PA headquarters, with Arafat trapped inside.

A Palestinian house destroyed by the Israeli army.

Jewish congregation in front of the Wailing Wall (the Buraq Wall, or west wall of al-Aqsa).

AH 1423
AD 2002

Anti-Semitism

One week after the international forum on Anti-Semitism was held on 3 January 2002, the Israeli army, in a punitive operation against innocent civilians, demolished 45 houses in Rafah. However, Hamas retaliated by killing four Israeli soldiers to the east of that same town, precisely where Gaza airport is now located. Imad Abu Riziq and Muhammad Abu Jamus, of the al-Qassam Brigades, Hamas' military wing, were killed in that confrontation.

Ra'id al-Karmi,
assassinated by Israel.

Wave of hijackings and destruction

In mid-January 2002, the Israeli army once again invaded Rafah (on sovereign PA territory). They destroyed the airport runways, kidnapped several members of Hamas and murdered the leader of al-Fatah and the leader of the al-Aqsa Brigades in Tulkarem, Ra'id al-Karmi, and his counterpart in Nablus, Khamis Ahmed Abdallah.

On 18 January 2002, Israeli tanks destroyed the headquarters of the Palestinian security forces in Tulkarem, killing one and seriously injuring ten of its members; they occupied a building near Arafat's personal office and used explosives to destroy the building housing Palestinian radio and television studios in Ramallah.

How did the outside world react to this barbarity? Japan froze bank accounts belonging to Hamas and the Islamic Jihad.

Prisoners set free by Palestinian crowds

Whenever the Palestinian Resistance mounted an assault in response to Israeli aggression, the Palestinian National Authority condemned it and imprisoned dozens of activists, who were systematically tortured. This aroused the people's anger and, on 22 January 2002, an enraged mob burst into Nablus jail and freed the prisoners. The police wardens opened fire on the crowds, killing one person and seriously wounding many more.

Collaborators and Israeli soldiers pay the price with their blood

On 5 February 2002, a group of hooded people burst into in a Palestinian National Authority criminal court hearing and executed three collaborators who were being tried.

A few days later, the al-Aqsa Brigades murdered an Israeli policeman, a soldier and an officer, while an undetermined number of people were wounded. The following day, the al-Qassam Brigade killed six Israeli soldiers in Nablus.

The Israeli response was not long in coming. Several Palestinian police stations were attacked, and six police officers were killed in the operation. Once again, Yasser Arafat asked President Bush to intervene to halt the escalation of violence.

The attacks continue

On 2 March 2002, the 'Atif Ubaydat Brigades murdered 11 Israeli settlers and seriously wounded 40 others in the centre of Old Jerusalem. That same day, they killed an Israeli army officer at Mar Saba, near Bethlehem.

The next day, the al-Qassam Brigades killed 10 Israeli soldiers in the northern district of Ramallah and suffered no casualties themselves.

Two days later, a young Palestinian man blew up a bus that was transporting soldiers to Jerusalem, leaving 50 Israelis dead.

This long list of assaults and counterattacks shows that reasoning and non-violence are the way and means of resolving conflict.

Graffiti in Gaza: "If you destroy our houses, you will not destroy our souls".

The impact of
a missile on Arafat's
headquarters in
Ramallah on
29/3/2002.

Yasser Arafat under
candlelight at his
destroyed
headquarters,
30/3/2002.

The "Bloody Friday" Operation

The Israeli government, unable to control the situation, launched a punitive and intimidatory operation, code-named "Red Friday" or "Bloody Friday", against the headquarters of the PA, where Arafat was living and working, and against the towns of Gaza, Nablus and Ramallah, using Apache helicopters, F16 fighters and armoured vehicles. This resulted in the death of 50 civilians.

The Israeli army
occupying part of
Arafat's headquarters,
29/3/2003.

The Arab Peace proposal

On 27 March 2002, an Arab summit was held in Beirut, although half the delegates failed to attend. Delegations from Iraq were reconciled with those from Saudi Arabia, as were those from Iraq and Kuwait. This was publicly sealed by the Saudi heir, Prince Abdullah, embracing the Iraqi vice-president, Izzat Ibrahim, and a warm greeting between members of the Iraqi and Kuwaiti delegations.

The summit produced agreement over the "Arab peace proposal", presented by the Saudi Crown Prince, Abdullah bin Saud.

Tightening the noose

On 29 March 2002, Israel intensified its attacks on Arafat's headquarters. Several of his collaborators were arrested and he was isolated from the outside world. At the same time, Bethlehem was occupied and the Church of the Nativity was surrounded, as a group of armed Palestinians had taken refuge inside it. On 15 May, diplomatic intervention by the European Union led to them being granted leave to emigrate to Europe.

Besieged Palestinians praying at the Church of the Nativity.

Intifada and peace

1 & 2. The Israeli army besieges the Church of the Nativity, Bethlehem, where a group of Palestinian gunmen were taking refuge (2/5/2002).

3. A Palestinian besieged in the Church of the Nativity eating tree leaves.

4. The besieged Palestinians sleeping in the Church of the Nativity.

5. Ibrahim Ubaydat, one of the Palestinians, was later exiled to Spain.

6. The Palestinians saying their farewells.

7. The besieged Palestinians leaving the Church of the Nativity, on 10/5/2002, after 38 days.

The Massacre of Jenin

On 3 April 2002, the Israeli army invaded the Jenin refugee camp in the northern part of the West Bank under the command of its Defence Minister, General Shaul Mofaz. A massacre took place inside the camp, but reports are scant as the Israeli army barred the press corps and ambulances from approaching the site of the destruction. Although the resistance killed 13 Israeli soldiers, the invading army physically crushed and flattened the whole camp. The aftermath of the military operation was a distressing scene of rubble and corpses.

The Arab world reacted in a spirit of revenge—Iraq paralysed its oil exports for a month, in an act of solidarity with the Palestinian people, while a synagogue on Jerba island in Tunisia was targeted by a car bomb attack that produced several German Jewish victims, and the Israeli embassy in Paris was set on fire on 23 May 2002.

General Shaul Mofaz, Israel's minister of defence.

The attack on a synagogue in Jerba (Tunisia).

The remains of Jenin after the Israeli invasion.

395

Arafat and the
US Secretary of State,
Colin Powell, at
Ramallah on
14/4/2002.

The "harvest" of the
Israeli raid on Jenin.

Sabri al-Banna (Abu Nidal).

Salah Shehadeh, the leader and
founder of the al-Qassam Brigades.

The US refuses an investigation

On 19 April 2002, the PA, together with some Arab countries, requested a UN investigation of the Jenin massacre, but the US refused and, on 5 May, announced its withdrawal from a signed committment to set up an International Criminal Court.

Israel assassinates Salah Shehadeh

On 5 July 2002, Yasser Arafat dismissed the head of security, Colonel Jibril Rayyub. On 23 July, the leader and founder of the al-Qassam Brigades, the military wing of Hamas, Salah Shehadeh, was killed outright by a rocket launched from a F16 jet fighter at the building where he was living. Fifteen other neighbours from the same building, of which nine were children, also died.

On 19 August 2002, the controversial Sabri al-Banna, alias Abu Nidal, a dissident of Fatah since the seventies, was assassinated in Baghdad.

USA recognizes occupied
Jerusalem as the capital of Israel

On 30 September 2002, President George Bush signed his country's recognition of occupied Jerusalem as the capital of Israel and, on 7 October, the Israeli army committed another massacre of civilians in Khan Yunis which left 14 dead and 110 wounded.

Ehud Barak, the Israeli prime minister, receives the Mitchell Commission, charged with investigating the Jenin massacre.

More operations and more organizations

On 28 November 2002, al-Qaeda claimed responsibility for the attack on a hotel frequented by Israelis in Mombassa, Kenya, which left 15 dead, of whom three were Israelis, and the unsuccessful attack on an airplane belonging to the Israeli company, Arkia, as it was taking off.

On 27 December 2002, the Islamic Jihad Movement responded to the assassination of the Hamas leader in Tulkarem, Tarek Abed Rabbo, and its leader in Bethlehem, Jadallah Musa Shawkat, by sending a guerrilla force of 2 soldiers to the Jewish Otniel settlement in southern Hebron. They opened fire, killing four people and seriously wounding eight others.

Jenin–Tel Aviv face to face

The Jenin massacre was avenged on 5 January 2003 by a double operation mounted by the al-Aqsa Brigades in the centre of Tel Aviv. Buraq
Abd ar-Rahman carried out the first suicide bomb attack at a bus station
located in Rothschild Street. Samir Imad an-Nuri perpetrated the attack
in the street opposite. The result of the massacre was 23 dead and over
100 wounded.

Faced with the magnitude of the losses, Israel launched an air and ground
attack on the civilian population of Gaza and the Jenin refugee camp.
However, on 23 January 2003, in an ambush outside the Bet Hagai settlement, Hamas killed three Israeli soldiers, without suffering any losses
themselves.

AH 1424
AD 2003

Israel declares dirty war

Israel declared its policy intention to kill the leaders of Hamas and other related organizations, including those of the PA. Indeed, on 8 March
2003, immediately after an operation by the Palestinian resistance
against the Kiryat Arba settlement near Hebron, which left 3 settlers
dead and 8 wounded, four of them soldiers, a squadron of Apache helicopters fired four remote-controlled missiles at the car in which
Ibrahim Makadme, a Hamas leader, and three escorts were travelling. It
killed them outright, in the heart of the Sheikh Radwan neighbourhood in Gaza.

Preparations for the war against Iraq

While skirmishes between the Israeli army and the Palestinian Resistance
were coming to a head, American and British troops began to concentrate
in the region, poised to invade Iraq, in spite of the fact that most world
countries were opposed to such an invasion and that the USA had failed
to secure authorization from the United Nations Security Council. Nevertheless, the USA declared that such permission was not necessary and
that it would go to war on account of the fact that the regime in Iraq possessed weapons of mass destruction which UN inspectors, however, had
not been able to locate in the course of 13 years of intense searching.

AH 1424
AD 2003

The world opposes the war

Despite the US, Britain and their satellite countries' attempts to internationalize the invasion of Iraq, their war camp was opposed by France, Germany and Russia. This did not, however, prevent the US from pressing ahead with its plans. Finally, on 20 March 2003, George Bush announced the beginning of the invasion by land, sea and air.

In spite of the heavy resistance encountered by the British in southern Iraq, the Iraqi army did not hold out for more than a month since the outbreak of hostilities, much to the surprise of military experts. When Baghdad fell, the end of the war was announced.

US marines during
the invasion of
Baghdad.

The collapse of Saddam's regime
and the Palestinian Problem

The fall of the Iraqi dictatorship affected the Palestinian problem and the balance of forces in the region. The Israelis took advantage of the presence of their ally, the world's superpower, in Iraq, and the serious warnings against Syria and Iran, to further pressure the Palestinian people in an attempt to weaken their will and fighting spirit.

The actual situation on the ground was quite different as resistance operations continued and collective punitive operations by Israel continued apace, according to a premeditated plan.

Saddam's statue in the centre of Baghdad is pulled down, marking the end of the Baath party's rule in Iraq.

Mahmoud Abbas, prime minister of the PA

In an attempt to establish a negotiated peace with Israel, Yasser Arafat appointed Mahmoud Abbas (Abu Mazen) to be prime minister of the PA, in compliance with a presidential decree he had signed.

On several occasions Abbas met with Israeli representatives in an attempt to find a way of implementing the Roadmap, but Israel wanted to introduce important changes in the topography of the map presented by the American mediator, in spite of its earlier commitment to the overall plan. Abbas tried to dispel Israeli misgivings by securing commitments from the Palestinian Resistance to call a halt to any military activity against Israel, providing Israel did the same. However, Israel rejected a mutual commitment and instead invaded several Palestinian camps, destroyed many of their houses and farmland and arrested several of their inhabitants. Abbas's failure in these two vitally important matters led him to tender his resignation.

US forces crossing a
bridge in Baghdad.

An unsuccessful attempt on the life of Arrantisi

On 10 June 2003, an Israeli helicopter fired a missile at one of the most distinguished leaders of Hamas, Dr. Abdul Aziz Arrantisi, in Gaza. Arrantisi sustained only light wounds but, unfortunately, a woman and her 8-year-old daughter were killed and 35 more were injured.

Israel threatens to deport Arafat

Israel announced it was considering banishing Arafat from Palestine, but this drew opposition and protest from many countries.

Meanwhile Arafat continued to perform his duties by appointing Ahmed Korei to succeed Abbas as leader of the Palestinian government.

Israel assassinates Abu Shanab

On 21 August 2003, an Israeli Apache helicopter launched five missiles at the car in which the engineer, Ismael Abu Shanab, a leader of Hamas, was travelling in Gaza, together with two of his assistants. All three were killed outright and several passers-by were injured.

Abdullah Aqel murdered by Israel

Israel's declared policy to murder Palestinian leaders continued unabated. This time it was the turn of the leader of the al-Qassam Brigades who was travelling with one of his companions on 30 August 2003. As in the case of Abu Shanab, he was assassinated by missiles fired from a helicopter.

Dr. Abdul Aziz Arrantisi.

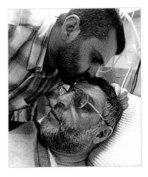

Arrantisi hospitalized after the attempt.

Ismael Abu Shanab.

Abdullah Aqel.

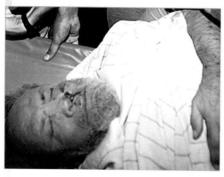

Mahmoud Azzahar,
wounded by the impact of
a missile fired from an F16 at
his Gaza apartment.

The US tightens the blockade on Hamas

The US declared Hamas to be a terrorist organization, confiscated its bank accounts and asked all countries in the world to follow its example. Some governments responded positively to the request from the Bush administration.

Israel attacks Syrian territory

To intensify the conflict and eliminate the possibility of a negotiated peace, Israel violated Syrian air space by shelling a post in the capital, Damascus, on the pretext that the Palestinian organizations were using it as a military base.

Many world capitals considered the unjustified Israeli aggression as an attempt to export the conflict beyond its borders. However, Syria submitted a formal complaint to the Security Council. The US threatened to veto any condemnation of Israel, so that, in the end, its action went unpunished. The Bush administration even declared that all Palestinian resistance groups were terrorist organizations.

Unsuccessful attempt on the life of Ahmed Yassin

On 6 September 2003, the Israeli air force fired missiles from an F16 at the building housing the elderly and paraplegic Ahmed Yassin, founder of Hamas, in the centre of Gaza. Yassin was slightly wounded, as were 17 other civilians.

Hamas announced a quick response. A few days later, two attacks were carried out in Jerusalem and Tel Aviv, leaving a death toll of 50 Israelis and dozens of wounded.

Another unsuccessful attempt

In a very similar attempt to the one on Yassin, on 10 September 2003, a leader of Hamas, Mahmoud Azzahar, survived an attack in which his eldest son, Khaled, and two of his bodyguards were killed. Dozens of civilians were injured too.

4th anniversary of the Intifada

The Islamic Resistance, wary of the sincerity of the peace proposals and aware of the fundamentalist mentality of the Israeli government, gave no credibility to the Peace process and decided not to waste time in sterile negotiations since, even the Roadmap, proposed by the US and ratified by Israel, had gradually been taken over by Israel. However Hamas gave the PA a free hand to continue negotiating, without the participation of the Resistance. At the same time, Hamas announced it would continue fighting, as long as Israel continued killing Palestinian civilians and destroying the infrastructure of the West Bank.

AH 1424
AD 28-09-2003

Homes demolished by
the Israeli army.

405

The West Bank Wall

Israel decided to implement a project it had kept secret which involved building a wall separating the territories that Israel chose to annex from those in the West Bank. The unusual thing about the wall is its direction and siting, because it is sited entirely on PA territory and its tortuous path encircles several citadels and Palestinian villages that have become isolated from the outside world. Even worse, many farmers have seen how their houses are on one side of the wall, while their land is on the other. This wall is a flagrant violation of the peace agreements signed by Israel and the PA. Consequently, the UN General Assembly voted by a majority to declare the project illegal and call for it to be dismantled immediately. However, the US once again threatened to veto any resolution taken by the Security Council in this respect.

The Resistance bursts into an Israeli military base

The al-Qassam Brigades, in a joint operation with the Jerusalem Brigades (the military wing of Islamic Jihad), managed to infiltrate security positions at the Israeli Netzarim settlement and kill 3 soldiers, seriously wounding several others.

On 26 October 2003, the Israeli army attacked the town of az-Zahra in southern Gaza and destroyed three residential blocks used to accommodate the relatives of the Palestinian police. Several citizens were arrested.

The PA fulfils its commitments

In accordance with its commitments before the international community, on 20 November 2003, the Palestinian Authority arrested the young man, Jabr al-Akhras, and accused him of taking part in an ambush in which two Israeli soldiers were killed.

The Resistance steps up its activity

On Friday 21 November 2003, the al-Qassam Brigades claimed responsibility for the destruction of an Israeli tank on the Palestinian-Egyptian border. The tank was blown up by a remote-controlled explosive device. The Israeli army responded by taking revenge on nearby "dwellings", three of which were demolished.

The West Bank Wall was condemned by most countries.

On 7 December 2003, the same al-Qassam Brigades launched a rocket attack on the Israeli Gahne Tal settlement near Khan Yunis. The following day they attacked the Netzer Hazani settlement, which they pounded with two howitzer cannons. A few hours later they hit an Israeli military post in Ghadiya, near Gaza.

With regard to these attacks, Yassin, the founder of Hamas, declared they proved that the occupation was untenable.

The Libyan president, Muammar Gaddafi.

Saddam is captured

On 14 December 2003, the American forces captured the deposed president of Iraq, Saddam Hussein. Reactions to his arrest were mixed—some could not conceal their joy, while others, specifically the Arab people, were not happy about the way the arrest had taken place, because it had been carried out by a force of occupation.

The statistics speak

On 16 December 2003, the National Palestinian Census Bureau conducted a survey on the attitude of Palestinians aged between 10 and 24 with regard to the Resistance and the best way of liberating their land. 60% voted in favour of the Intifada as the only way to liberate their homeland, and 91% agreed that it was the young people who should decide on the strategy to be followed.

AH 1424
AD 2004

The West Bank Wall

Contrary to international law and the will of most states in the world, on 5 January 2004, Israel began surveying the land prior to the construction of the "wall of racial segregation" (the separation wall) to the northeast of Jerusalem. The land earmarked for the 720-km-long wall was expropriated from its Palestinian owners, and shafts with signs saying "Military Zone" were immediately installed by sappers. Strangely enough, the land wrested from the Palestinians was the most fertile in the whole area.

Libya changes attitude

On 6 January 2004, the Libyan leader, Muammar Gaddafi, announced his intention to compensate Libyan Jews for the properties they had abandoned in Libya when they left to settle in Israel. In response, Libyans were at leave to visit Israel. The US president praised the measures taken by Libya with regard to the Palestinian problem, which were deemed positive. However they were insufficient for the USA to lift the embargo on Libya, which was extended for another period.

Israel accuses France

At a press conference held on 7 January 2004, the Israeli government accused France of being the most anti-Semitic Western nation. France hastily responded that acts of sabotage against Jewish properties in France had decreased by 36% in 2003. At the same time, it announced its aim to implement measures against French Muslims, including a prohibition on wearing the *hijab* (headscarf) in public schools and administrative buildings, a move deplored by Muslims and a large part of French society.

Demonstration
in Ramallah.

Temporary truce

On 10 January 2004, Israel claimed to have accepted a truce negotiated with the Resistance, but Yassin denied the existence of any prior negotiations to reach a ceasefire with Israel. He said that what he had received was an informal offer of a ceasefire for one year, presented through Egyptian mediators, which he had rejected, as he considered it was merely an Israeli ploy to delay issues until they had the situation under control. In any case, he said, the Resistance would accept a temporary truce in exchange for a serious commitment by Israel to recognize an independent Palestinian state in Gaza and the West Bank, without in return asking for recognition of the state of Israel by the Resistance.

The battle continues

On 19 January 2004, the al-Qassam Brigades launched an operation which involved firing three Qassam missiles at the Atzmona settlement, and a Battar missile at Rafah Yam.

Exchange of Prisoners

On 29 January 2004, an exchange of prisoners-of-war took place in Germany between Israel and the Lebanese Hezbollah. This involved handing

over the mortal remains of three Israeli soldiers and a Mossad prisoner, in exchange for thirty-five Palestinian civilians, with an Israeli pledge to later release another four hundred Palestinian detainees, and to repatriate the mortal remains of fifty-nine Lebanese citizens, but this commitment was not, however, fulfilled.

The Separation Wall before the International Court

In November 2004, the PA announced it was mounting a public relations campaign against the building of the West Bank Wall that Israel had begun to erect, and that legal commissions had been set up to file a lawsuit, which the UN transferred to the jurisdiction of the International Court of The Hague.

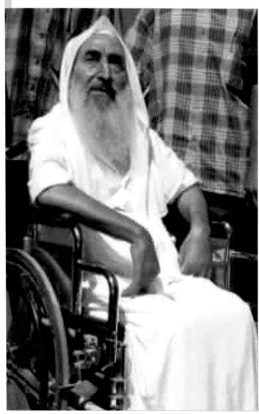

A chilling toll

At the beginning of January 2004, the Israeli Settlement Council issued several reports indicating that the Intifada of al-Aqsa had caused the death of 1,212 Israelis, and that the al-Qassam Brigades and the Islamic Jihad Movement had carried out most of the Palestinian Resistance operations.

A Joint Operation

On 6 March 2004, the Aqsa, Qassam and Jerusalem Brigades conducted a joint operation at a border post which resulted in the destruction of two Israeli armoured cars. The next day, as was to be expected, Israeli forces took revenge on the civilians at the refugee camps of Bureij and Nuseyrat in the Gaza Strip, leaving 13 dead and 55 innocent people injured.

The elderly Yassin, murdered

On 22 March 2004, an Israeli military aeroplane fired a missile at the car of the elderly and paraplegic Ahmed Yassin as he was about to get into the car that was to take him home from the mosque where he had been saying dawn prayers. Yassin was burnt to death inside the car.

3. The Death of Arafat

On Thursday, 11 November 2004, in an official communiqué from the Palestinian Authority, it was confirmed that Yasser Arafat had died in Paris, where he had been receiving treatment at a military hospital. Arafat, who the Israelis had not allowed to leave his official residence for three years, had sunk into an irreversible coma from which he never recovered. His coffin was first taken to Cairo where a military funeral parade was held before more than 50 state and government leaders. It was then taken to Ramallah where he was buried, surrounded by tens of thousands of Palestinians.

There are many hypotheses about the cause of Arafat's death. One such theory, put forward by Faruk al-Kadumi, claims that he was poisoned

AH 1425
AD 11-11-2004

Homage to the
Palestinian president,
Yasser Arafat, at a
French air base.

Intifada and peace

Residents to the Old City in Jerusalem praying for Yasser Arafat.

and that the US refused to provide the necessary antidote for his recovery. However, the French authorities have refused to hand over the medical report concerning his death to anyone except his wife, Suha, who keeps it in secret and will not reveal any of its content to the press.

Arafat's enigmatic finance accounts

The British Broadcasting Company reported that, on Arafat's deathbed, the destiny of the millions of dollars that had passed through Arafat's hands had been discussed. Israeli experts claimed that the funds Arafat had been "amassing" since taking over the PLO leadership had come from financial aid, taxes and transactions he had negotiated, which were credited directly in his bank accounts.

The International Monetary Fund made public that, in the year 2000 alone, the international aid awarded to the Palestinian Authority exceeded one hundred thousand dollars. Palestinian sources declared that it was almost impossible to separate the sums transferred directly to Arafat as the declared beneficiary from the money deposited in accounts allocated for Palestinian funding.

4. US Pledge to Israel

A.H. 1426
A.D. 2005

In an official communique of 4 February 2005, the US Secretary of State, Condoleezza Rice, promised Israel the financial backing of the World Bank, the political support of the European Union and recognition of the state of Israel by at least ten Arab states, including full normalization of political and diplomatic relations, in exchange for its withdrawal from Palestinian enclaves and alterations in the route of the separation wall built by Israel.

Massacre at Bet Laha

On 4 February 2005, the Israeli army perpetrated a massacre of civilians in this town. Eight people were killed, including Muhammed Kamal Ghubun and his two brothers.

Israel Rewards the Mauritanian Regime

In exchange for the Mauritanian regime's pledge of neutrality, the Israeli Minister of Foreign Affairs, S. Shalom, announced on 6 april 2005 his intention to visit Mauritania with a view to cementing their bilateral relations, which includes the delivery of economic aid as a token of Israel's recognition of Mauritania's negative stance towards the Intifada.

Condoleezza Rice.

Legislative Elections in Palestine

On 9 August 2005, Mahmoud Abbas, Palestinian Authority President, postponed the general elections to between 17 July 2005 and 25 January 2006, against the consensus of representatives of the Palestinian associations.

Israel withdraws from Gaza

On 15 August 2005, the Israeli army, under pressure from resistance operations, began its withdrawal from the Gaza Strip announced in late 2003.

The Gaza Strip, with a surface area of 365 km^2 and a population of 1,390,000 inhabitants, was occupied 38 years ago.

The Palestinians celebrated the withdrawal in a spirit of jubilation and the hope of recovering their capital, Jerusalem, together with other occu-

413

Mahmud Abbas.

pied territories, in accordance with previously signed agreements.

Assassination of General Musa Arafat

For several hours, a group of eighty hooded Palestinians assaulted the official residence of the head of military intelligence and of the Palestinian president's military guard, the 66-year-old Musa Arafat, killing him and seriously wounding three of his bodyguards. Musa Arafat's son, Manhal, was kidnapped for several hours and later released unharmed.

General Arafat was known for his severe treatment of the Palestinian resistance.

Israel Dismantles its Gaza Settlements

The Israeli withdrawal from Gaza culminated on 12/9/2005 with the demolition of buildings and infrastructure making up the 17 Jewish settlements founded up to that time. The Palestinian flag was again raised on the territory occupied 38 years previously.

Four-Member Commission Manifesto

All Palestinian forces rejected the manifesto of the four-member commission (USA, Russia, European Union and United Nations), issued on 22/9/2005, which urged the Palestinian Authority to disarm the resistance, considering it an interference in internal affairs and linking this procedure to the result of the general elections and the simultaneous disarming of Jewish settlers.

Israel Strikes again

At a crowded celebration held by Hamas on 23/9/2005 at the Jabaliya refugee camp in the Gaza Strip, Israel wrought havoc among crowd members, with an outcome of 20 deaths and over a hundred injured, many of them children and elderly people.

5. Consequences of Second Intifada

The Palestinian National Information Centre issued a report on the losses sustained by both the Israelis and Palestinians as a result of the second Intifada operations, which erupted after Sharon's intrusion at the al-Aqsa Mosque. The results were as follows:

FROM 29 - 09 - 03
TO 30 - 12 - 03

Palestinian casualties	
Death toll	3.443
- Aged under 18	526
- Women	188
- Policemen	344
- Sick and handicapped people	103
- Doctors, health officers and members of Civil Protection	29
- Journalists	9
- Sportspeople	220
- Due to shelling	733
- Due to assassination	300
- At the hands of settlers	42
- Total number of injured	46,679
- Total number of detainees at 22 concentration camps	11,112
- Students - both sexes	1,554
- Teachers	162
- Wounded and disabled	767
- Women	68
- Total number of fruit-bearing trees felled	982,154
- Total amount of agricultural area destroyed	62,203,000 m²
- Total number of administrative headquarters destroyed	570
- Total number of houses demolished	4,783
- Total number of dwellings destroyed	114,017
- Number of schools and universities closed on military orders	12
- Number of schools closed due to inability to provide schooling	1,125
	→

→ **Palestinian casualties**

- Number of schools destroyed by Israeli army	302
- Number of schools temporarily occupied by Israeli army	60
- Number of schools turned into barracks by the Israeli army	43
- Number of students shot dead by the Israeli army	646
- Number of students under the age of 18 wounded by shots from the Israeli army	4,324
- Total number of food stores destroyed	401
- Number of poultry farms destroyed	162
- Number of stables destroyed	92
- Number of sheep killed	4,095
- Number of cattle killed	688
- Number of beehives ruined	8,825
- Number of water pumps	243
- Number of farmhouses	207
- Number of battery poultry killed	1,429,737
- Area of farmland laid wasted by destruction of irrigation networks	17,108,000 m²
- Number of water tanks destroyed	908
- Length of broken water pipes	687,744 m
- Length of separation wall on damaged properties	1,466 m
- Number of farmers affected	10,021
- Number of nurseries destroyed	6
- Number of tractors destroyed	3
- Length of metal fencing separating farms	253,651 m
- Number of industrial units destroyed	7,768
- Number of forced unemployed	302,000 (43.7 %)
- Percentage of families depauperised because of military siege	60%
- Number of assaults on journalists	668
- Number of shellings in residential neighbourhoods	23,684
- Number of military control posts installed	2,002
- Total amount of Palestinian land expropriated and annexed to Israeli settlements	184,883 m²

29-09-2000
31-01-2003

Human casualties sustained by Israel

Casualties	Settlers	Military personnel	Total
Dead	506	218	724
Wounded	3.593	1.469	5.062

List of Israeli dead and method of attack used by the Resistance

Methods	Settlers	Military personnel	Total
- Stone-throwing	2	-	2
- Knifings	5	-	5
- Car crashes	1	7	8
- Other means	14	2	16
- Shootings (in clashes)	83	80	163
- Drive-by shootings	27	9	36
- Car shootings	53	10	63
- Mortar shelling of settlements	13	3	16
- Mortar shelling of military facilities	22	22	44
Explosives	23	30	53
Suicide bomb attacks	269	28	297
Car bombs	15	23	38
Mortars	-	1	1
Others	1	3	4
Total	506	218	724

Effects of the Intifada on Palestinians

- Greater Arab and Islamic support for the Palestinian Resistance, to the detriment of support for the PA.
- Many people are still convinced of the efficiency of a military solution to the Palestinian problem, including the PA.
- Al-Fatah becomes involved in the armed resistance.
- Unease expressed by the international community when faced with the brashness of the Israeli government.
- Greater presence of the Arab media in the international arena.
- For the first time ever, a spontaneous, grass-roots refusal by young Arab boys to consume products manufactured by companies known to provide financial support to Israel, such as Kuntaki, whose sales in Saudi Arabia have dropped by approximately 80%, and Pepsi Cola, with a 46% sales slump in Egypt. To avoid lower sales, MacDonald's put up posters at the entrances to their establishments announcing they would donate one Saudi riyal per menu for those injured in the course of the Intifada.
- The incorporation of most members of Palestinian political trends into Intifada activities.
- The cruelty of Israeli reaction to any Resistance action has become clear to the international community and has drawn condemnation. This is something Israel falsely attributes to a resurgence of anti-Semitism promoted by Muslims in the West.
- An escalation of armed confrontation between Israeli forces and Palestinian police, as the latter become less tolerant of inhumane aggression against their innocent citizens.
- Since 1948, Palestinians resident in Israel have taken part in military action as part of the Intifada.
- The Intifada, which started as a grass-roots protest movement, has spawned a number of highly operative and effective political–military groups.

Effects of the Intifada inside Israel

- Israelis in every part of the country have become panic-stricken.
- The feeling prevails in intellectual Zionist circles in Israel that the Arab-Israeli conflict is a clash between civilizations and that there should therefore be a merciless crusade against Islam involving the use of all available means on a world scale.
- Loss of credibility in Israeli political circles by the Israeli pacifist sector.
- A recession in tourism, with a 30% drop in revenues, leading to 70,000 layoffs in this sector.
- A recession in Israel's foreign trade, causing daily losses of US$16 million, a rate of US$4,000 million a year.
- For the first time, the trend in Jewish immigration has been reversed, with a balance of people emigrating from Israel, a figure currently estimated to be 1 million Jews.
- Demographic investment in the "Greater Israel": 5 Arabs to 2 Israelis.
- The transformation of Resistance operations from guerrilla warfare to a war of attrition against the Israeli army.

وداعاً
سيدي ...

PART FIVE
Intifada and peace

CHAPTER FIVE
Analytical assessment
of the future of Palestine

Analytical assessment of the future of Palestine

Clearly, Jerusalem is the real bone of contention because it is the Holy City, not only of Muslims, but also of Christians and Jews. Nevertheless, Israel claims it exclusively, with the aim of turning it into the state capital. Control and possession of the city has always been the reason for dispute, and regional and international wars, and will continue to be if the state of Israel pursues its hegemonic and excessively patriotic doctrine, oblivious to the realities of the region and the rights of others.

An example of Israeli machinations in the course of hypothetical peace negotiations is its slow but steady expansion into municipal areas of Jerusalem: in 1967, the surface area of this municipality was only 6 km². In 1990, it had reached 23 km², and the current municipal plan is for it to reach 840 km²—that is, 15% of the total area of the West Bank.

Repeated and incessant peace proposals have always met with Israeli arrogance and with previously undeclared new claims and conditions, so that various foreign delegations have reached the conclusion that Israel does not want a negotiated peace but an imposed peace plan in which Jerusalem's status as the capital of Israel is not negotiable.

In a move to present its case for Jerusalem as a fait accompli, Israel has built a belt of 10 settlements around the Holy City, accommodating 190,000 Israeli immigrants from different countries, while another belt of 17 settlements for new immigrants is nearing completion.

Registered citizens in Jerusalem in 1967 were mainly Muslims. At present, the city's residents amount to 650,000, of which 450,000 are Jewish Israelis.

As part of its Judaization plan, the Jerusalem City Council has divided the municipal area as follows:

81% for Jews
4% for Arabs
10% for future projects

Demolishing Palestinian houses.

The plan to make Jerusalem an exclusively Jewish city is not new at all because the first thing that the Israeli army did after the occupation in 1967 was to eliminate the Maghrebian neighbourhood adjoining the Wailing Wall. Since then, they have continued to search for signs to confirm that the site of Solomon's Temple lies under the al-Aqsa Mosque. It is all in vain, as everything confirms the Islamic identity of the Holy Mosque of Jerusalem.

On various occasions, Jewish extremists have attempted to blow up al-Aqsa. From 1967 to 1990, al-Aqsa suffered 40 attacks and, from the beginning of the Oslo negotiations in 1993 until 1998, that number has increased to 72.

On 30 January 1980, in the UN Security Council resolution, which was passed with 14 votes in favour and one abstention (that of the USA), all changes wrought in the demography of Jerusalem by the Israeli occupying power were declared illegal. Nevertheless, the state of Israel did not

The pictures speak for themselves.

accept this resolution, nor any earlier or later ones. The UN has not taken any measures to bring pressure to bear on Israel to respect the international legal system and the UN resolutions. The Arabs, on the other hand, have been obliged to accept everything by force.